Progress to Proficiency

New Edition
Student's Book

Leo Jones

CAMBRIDGE
UNIVERSITY PRESS

Published by the Press Syndicate of the University of Cambridge
The Pitt Building, Trumpington Street, Cambridge CB2 1RP
40 West 20th Street, New York, NY 10011–4211, USA
10 Stamford Road, Oakleigh, Melbourne 3166, Australia

© Cambridge University Press 1986, 1993

First published 1986
Seventh printing 1991
Second edition 1993

Printed in Great Britain at the
University Press, Cambridge

ISBN 0 521 42575 1 Student's Book
ISBN 0 521 42574 3 Teacher's Book
ISBN 0 521 42542 5 Set of 3 cassettes

Contents

Thanks

I'd like to thank everyone who generously gave their advice and made comments and suggestions which have helped to shape this New Edition of *Progress to Proficiency*.

Heartfelt thanks to Jeanne McCarten, who started the ball rolling and kept the project moving along. Her discerning ideas and wise advice encouraged me to incorporate countless improvements.

Thanks to the teachers who provided feedback on the first edition:
Craig Andrew, C.A.R.E.L., Royan   Liz Charbit, Geos Academy, Hove
Anne Cosker, MPT Harteloire, Brest   Marina Donald & Margery Sanderson,
Stevenson College, Edinburgh   Shirley Downs, British Institute, Rome
Brian Edmonds, British Institute, Paris   Hilary Glasscock & Jenny Henderson,
Cambridge Centre for Advanced English   Cecilia Holcomb, Scanbrit School of
English, Bournemouth   Ian Jasper, British Council, Bilbao   Anne Koulourioti
& Ourania Petrakis, Asimenia Featham School of English, Rethymnon, Crete
Sheila Levy, Cambridge Academy of English   Vicki Lynwoodlast, English
Language Centre, Hove   P.L. Nelson-Xarhoulakou, Athens
Steve Norman, Cambridge School, Barcelona   Bruce Pye, VHS
Spracheninstitut, Nuremberg   Michael Roche, Academia de Idiomas
Modernas, Valladolid   Cristina Sanjuan Alvarez, Escuela Oficial de Idiomas,
Zaragoza   Jennie Weldon, The English Centre, Eastbourne

I'm particularly grateful to everyone who wrote detailed reports on the first edition, and recommended particular improvements and changes:
Margaret Bell, International House, London   Jennie Henderson, Cambridge
Centre for Advanced English   Ruth Jimack, British Council, Athens
Jill Mountain, British Institute, Rome   Clare West, English Language
Centre, Hove

The New Edition was greatly enriched with ideas, criticisms and suggestions from:
Ruth Jimack   Jenny Johnson   Rosie McAndrew   Laura Matthews
Pam Murphy   Jill Neville   Madeline Oliphant   Alison Silver
Bertha Weighill   Clare West

And thanks to the following people for their contributions and assistance:

Peter Taylor, who devoted so much time and effort to collecting the authentic interviews, who produced the studio recordings and edited all the recorded material, with the help of Peter, Leon, Andy and Di at Studio AVP.

The actors who took part in the studio recordings, and who talked about their own experiences and attitudes:
Ishia Bennison   Tim Bentinck   Amanda Carlton   Elaine Claxton
Charles Collingwood   Karen Craig   Rupert Farley
Michael Fitzpatrick   Gordon Griffin   Tim Monro   Jacqui Reddin
Anne Rosenfeld   Chris Scott   Kerry Shale   Ken Shanley
Coralyn Sheldon   Steve Tomkinson

The people who generously agreed to be interviewed:
Steve Abbott   Fiona Bristow   Vince Cross   Ray Gambell
Kate Gooch   Abdulrazak Gurnah   Stephen and Susan Hill
Amanda Hooper   Karen Lewis   Christine Massey   Alastair Miller
Jilly Pearson   David Reindorp   Sarah Springman   Lisa Wood

Lindsay White who coordinated the production of the book with friendly aplomb, tact and skill

Amanda Ogden for her impeccable, resourceful work on researching the photographs, cartoons and reading texts

Ruth Carim for proof-reading the material so carefully

Nick Newton for his tasteful ideas for the design of the book

Peter Ducker for his stylish, meticulous work on the design and layout of each page of the book

Alison Silver guided the project smoothly, efficiently and cheerfully towards its publication. Her eye for detail, thoroughness and discernment enhanced the book enormously. Working with her was, as always, such a pleasure.

Finally, thanks to Sue, Zoë and Thomas for everything.

From the first edition

My special thanks to Christine Cairns and Alison Silver for all their hard work, friendly encouragement and editorial expertise.

Thanks also to all the teachers and students at the following schools and institutes who used the pilot edition of this book and made so many helpful comments and suggestions: The Bell School in Cambridge, the British Council Institute in Barcelona, The British School in Florence, the College of Arts and Technology in Newcastle upon Tyne, the Eurocentre in Cambridge, Godmer House in Oxford, the Hampstead Garden Suburb Institute in London, Inlingua Brighton & Hove, International House in Arezzo, Klubschule Migros in St Gallen, The Moraitis School in Athens, the Moustakis School of English in Athens, the Newnham Language Centre in Cambridge, VHS Aachen, VHS Heidelberg, VHS Karlsruhe, the Wimbledon School of English in London and Ray Thomson in Switzerland. Without their help and reassurance this book could not have taken shape.

Introduction

Progress to Proficiency is for students who are preparing for the University of Cambridge Certificate of Proficiency in English examination (the 'Proficiency' exam), or for an examination of similar level and scope. Each of the eighteen units is based on a different topic, and contains sections which will help you to develop and improve your reading, writing, listening and speaking skills in English.

Using *Progress to Proficiency* . . .

- will make your learning an enjoyable experience
- will be intellectually stimulating and thought-provoking
- will help you do your very best in the exam
- will enable you to perfect your English for professional, academic and social purposes – not just for an exam, but for real life

These criteria are reflected in every unit of *Progress to Proficiency* through a wide variety of exercises and activities, which focus on different aspects of English:

- developing and increasing your vocabulary
- helping you to understand, enjoy and appreciate reading passages
- revising grammar
- studying more advanced grammar points
- improving your writing skills and composition writing
- developing your summary writing skills
- idioms and phrasal verbs
- improving your listening comprehension
- developing your oral communication skills
- Proficiency examination skills

As you work through the units, you'll be building your proficiency in English PROGRESSIVELY. You'll notice a gradual change in the nature and style of the exercises and activities as you progress through the book. At the beginning, they help you to improve your English by giving you guidance, encouraging you to enjoy learning and giving you opportunities to use English creatively; towards the end, you'll be concentrating more on acquiring and refining the special skills needed for the examination.

Many of the exercises and activities are designed to be done in cooperation with other students, working in pairs or small groups. You'll find that by sharing ideas you can learn a great deal from each other. Working in pairs or small groups really will help you learn more effectively – and more enjoyably.

Working through *Progress to Proficiency* will help you to make progress, but it's YOUR TEACHER who can help you to improve the specific aspects of English that you're weakest in and can guide you towards particular exercises that seem most valuable for you and your class. Your teacher may decide to leave out some exercises if the limited amount of time available can be more profitably devoted to other exercises – you may decide to do some of these omitted exercises as extra homework.

Remember that YOU are the most important person in the learning process. You are the person who is most responsible for your progress: by asking questions, seeking advice, continuing to expand your vocabulary (see page 7), reading English for pleasure, talking English and listening to English whenever you can, you should be in control. Improving your English takes time and practice – and hard work too.

A lot of this work will need to be done on your own outside class: preparing material for each lesson, regularly reviewing what you have covered in class, learning new vocabulary, and doing all the written tasks that you are set.

While working with *Progress to Proficiency* you'll need a good English–English dictionary beside you, as well as a comprehensive grammar reference book – no coursebook can answer all your questions on vocabulary and grammar, and your teacher is only available when you're in class.

Symbols

indicates that you should use a fluorescent highlighter to highlight useful words or expressions in a text or exercise.

indicates Communication Activities. In these activities you and your partner(s) are given different information which you have to communicate to each other. These are printed at the end of the book in random order, so that you can't see each other's information.

indicates recorded material on the cassettes.

★★   indicates examination advice and study tips.

⚠   indicates a warning.

Enjoy using Progress to Proficiency!

1 Free time

A   Work in pairs. Discuss these questions with your partner:
- What's going on in the photos? What are the people doing?
- How much 'free time' do you have in an average week?
- What kinds of things do you enjoy doing in your spare time, when you have any?
- If you had more time for hobbies or sports, what might you take up?
- What's your favourite sport and why?
- What's your main hobby? Why do you enjoy it?

B   Work in pairs. Before you listen to the recording, find out what your partner thinks are the attractions (or otherwise) of these hobbies and interests:

⟫→

3

C 🖭 You'll hear five people describing their hobbies or leisure interests: Karen, Tim, Jacqui, Mike and Ishia.

1 As you listen, note down what each speaker's hobby or interest is and the reasons why they enjoy it or find it rewarding.
2 Compare your notes with a partner. Listen to the recording again to settle any points of disagreement, or to fill any gaps in your notes.
3 Discuss which of the activities sounded most and least attractive.

D Work alone. Evaluate each activity as follows:

✓ beside the sports and pastimes you participate in, are interested in, or watch
F beside the ones that other members of your family take an interest in
✗ beside the games and pastimes you dislike or disapprove of
? beside the ones you might take up or get interested in one day
Underline your favourite activity in each category and add any which are missing.

Team sports: soccer ☐ American football ☐ baseball ☐ hockey ☐ rugby ☐ volleyball ☐ basketball ☐ ice hockey ☐

Individual competitive and non-competitive sports: boxing ☐ motor racing ☐ tennis ☐ badminton ☐ golf ☐ squash ☐ cycling ☐ sumo ☐ field and track athletics ☐ swimming ☐ cross-country skiing ☐ downhill skiing ☐ skating ☐ aerobics ☐ windsurfing ☐ surfing ☐ sailing ☐ jogging ☐ fitness exercises ☐ water-skiing ☐

Outdoor activities: birdwatching ☐ fishing ☐ hiking ☐ gardening ☐ walking the dog ☐ hunting ☐

Indoor games: chess ☐ draughts ☐ backgammon ☐ board games: Scrabble, Trivial Pursuit, Monopoly, etc. ☐ card games: bridge, poker, etc. ☐

Hobbies: collecting things – stamps, antiques, etc. ☐ reading books ☐ carpentry ☐ listening to music ☐ playing a musical instrument ☐ photography ☐ cooking ☐ doing crossword puzzles ☐ sewing ☐ knitting ☐ painting ☐ car maintenance ☐ do-it-yourself ☐ dancing ☐ singing ☐ cinema ☐ drama ☐

Work in groups and compare your lists. Find out the attractions (or otherwise) of the sports, games and hobbies that your partners have marked. Use a dictionary to look up any vocabulary you're unsure of, or ask your teacher.

★★ When you meet someone for the first time (and in the Proficiency Interview), you may well be asked about your hobbies and interests. Saying 'I don't have time for any' is a conversation killer. It may be better to pretend that you *are* interested in a couple of sports or hobbies, adding later that you regret how little time you have to pursue them.

A   Work in groups and discuss these questions:

- Do you know anyone who plays any of these instruments?
- Which of them would you like to be able to play? Give your reasons.
- What are the rewards of learning a musical instrument?

B   Read this article and then answer the questions that follow.

Tinkling the ivories, jangling the nerves

1   EXCEPT perhaps for learning a foreign language and getting your teeth properly sorted out once and for all, there is nothing more rewarding than learning a musical instrument. It provides a sense of accomplishment, a creative outlet and an absorbing pastime to while away the tedious hours between being born and dying. Musical "At Homes" can be a fine way of entertaining friends, especially if you have a bitter grudge against them. Instrumental tuition is widely available publicly, privately and by post.

2   Before choosing an instrument to learn you should ask yourself five questions. How much does it cost? How easy is it to play? How much does it weigh? Will playing it make me a more attractive human being? How much does it hurt? All musical instruments, if played properly, hurt.

3   The least you can expect is low back pain and shoulder strain, and in some cases there may also be bleeding and unsightly swelling. Various relaxation methods, such as meditation and the Alexander Technique, can help.

4   The most popular instrument for beginners is the piano, though I don't know why this should be so. The piano is expensive, it's fiendishly difficult to play, it weighs a ton and it hasn't been sexy since Liszt died. If you sit at the keyboard in the approved position for more than a few minutes, the pain is such that you are liable to break down and betray the secrets of your closest friends. The only good thing you can say about the piano is that it provides you with a bit of extra shelf space around the house.

5   Being difficult to play means that learning the piano could make you vulnerable to a syndrome known as Lipchitz's Dilemma. Lipchitz was an Austrian behavioural psychologist who observed that setting out to acquire a difficult skill leads to one of just two alternative results.

6   Either, because of lack of talent or lack of application, you reach only a low to average level of attainment, which leads to general dissatisfaction and maudlin sessions of wandering aimlessly about the house, gently kicking the furniture and muttering, "I'm hopeless at everything."

7   Or you reach a very high attainment level but, because you spend anything up to 18 hours a day reaching and maintaining this level, other aspects of your personality do not develop properly, which leads to general dissatisfaction and maudlin sessions of wandering aimlessly about the house, gently kicking the furniture and muttering, "Up the Villa."

8   Having thus established that no good at all can come of any sort of endeavour, Lipchitz himself gave up behavioural psychology and took a job in a Post Office as the person who runs out of things.

The violin is definitely a Lipchitz's Dilemma instrument, but it does have certain advantages over the piano. It is portable and need not be all that expensive to buy. You might not be able

9 to get as good a sound out of a cheap instrument as an expensive one but since it is notoriously difficult to get much of a sound out of any sort of violin your best advice is to forget the whole idea and take up something easier.

10 The maraca is a hollowed out gourd half filled with beads or dried lentils or some such. Shaken, it makes a rattling sound. Small babies find this mildly entertaining but nobody else is interested.

11 The harmonica is similar. You buy it. You blow it. You suck it. You put it in a drawer. You lie on the sofa and you turn the telly on.

Some people think that the drums are easy to play and assume it must be fun, thrashing about like that. Do not be misled. Even basic rock 'n' roll drumming requires a high level of musical understanding and physical coordination. Years of practice are needed to acquire a

12 fluent technique, sufficient stamina and command of rhythmic and dynamic nuance and yet, after all that trouble, people still come up and say, "Must be fun thrashing about like that." This is why drummers often contract some of the more amusing personality disorders from the Encyclopaedia Psychopathics.

An evening out with a drummer can be diverting, but be prepared for it to end with lines such as, "Leave it, Terry!" "For

13 God's sake, he was only joking!" and "OH, CHRIST, WHAT A MESS!" Otherwise, take my mother's advice and don't have anything to do with drums or drummers.

Brass instruments are much more fun. Professional brass players always wear an expression of bewildered good cheer. This is because they have discovered one of life's most wonderful secrets: you can

14 earn a living making rude noises down a metal pipe. It is a secret that enables them to steer through all life's uncertainties and absurdities with unruffled equanimity.

I have played the guitar for more than 30 years, but I would not advise others to do the same. Far too many other people

15 play the guitar and you will probably find, as I have, that they do it better than you.

A friend once invited me for tea. He had also invited a chap from the pub. The chap from the pub brought his accordion with him. It was an electric accordion which plugged into an amplifier. The

16 living room was small, the amplifier large. He played Lady Of Spain and The Sabre Dance. The International Court of Human Rights has my report on the incident and is considering my recommendations.

For sheer sex appeal you can't do better than a saxophone. Just holding a saxophone gives you a late night charisma, enables you to drink whisky and smoke with authority. But if you wish to maintain credibility, it's as well to have a good stock of excuses ready for when

17 you're asked actually to put the thing to your lips and blow, especially if your best shot is "Oh, The Camptown Ladies Sing This Song, Doo Dah Doo Dah." Otherwise, be prepared for maudlin sessions of aimless wandering, gentle furniture kicking, and muttering, "I'm hopeless at everything."

David Stafford

Note down your answers to these questions, or highlight the relevant information in the passage.

1 Nine instruments are mentioned: what are they?
2 Three rewards of learning an instrument are mentioned: what are they?
3 Four kinds of pain are mentioned: what are they?
4 What is the difference between the two symptoms of Lipchitz's Dilemma?
5 What reasons does the writer give for advising the reader *not* to take up eight of the nine instruments he mentions?

Write your answers to these questions in note form:

6 Which of the instruments seems to have the fewest drawbacks?
7 What happened at the end of the imaginary evening out with a drummer?

➡ Compare and discuss your answers with a partner.

A   Working in pairs, explain the difference in meaning (or emphasis) between
these pairs of sentences:

1   Standing at the top of the hill, I could see my friends in the distance.
    I could see my friends in the distance standing at the top of the hill.

2   Before preparing the meal he consulted a recipe book.
    After consulting a recipe book he prepared the meal.

3   Finding the window broken, we realised someone had broken into the flat.
    We realised someone had broken into the flat, finding the window broken.

4   While preparing the meal, he listened to the radio.
    While listening to the radio, he prepared the meal.

5   Crawling across the road, I saw a large green snake.
    I saw a large green snake crawling across the road.

B   Study these examples before doing the exercises on the next page:

1   There are two forms of **active participles**:

> On TV all you get is a row of heads *bobbing* along in the water . . . You find
> yourself *thinking* about what you are going to have for dinner or *singing* to
> yourself.
> *Having* thus *established* that no good at all can come of any sort of endeavour . . .

and three forms of **passive participles**:

> *Being warned* about the approaching storm, they made for the coast.
> *Warned* about the imminent storm, they prepared for the worst.
> *Having been warned* about the impending storm, they foolishly pressed on.

2   Participles are used to describe **simultaneous** actions:

> We sat on the beach *watching* the windsurfers *falling* into the water.
> . . . maudlin sessions of *wandering* aimlessly about the house, gently *kicking* the
> furniture and *muttering*, "I'm hopeless at everything."
> *Dressed* in her smartest clothes, she arrived early for the interview.

and to describe **consecutive** actions:

> *Getting* to the beach, we looked for an uncrowded spot.
> (BUT NOT: We looked for an uncrowded spot, getting to the beach. ✗)
> *Having got* to the beach, we found a parasol to sit under.

and to explain **reasons** or causes:

> *Not being* an expert, I can't teach you how to use a sailboard.
> *Being* a poor swimmer, I don't go out beyond my depth.

3   Participles can also be used after these words:
after   as   before   if   on   once   since   when   whenever   unless   until

> *After consulting* her parents and erstwhile coach, she started training again.
> *Once opened*, this product should be consumed within 24 hours.
> All musical instruments, *if played* properly, hurt.

⟫→

15

Passive participles and *having...* tend to be used more in formal style than in colloquial English. Normally the **subject** of a participle is the same as the subject of the main verb:

> *Waiting* for the bus, *I* saw him in his new car. (= I was waiting for the bus)

But in some cases the context makes the meaning clear:

> *Being* difficult to play means that learning *the piano* could make you vulnerable to a syndrome known as Lipchitz's Dilemma.

C Using participles of the verbs below, complete these sentences:

1 As .... , we'll meet outside the cinema at 8 o'clock.
2 He has been feeling terribly homesick ever since .... in this country.
3 On .... home, I went straight to my room.
4 .... by her indifference, he burst into tears.
5 Having .... the game, they shook hands.
6 Unless .... later, the key should be returned to the reception desk.
7 Remember to use block capitals when .... the application form.
8 Remember to bend your knees, not your back, whenever ....

arrange   arrive   complete   finish   lift   reach   require   shake

D Finish the sentences, with each one still meaning the same as the one before it.

1 I haven't got a car, which is why I usually travel by bus.   Not ....
2 The demonstrators chanted loudly as they marched into the square.   Chanting ....
3 They turned back when they found their way blocked by the police.   Finding ....
4 After she watched the match on TV, she's wanted to take up golf too.   Ever since ....
5 I heard that he collects butterflies and asked him to tell me about it.   Having ....
6 None of her friends turned up outside the cinema, so she went home.   Finding ....
7 As I don't know much about art, I can't comment on your painting.   Not ....
8 Three old men were sitting smoking at the back of the room.   Sitting ....
9 If you drink coffee too quickly, it can give you hiccups.   Drunk ....
10 I went to bed early because I felt a bit under the weather.   Feeling ....

E Having spotted the mistakes in these sentences, rewrite them correctly

1 Looking out of my window, there was a crowd of people in the street.
2 Wearing bright yellow trousers, we thought he looked ridiculous.
3 Being rather tall for his age, his father treats him like an adult.
4 Having been giving such a warm welcome he felt very pleased.
5 If washing in hot water this garment will shrink.

F Add suitable participles to this story.

On .... my eyes, I knew that I was in a strange, dark room. .... that I might still be dreaming, I pinched myself to see if I was still asleep, but, ... that I really was awake I began to feel afraid. I found the door in the darkness, but it was locked. I decided to call for help but, after .... for several minutes, I knew no one could hear me. I went to the window, and cautiously .... the shutters, I discovered that the window was barred and, ... outside, all I could see was darkness. My heart sank. .... with an

apparently hopeless situation, I sat down .... what to do. I remained there
.... on the bed in silent desperation for several minutes.

Suddenly, ... a key being turned in the lock, I . . .

➡ Add three more sentences, continuing the story with your own ideas.

A   Work in groups. Rearrange these steps into a more sensible order, deciding which of them you would omit. If any vital steps are missing, add them to the list.

GOLDEN RULES FOR WRITING A COMPOSITION

Jot down all the points you might make
Take a break
Analyse your notes, deciding which points to emphasise and which to omit
Show your first draft to someone else and get feedback from them
Edit your first draft, noting any changes you want to make
Proof-read the first draft: eliminate errors in grammar, spelling and punctuation
Do any necessary research
Proof-read your final version, eliminating any mistakes you spot
Discuss what you're going to write with someone else
Write a first draft, perhaps in pencil
Look carefully at the instructions
Write a plan, rearranging the points in the order you intend to make them
Use a dictionary to look up suitable words and expressions and write them down
Think about what you're going to write
Get feedback from other students on your final version (they are 'your readers')
Look again at the instructions
Have a rest
Write your final version

B   Write down your own 'golden rules' for writing a composition, to remind you of the steps *you* should follow every time you do a piece of written work.

Try to follow these steps every time you do written work during this course.

➡ Which of the steps would not be feasible when working against the clock under exam conditions? Adapt your 'golden rules', bearing in mind how you performed in the composition paper of the last English exam you took.

C   Read this composition, based on what Mike said about playing squash in 1.1 C.

You don't have to be a yuppie to play squash: if you play at a
public sports centre, rather than a private club, you soon
discover that it's a game that everybody plays. Taking part in a
league, you can meet people from all walks of life, and it's
quite normal for men and women to play each other. However,
unlike tennis, you can't play doubles, so it's not such a
sociable game.

     The reason why squash is such fun is that it's so easy to
play. Beginners can have an enjoyable game right away and can

get involved in the tactics and strategy of the game. With tennis, where it's a major achievement for a beginner even to hit the ball back over the net, you have to be quite proficient before you can do this. With squash, returning the ball is easy and you don't have to waste time retrieving all the balls that have been hit out — you only need one ball to play with and you can play at any time of the day or night and in all weathers. You don't even need to be strong to play: a soft, cunning service can be just as effective as a powerful, fast one. It does help to be fit and agile, though, because even though a game only lasts half an hour or so, during that time you're constantly using your energy and you don't have time for a rest while your opponent is off the court hunting for lost balls.

Perhaps it's because squash is such an energetic game that it's thought to be dangerous, and admittedly there is a risk of minor injuries like strains and sprains, or getting hit by your opponent's racket, because both players have to cover the whole court and sometimes get in each other's way. But if you're careful, and don't overdo it, it's no more dangerous than any other sport.

Discuss these questions with a partner :

- What further information would you like to be given, which is not given above ?
- What information has the writer assumed you already know about the game ?

Highlight the features that you find most effective, looking in particular at:

the choice of vocabulary   style and sentence structure

D *Write a description of your own favourite hobby or sport, mentioning its attractions and drawbacks.* (about 300 words)

If you don't take part in a sport or hobby, write about one that you'd like to take up one day – when you eventually have enough time.

Follow the 'golden rules' you discussed earlier. Before you begin writing, MAKE NOTES of the points you might make. In 300 words, you're unlikely to have enough room to mention them all, so you'll have to select the most important or most interesting ones.

➡ Show your finished composition to a partner and ask for feedback.

★★ When writing a composition, leave a wide margin on either side of your work and leave a line or two between each paragraph. This will leave you room to add extra ideas, and even to rewrite complete sentences later if necessary. There's also more space for your teacher to add comments later too.

2 Adventure

A   Work in groups. Discuss these questions with your partners:
- Are you an adventurous person – or do you tend to play safe and avoid risks?
- What kinds of adventures or dangerous activities do you avoid at all costs?
- What kind of people do adventurers or travellers need to be? Which do you think are the ten most important qualities – and why?

  *arrogance   boldness   charisma   compassion   confidence   courage
  curiosity   dedication   determination   dignity   a good sense of direction
  enthusiasm   fearlessness   humility   a sense of humour   intelligence
  knowledge   linguistic skills   modesty   obstinacy   patience   persistence
  resilience   resourcefulness   ruthlessness   stamina   tolerance   willpower*

- Look at the people in this photo – what kind of people do they appear to be?

Dervla and Rachel Murphy

B   The passage on page 20 is a review of *Eight Feet in the Andes* by Dervla Murphy. As you read it, find the answers to these questions:

1 Whose were the eight feet?   3 How long was the journey?
2 Who is the heroine of the story?   4 Where did they sleep?

C   [icon] Highlight these words and phrases in the article – ¶ indicates the relevant paragraph:

  saunter ¶ 1   *madcap schemes* ¶ 3   *frolic* ¶ 4   *heartening* ¶ 4
  overenthusiastically ¶ 6   *day one* ¶ 6   *fretting* ¶ 7   *coveted* ¶ 7
  homespun ¶ 9   *sticky moments* ¶ 12   *trusting soul* ¶ 13

Match their meanings to these words and phrases:

  amusing game   crazy plans   stroll   encouraging   without restraint
  the beginning   someone who believes other people are honest   unsophisticated
  dangerous incidents   fussing and worrying   envied and wanted

ONCE upon a time, with travel writing, the rewards won related to the risks taken. No longer. Travel writers travel by public transport; often they just hop in the car. They travel round British seaside resorts; they saunter up low mountains in the Lake District. Greatly daring, they visit islands off the coast. There is no point in travelling hopefully; far better to arrive as quickly as possible and collect your multi-national publisher's advance.

Dervla Murphy had never heard of such a thing when she decided, after the death of her invalid mother, to travel from Ireland to India – on a bicycle.

Motherhood usually puts paid to such madcap schemes but for Miss Murphy only temporarily. She waited for the child to reach a reasonable age and then took it with her.

Rachel was five when they travelled together in South India, six when they went through Baltistan with a pony, and nine when, in this book, she crossed the Peruvian Andes from Cajamarca to Cuzco with her mother and a mule – a 2,000 kilometre journey of which she did 1,500 on foot. This Andean frolic – her mother's term – was to be her last before settling down to school, though it is hard to see what there can be left for her to learn. To read about Rachel is heartening for parents of a generation which seems to be losing the use of its legs.

She is an ideal travelling companion, settling down on a ledge overlooking the world to read *Watership Down* or write poems after ten hours up one mountain and down the next. "We're seeing clouds being born," she says once. She is thrilled to find a baby scorpion under her sleeping bag. After three months of travelling up and down vertical slopes of 3,300 metres her mother notes almost absently that she never once complained; and she herself only once questions the wisdom of asking a nine-year-old to walk 35 kilometres at an altitude of 4,000 on half a tin of sardines.

Rachel confides in her diary: "I got the whole of my upper left arm punctured by lots of slightly poisonous thorns ... Mummy is in an exceedingly impatient mood ... I think this is a very pretty place, at least in looks ...We had to sit down while we thought about what to do next ..." She has a much better sense of direction and indeed of responsibility than her mother who tends to join overenthusiastically in all religious festivals and who has dreadful blisters from day one in a hopeless pair of walking shoes.

The Murphys clearly see not Rachel but Juana, their beautiful glossy mule, as the heroine of the story. She cost £130 and they fuss over her like a film star, fretting about her diet, her looks, her mood. Juana is coveted by all; as the journey proceeds it is shadowed by the parting from her. There is a terrible moment when she falls over a precipice to certain death but for a divinely placed single eucalyptus tree in her path.

From Cajamarca to Cuzco they follow in the hoofprints of Pizarro and the *conquistadores*, often camping in the same place, almost always surveying the same timeless unchanging scene.

Miss Murphy's philosophy may be homespun – "I know and always have known that we twentieth-century humans need to escape at intervals from that alien world which has so abruptly replaced the environment that bred us" – but she has an enviable gift for communicating her passion for the road. No heat or cold is too extreme, no drama too intense for her to sit on the edge of some mountain and tell us about it that evening in her diary. Sometimes the view is too exciting for her to eat her raw potatoes and sardines.

There is very little food; everyone goes hungry. The pair arrive at sizeable towns and find nothing to buy but noodles and stock cubes and bottles of Inca Cola; the restaurant offers hot water to add to your own coffee. There is always worry about alfalfa for the choosy Juana. They are shocked at the poverty they see, and find it mystifying that the Indians can tolerate such a life.

She and Rachel share it wherever possible. They stop, make friends, join in. They accept all invitations, are ready to sleep with hens roosting on their legs, eat anything, drink anything no matter what floats on top of it and they repay hospitality (when permitted) with tins of sardines. She worries that religion is so little comfort to the Peruvian Indian, that the babies chew wads of coca, that the boys Rachel plays football with on their sloping pitches have no future, that she cannot repay kindnesses: the ancient shepherdess who shared her picnic lunch of cold potato stew on a cabbage leaf, the old man who set his dog to guard their tent at night.

There are sticky moments, always near towns. Within a day of Cuzco, Juana is stolen but all ends happily and they reach the Inca city with feelings of anti-climax at journey's end. They took a week less than the *conquistadores* but then the *conquistadores* had battles to fight.

The Murphys, mother and daughter, know no fear just as they know no discomfort, and their remarkable journey shows that the trusting soul is still free to wander at will.

Maureen **CLEAVE**

D Now answer these questions, referring back to the article as necessary.

1 What is the writer's attitude to modern travel writers?
2 How many journeys had the mother and daughter team made before this one?
3 Why was this to be their last one together?
4 How did Dervla behave in a less grown-up way than her daughter?
5 When the writer describes Miss Murphy's philosophy as 'homespun' (¶ 9), is this pejorative or complimentary?
6 What did they eat on their journey?
7 What happened to Juana at the end of their journey?
8 What were their worst and best experiences?

E Work in pairs. Looking at the first paragraph again, highlight the words or phrases which show SARCASM or IRONY.

Which of these, if any, do *you* actually find amusing?

F Work in groups and discuss your reactions to the passage:
• What risks was Dervla Murphy running by taking Rachel on her journey?
• What aspects of their journey would you find most difficult or rewarding?
• Where in the world is it safe for 'the trusting soul' to 'wander at will'?

A Work in pairs. Match the sentences that mean the same as each other.

1 What was the mule like?   What is a mule like?
   What are mules like?   Could you describe their mule?

2 Do you like tea now?   Is the tea all right for you now?
   Do you like the tea now?   Have you overcome your dislike of tea?

3 Would you like some coffee now?   Would you like your coffee now?
   Would you like a coffee now?   Would you like the coffee now?

4 Every difficulty was foreseen.   Some of the difficulties were foreseen.
   Some difficulty was foreseen.   The difficulty was foreseen.
   No difficulty was foreseen.   Each difficulty was foreseen.
   We didn't expect any difficulty.   We expected a particular difficulty.
   All the difficulties were foreseen.   Not all of the difficulties were foreseen.
   We expected a certain amount of difficulty.

5 He's not *the* Michael Jackson.   He's not the famous Michael Jackson.
   He's not Michael Jackson.   Michael Jackson is not his name.

6 Who's coming to dinner?   Who's coming to the dinner?
   Who has been invited to the banquet?   Who has been invited to eat with us?

B Some nouns are normally uncountable:

   *advice   applause   behaviour   clothing   fun   information   laughter
   luggage   music   news   progress   rain   research   snow   spaghetti
   teaching   transport   travel   wealth*

   Music *helps me to relax.*   **Travel** *broadens the mind.*

If we are referring to a **particular** example of each, a different countable word
or phrase must be used:

   What a pretty **song***!   What a catchy* **tune***!   What a lovely* **piece of music***!
   Did you enjoy your* **trip***?   We had a great* **journey***.*

Match the uncountable nouns above to these countable words or phrases:

   a/an action   analysis   article   asset   car   chuckle   class   coat   fact
   fortune   game   hint   improvement   joke   journey   laugh   lesson
   possession   report   shirt   song   suitcase   tip   train   trip   tune

   a/an article   drop   fall   flake   item   means   piece   plate   round   **of**

★★ These Grammar review sections will help you to revise the main 'problem areas' of
English grammar, giving you a chance to consolidate what you already know and to
discover what you still need to learn. The Advanced grammar sections will
introduce you to more advanced structures.
   But they are no substitute for a good, comprehensive grammar reference book, to
which you should refer for more detail and further examples.

22

C Some nouns are uncountable if used with a **general** meaning:

ABSTRACT NOUNS *adventure   atmosphere   business   confidence   death education   environment   experience   failure   fear   history   imagination industry   kindness   knowledge   life   love   philosophy   pleasure   success thought*
MASS NOUNS *butter   cheese   coffee   juice   metal   milk   pasta   plastic poison   soup   sugar   tea   wine   wood*

> *Business is **booming**.   Do you know much about **business**?*
> *I have orange **juice** and **coffee** with **milk** for breakfast.*

But they are countable if they refer to **particular** things or examples:

> *She runs her own **business**.   Running a **business** is a great responsibility.*
> *I'd like an orange **juice** please.   Lead is a heavier **metal** than aluminium.*

Fill the gaps with suitable nouns from the lists above.

1 A thorough .... of English is required.
2 It was an unforgettable ....
3 The journey was a great ....
4 Oak is a harder .... than pine.
5 She had a thrilling ....
6 It was a great .... to meet them.
7 He has a very vivid ....
8 The trip was an utter ....
9 This is a very salty ....
10 Cheddar is a very tasty ....
11 He has a great .... of music.
12 I'd like a strong black .... please.

➡ Write sentences using ten of the words listed above as uncountable nouns.

⚠ The use of articles is often determined by the context, and depends on information given earlier in a text or conversation, as in this example:

> I bought *a* computer from *a* mail order catalogue. *The* computer has gone wrong and I can't get it fixed because *the* company's gone out of business.

D Fill the gaps in these extracts with *a*, *an*, *the*, *his*, *her*, *their*, or Ø (no article) – in some cases more than one answer is possible. Afterwards, refer back to paragraphs 7 and 11 of the article in 2.1.

> **The**............... Murphys clearly see not Rachel but Juana, ... beautiful glossy mule, as .... heroine of .... story. She cost £130 and they fuss over her like .... film star, fretting about .... diet, ... looks, ... mood. Juana is coveted by all; as .... journey proceeds it is shadowed by .... parting from her. There is .... terrible moment when she falls over .... precipice to .... certain death but for .... divinely placed single eucalyptus tree in .... path.
>
> She worries that .... religion is so little comfort to .... Peruvian Indian, that .... babies chew .... wads of .... coca, that .... boys Rachel plays .... football with on .... sloping pitches have no future, that she cannot repay .... kindnesses: .... ancient shepherdess who shared .... picnic lunch of .... cold potato stew on .... cabbage leaf, ... old man who set .... dog to guard .... tent at night.

E   Correct the errors in these sentences:

1   Politics don't interest him, except when election takes place.
2   Grapefruits are my favourite fruits, but I don't like the banana.
3   The news are depressing today: two aircrafts have crashed.
4   There are crossroads at top of hill.
5   Mathematics were most difficult subject at the school for me.
6   Hague is capital of Netherlands, but Amsterdam is largest city.

F   🗣️ Work in pairs. One of you should look at the photograph in Activity 3, the other at Activity 22. Find out about your partner's picture by asking questions.
   Write a paragraph about your partner's picture, based on the answers you received, but WITHOUT looking at the photograph.
   Read each other's paragraphs and check the use of articles and determiners. Finally, compare your description with the original picture.

2.3   Climbing mountains   Listening

Alastair Miller

A   Before you listen to the interview with Alastair Miller, a member of the British Combined Services expedition to Everest, look at the questions he was asked. Discuss with a partner what answers you think he gave.

1   What do you enjoy about climbing mountains?
2   Do you ever find yourself in situations where you're frightened?
3   What is it like taking part in an expedition to climb Everest?
4   What is there left for you to do now, after going to Everest?

B   📼 In the first part of the interview, Alastair deals with the first two points. Note down your answers to these questions.

1   What are the four things he says he enjoys about climbing – and what are the reasons he gives for enjoying each of them?
2   What are the two kinds of fear he describes?
3   Why was the accident in Yosemite Valley, California, more frightening for his companion than for Alastair himself?
4   Why did he have to be 'philosophical' during the thunderstorm on the Aiguille du Midi in the French Alps?
5   Why didn't they go back down the mountain when the storm broke?

C 🔲 The second part of the interview is about the Everest expedition. Fill the gaps in these sentences with information from the interview.

1 On a large expedition there is a '................ effect': there are .... people at the bottom of the mountain and .... or .... people trying to reach the summit. This means that .... have to be carried up the mountain.
2 Approaching Everest from the .... , there were no .... to carry their equipment. So it was carried by yaks, and above Camp One, by ....
3 It was exciting for Alastair when he went above .... for the first time, even though he was on .... ropes and was entirely .... He was properly .... not just ....
4 Above Camp One they didn't .... or .... , they only cleaned their ....
5 Snow holes are .... but they are .... and ....

D 🔲 The final part of the interview deals with question 4 in A. Answer these Yes/No questions.

1 Does he want to climb again in the Himalayas?
2 Does he want to be a member of another large Everest-style expedition?
3 Has he done any climbing in the Andes?
4 Has he done any climbing in North America?

E Work in groups. Compare your reactions to the interview. What impressed you most? What surprised you most? Would you like to be a mountaineer and rock-climber? Give your reasons.

"No one's actually ever bothered to climb the East Face before."

BANX

A Find the answers to these questions in the text.

1 Apart from the writer, how many other people are mentioned in the passage?
2 Which of them did the writer trust most – and who did he trust least?
3 How confident was the writer that the expedition would ever leave London?
4 Did Major Pingle really exist?

OUTLOOK UNSETTLED

THERE are, I suppose, expeditions and expeditions. I must say that during those six weeks in London it looked as if ours was not going to qualify for either category. Our official leader (hereinafter referred to as Bob) had just the right air of intrepidity. Our Organizer, on the other hand, appeared to have been miscast, in spite of his professional-looking beard. A man of great charm, he was 5 nevertheless a little imprecise. He had once done some shooting in Brazil, and we used to gaze with respect at his photographs of unimaginable fish and the corpses (or, as it turned out later, corpse) of the jaguars he had killed. But when pressed for details of our own itinerary he could only refer us to a huge, brightly-coloured, and obsolete map of South America, on which the railway line between 10 Rio and São Paulo had been heavily marked in ink. 'From São Paulo,' he would say, 'we shall go up-country by lorry. It is cheaper and quicker than the train.' Or, alternatively: 'The railway will take us right into the interior. It costs less than going by road, and we shall save time, too.' It was clear that Bob, for all his intrepidity, viewed our Organizer's vagueness with apprehension. 15

At the other end – in Brazil, that is to say – the expedition's interests were said to be in capable hands. Captain John Holman, a British resident of São Paulo whose knowledge of the interior is equalled by few Europeans, had expressed his willingness to do all in his power to assist us. On our arrival in Brazil, as you will hear, this gentleman proved a powerful, indeed an indispensable ally; but at this 20 early stage of the expedition's history our Organizer hardly made the most of him, and Captain Holman was handicapped by the scanty information which he received with regard to our intentions. In London we were given to understand that the man who really mattered was a Major Pingle – George Lewy Pingle. (That is not his name. You can regard him as an imaginary character, if you like. 25 He is no longer quite real to me.)

Major Pingle is an American citizen, holding – or claiming to hold – a commission in the Peruvian army. He has had an active and a varied career. According to his own story, he ran away from his home in Kentucky at the age of 15; joined a circus which was touring the Southern States; found his way across 30 the Mexican border; worked for some time on a ranch near Monterey; accompanied an archaeological expedition into Yucatan, where he nearly died of fever; went north to convalesce in California; joined the ground staff of an aerodrome there and became (of all things) a professional parachutist; went into partnership with a German, whose ambition it was to start an airline in South 35 America; and since then had travelled widely in Colombia, Peru, Chile and

A Work in pairs. Discuss the differences in meaning or emphasis in these sentences:

1 Tricia only wants to help.   Only Peter wants to help.
2 Paul just doesn't like flying.   Olivia doesn't just like flying . . .
3 Pam doesn't really feel well.   Jack really doesn't feel well.
   Anne doesn't feel really well.
4 Tony and Jane still aren't married.   Still, Sue and Bob aren't married.
   Olivia and Paul aren't still married, are they?
5 I don't particularly want to see Lisa. I particularly don't want to see Tim.
6 I enjoy eating normally.   I normally enjoy eating.   Normally, I enjoy eating.
7 Carefully, I lifted the lid.   I carefully lifted the lid.   I lifted the lid carefully.

B Work in pairs. Look at the examples and fill the gaps with suitable adverbs or phrases from the lists.

1 Some adverbs are almost always placed in front of the main verb in a sentence (or after the verb *to be*) – but not usually at the beginning or end of the sentence:

*almost   already   always   ever   hardly ever   just   nearly   never   often
practically   quite   rarely   seldom   utterly   virtually*

Have you *ever* been to South America?   We have .... finished our work.
I .... disagree with what you said.   It is .... as cold as this usually.

2 Some adverbs are usually placed in front of the main verb OR after the object (but not normally at the beginning of the sentence):

constantly   continually   perpetually   regularly   sporadically
*absolutely   altogether   completely   enormously   entirely   exactly
   greatly   more or less   perfectly*

He *constantly* asks questions.   He asks questions *constantly*.
I don't .... agree with her.   Your work has .... improved.
He isn't .... brilliant.   I enjoyed the show ....

3 Adverbs consisting of more than one word are usually placed at the end of the sentence, or at the beginning (but NOT in front of the main verb):

*again and again   all the time   every so often   from time to time
   many times   most of the time   once a week   once every four years
   once in a while   over and over again   several times   twice a day*

*at the moment   at one time   a fortnight ago   before breakfast
   before long   every day   in a moment   in the evening   in the past
   the following week   the previous day   within the hour*

Most of the time I try to avoid risks.   I try to avoid risks *most of the time*.
The Olympics take place ....
I've warned you .... to take care.
I don't have the information ...., so I'll call you back ....
.... I agree with what she says, but .... we don't see eye to eye.
Although she had washed her hair ...., she washed it again ....

⟫→

4 Many adverbs are usually placed at the beginning of the sentence, or in front of the main verb, or after the main verb or the object:

normally   occasionally   periodically   sometimes   usually
afterwards   at once   clearly   eventually   immediately   later   obviously
presently   presumably   probably   shortly   soon   suddenly

Usually I wash my hair twice a week.   I *usually* wash my hair twice a week.
I wash my hair twice a week *usually*.
I can't give you my answer ...., but I'll let you know ....
Let me know .... what you thought of the film.
It will .... be time to go home, so you'll have to finish the work ....

5 Most **adverbs of manner** are commonly placed after the main verb or its object – though other positions are often possible:

accidentally   anxiously   apprehensively   automatically   carefully
discreetly   easily   fiercely   fluently   foolishly   frankly   gently   gloomily
gratefully   hurriedly   independently   innocently   instinctively   lovingly
mechanically   oddly   proudly   reassuringly   reluctantly   sensibly
sincerely   strangely   systematically   thoughtfully   violently   warmly

He reacted *violently* to my comments.
She was behaving very ....   They congratulated him ....
He held up the prize .... and thanked everyone ....
I raised my hand .... to protect my face.
She took his hand .... and looked .... into his eyes.

6 Adverbs which '**comment**' on the whole sentence are usually placed at the very beginning of a sentence before a comma, though other positions are often possible.

Amazingly   Fortunately   Funnily enough   Hopefully   Luckily
Strangely enough   Surprisingly   Unfortunately

Unfortunately, Elizabeth lost the race.   Elizabeth *unfortunately* lost the race.
............., I found my wallet in the car.   ...., I'll have finished the work soon.
............., she didn't get the job.   ...., they're getting married.

➡ Compare your answers with another pair's.

⚠ Remember that adverbs almost never go between a verb and a direct object:
He ate quickly his sandwiches. ✗   She took gently his hand. ✗

C Rewrite the sentences using the words given, but without changing the meaning:

1 They eventually replied to my letter.	**after a while**
2 I'm afraid that's a mistake I frequently make.	**again and again**
3 There are many occasions when I eat out in the evenings.	**often**
4 Soon I'll have finished writing this report.	**practically**
5 They helped me although they seemed unwilling.	**reluctantly**
6 There's nothing I'd like to do less than go for a walk.	**particularly**
7 Each branch of the company is a separate operation.	**independently**
8 I expect that he will be feeling apprehensive.	**presumably**
9 You should pay constant attention to your spelling.	**always**

10 She gave me a worried look.
11 All enquiries will be handled with discretion.
12 He does occasionally lose his temper.

anxiously
discreetly
from time to time

⚠ Adverb position is a very difficult area of English usage, and it's often best to
rely on your *feelings* for what seems right and what seems wrong. Pay special
attention to any corrections you are given.

There are no hard and fast rules, unfortunately.

2.8 Going for a walk?

A Work in pairs or alone. Before you listen to the recording, try to guess or
deduce what information seems to be missing here:

PRECAUTIONS

1 DO have at least .... people in your party.
   – DON'T go .**alone**.....
2 DO be ....
   – DON'T do anything you're not .... to do.
3 DO expect the weather to ....
   – DON'T rely on ....
4 DO allow yourself plenty of ....
   – DON'T let .... catch up with you.
5 DO walk at the .... of the .... member of the group.
   – DON'T leave anyone ....
6 DO .... if fog or low clouds come down, and find .... where you can sit and wait
   for ....
   – DON'T .... in case you walk over a ....!

EQUIPMENT

1 A .**map**..... – You must .... your .... before setting off.
2 A .... in case there are no .... or the sun is obscured , and make sure you know
   .... – Don't just follow .... and rely on your ....
3 A rucksack, containing .... and .... clothing.
4 Footwear: ...., not .... or ....
5 Emergency .... in your rucksack: ...., ..., ...
6 A .... in case you get caught in the dark.
7 A .... or a .... in case you have to spend the night in the open.

And ... Before setting out DO .... and ....
and DON'T forget to .... when you get back.

B [▭] Listen to the recording, filling in the missing information above.

C After listening to the recording, discuss these questions with your partner:
  • What important advice did the speaker leave out?
  • Which of his advice do you disagree with?

≫→

D Work in groups. Make a list of your own safety rules for TWO of these activities:
sailing   windsurfing   swimming in the sea   skiing   driving in remote areas
going out at night alone   cycling in heavy traffic   climbing a ladder

E *Make up a fictional story about a walk in the mountains where you ignored the advice given in the recording but where, despite a number of close shaves, you arrived home safely.*   (about 300 words)

(If you prefer, you could write about one of the activities you discussed in D, where you ignored your own rules of safety.)

➡ Make notes before you start writing.

F Show your completed story to another student and ask for feedback.

★★ In the Proficiency exam, you'll be given a narrative composition title to write about –
a fictional or semi-fictional story is often easier to control, and may be more
interesting than a rather uneventful true story.
    Many storytellers narrate stories using an 'I' narrator. It's usually more convincing
to imagine yourself as the protagonist of a story than to create a main character.

A Which of the following would you KEEP and which would you HOLD?

  a diary   a job down   a meeting   a promise   a straight face   your breath
  in touch with someone   someone company   your head high   yourself to
  yourself   someone in the dark   someone responsible   your fingers crossed

B Find synonyms for the phrases in italics, or explain their meaning. Use a
  dictionary if necessary.

  1 She walked so fast that I couldn't *keep up with* her.
  2 There's no point in trying to *keep up with the Joneses*.
  3 You've done a lot of good work this month. I hope you can *keep it up*.
  4 They're getting married next month! *Keep it to yourself*, though.
  5 I'll *keep my fingers crossed* for you on the day of your interview.
  6 I'm sorry for what I did, I hope you won't *hold it against* me.
  7 Their reasoning just didn't *hold up*.
  8 *Hold on* a moment, I haven't got a pen. Could you *hold the line*, please?
  9 We got *held up* in the traffic.
  10 They explained what happened, but I feel they were *holding something back*.

C Fill the gaps in these sentences with suitable phrases from the list below. You
  may need to change the form of the verbs.

  1 The clouds look pretty ominous, I don't .... much hope of sunny weather.
  2 Fortunately, their supplies .... till the rescue party got to them.
  3 You'd better .... the subject of his first marriage, otherwise he'll get upset.
  4 They managed to .... their costs .... by employing part-time workers.
  5 It was a private argument, so I thought it best to .... it.
  6 She felt that her boss's attitude was .... her .... in her career.
  7 If she wants to get on, she'll have to .... her boss, not disagree with him.
  8 Tell me exactly what you think – don't .... anything ....
  9 They didn't think our offer was high enough, so they .... more.
  10 As they climbed up the cliff, the leader told them to .... tight.

  hold back   hold back   hold on   hold out   hold out   hold out for
  keep down   keep in with   keep off   keep out of

D Write the first paragraph of a story, using as many of the verbs and idioms from
  above as possible. Begin like this:

  I didn't realise I'd be held up for so long but . . .

3 People

A Work in groups and discuss these questions:

- Do you like being alone – or do you feel lonely when you haven't got company?
- Do you enjoy the pace of life in a big city? Or do you find it stressful?
- If you wanted to 'get away from it all' where would you go?

B Read this article, preferably alone before the lesson, and then do the tasks on the next page.

The great escape

1 LOOKING around the small wooden cabin, I counted seven people. Or it might have been eight. The lighthouse keeper's wife was the last to arrive. She dropped out of the sky, unannounced, courtesy of a Coast Guard helicopter that landed on the gravel beach right in front of the cabin.

2 "Hi, I'm Lise," she shouted as the chopper disappeared. "I thought I'd drop in for a visit." Looking around, she added: "Hey, I thought you were here on your own!"

3 I'd stopped thinking that days ago.

4 "I want to be alone," I had declared on leaving London. I was tired, dog tired, of people and telephones and deadlines and crowds. So I planned a great escape, a Big Sleep, a magnificent foolproof Fortress of Solitude, where for three whole weeks I planned to hibernate like a bear in the middle of nowhere.

5 Everything seemed perfect. A friend in Canada needed a house-sitter for his remote homestead on the far coast of Vancouver Island, the silvery western edge of Canada. Here, the map ends and the open Pacific begins. Huge silent forests swell in the heavy winter rains, growing dense and impenetrable right down to the water's edge.

6 I knew I could be entirely alone here. No roads go near this part of the coast. The only way in is by boat or small plane. I would have no telephone, no electricity, no television, no interruptions. I felt unassailable. Friends and family were outraged. "What do you mean, you want to be alone? Out in the bush like that? No one wants to be that alone."

7 "Oh yeah?" I thought. I said nothing. They kept talking.

8 And then came the unsolicited offers. No fewer than 15 people offered to come and stay with me. For my own good, of course.

9 Some of the offers were positively scary. "Is it OK if I bring the boys?" These boys are aged two and four, television junkies from the womb. Their mother has never lived out of range of a washing machine or a dishwasher in her entire life.

10 "Frank and I will both come – he's much better after his operation."

11 "I'll bring my guitar."

12 "I've been really depressed, I need solitude too."

13 But despite all these offers, when the tiny float plane at last landed in the inlet near the cabin, and I clambered out with my heavy boxes of books and groceries, I was blissfully alone. My first few days were entirely peaceful. A long-dreamed-of silence surrounded me, and vast space. It didn't last long.

14 The depressed friend arrived first. She was heroically prepared to stay for 10 days. "Don't worry about me – I won't get in your way."

15 "Oh yeah?" I thought. This friend had been egged on by numerous other friends. "What is that woman doing out there they're all asking? I'm supposed to report back."

16 It was really very simple. I wasn't doing much at all. I was sleeping and reading and chopping wood and beachcombing and watching the eagles and looking out for other wildlife. The problem for everyone else seemed to be that I was doing it alone. Human nature, I decided, abhors a vacuum. It was clear that I would have to settle for semi-solitude. And in the end I found I didn't really mind. Which is just as well.

17 No one else arrived from "outside". The threat of "the boys", the guitar and the post–operative Frank came to nothing. But as the days passed I was astonished to find myself meeting more and more people.

My nearest neighbours turned out to be

Dave and Diane, living in a deserted Indian village 15 miles up the coast. Diane called me on the marine radio. "Don told us you were there all alone, so we thought we'd check in to see how you're getting on."

"Don?" I thought. I didn't know any Don.

Dave and Diane and their children came to see me in their boat. They told me where to dig for clams and that the herring run had started and that hundreds of sea lions were playing further out in the bay and that the grey whales had arrived on their annual migration.

That was the day Lise from the lighthouse arrived. All day long, the coffee pot spluttered on the woodstove and conversation never flagged. I learned about light-keeping and edible seaweeds and how to smoke mussels and where the gooseneck barnacles grow.

"Here I was worrying about you," said Lise cheerfully. "I never thought you'd have so much company."

Neither did I. But it was good company. On the day of the crowded cabin, we went out in the boat to see the grey whales spouting. Later on, we went all the way to the lighthouse, riding on the huge swells of the open Pacific, in Dave's small boat.

My depressed friend became alarmingly cheerful after all this and thought she might stay even longer. She had, however, to get back to work. As her plane took off from the water, silence returned. The guests had all left.

"Ah, solitude," I thought, tentatively. Just me and the whales and the sea lions and the eagles and the herring. The solitude lasted precisely two more days before a large, friendly person emerged from the forest announcing that he was Bob, from the logging camp down in the next inlet. He'd hiked over to see how I was doing. "Just thought I'd check in. Bill told me you were here all alone."

"Bill?" I thought, and, "All alone?" Bob stayed and drank a pot of coffee. I learned a lot about trees.

A few days later, a strange boat anchored in front of the house and three men made their way to shore. They were from the Department of Fisheries, monitoring the herring run. "Liz told us you were out here on your own. How's it going? Aren't you lonely?"

"Liz?" I thought, and, "Lonely?" as I put the coffee pot on. That day I ran out of coffee and learned more about herring.

I had visitors on 14 of my 21 days of solitude. I learned a lot, not just about herring and trees and whales, but about solitude and loneliness. In such a remote landscape, people are very aware of each other. The presence of a person – any person – matters. People are assumed to be interesting creatures, and important. In the exhausting bustle of Central London, that doesn't always seem to be the case. I have been lonely in the rush hour at Oxford Circus. I was never lonely in my days of solitude on the far coast of Canada.

Next year I've been asked to go back to that coast, to house-sit once again in that green, silent place. I'll go, of course. And I'll know, next time, to take more coffee.

Margaret Horsfield

C 1 Make notes on each of the visits to the homestead, in the order the visitors arrived – the writer's information is given as an example:

Names	Who they were	Means of transportation
a) Margaret	the writer	float plane
b)		
c)		
d)		
e)		
f)		

2 Who were the friends or acquaintances who didn't come to visit – and why do you think the writer was relieved?

a) .... b) .... c) ....

3 Who were Don, Bill and Liz?

4 Why is the friend described as *heroic* (¶ 14) and *alarmingly cheerful* (¶ 24)?

5 What were the most rewarding aspects of her stay?

D   Highlight the following words and phrases in the article (¶ shows the paragraph number):

foolproof ¶ 4   *unassailable* ¶ 6   *outraged* ¶ 6   *the bush* ¶ 6
unsolicited ¶ 8   *positively* ¶ 9   *blissfully* ¶ 13   *egged on* ¶ 15
abhors a vacuum ¶ 16   *came to nothing* ¶ 17   *flagged* ¶ 21
tentatively ¶ 25   *bustle* ¶ 29

Then match them to their OPPOSITES below:

calm   civilisation   confidently   continued   did happen   discouraged
invited   loves an empty space   not in the least   precarious   unhappily
unruffled   vulnerable

E   Work in groups. Discuss these questions with your partners:

- When have you been alone for a long time? Describe your own experience of solitude, loneliness or isolation.
- Have you ever lived in a small community or village? What was it like?

3.2   Reporting – 1

A   Match these reporting verbs with the verbs with similar meanings below:

*complain   confess   disclose   emphasise   forecast   infer   insinuate   order
promise   reiterate   remember   suppose   yell*

*admit   gather   grumble   guarantee   guess   imply   predict   recall   repeat
reveal   shout   stress   tell*

B   Decide which of the endings below fit comfortably with these beginnings:

They . . . accused   admitted   advised   agreed   allowed   apologised
asked   couldn't decide   discovered   dissuaded   didn't expect   explained
forbade   forgave   hoped   imagined   implied   didn't know   learned
mentioned   persuaded   pretended   promised   never realised   reckoned
refused   didn't remember   reminded   didn't reveal   didn't say   shouted
suggested   didn't tell   threatened   wanted   warned   wished

. . . **that we had done it.**	. . . **that we should do it.**
. . . **to do it.**	. . . **when to do it**
. . . **us to do it**	. . . **if we had done it.**
. . . **when we should do it.**	

Five verbs don't fit with any of the endings – which are they?

➡ Note down any combinations you're unsure of and discuss these as a class later. Write sentences using any words in A and B that you were unsure of.

C   Change each sentence into reported speech, using a suitable verb from the list in B above. Imagine that they were said to you by different people last week.

1 'I'll certainly give you a hand tomorrow evening.'
    She promised to help me the next evening.
 or   *She promised that she would help me the following evening.*
2 'I'm not going to help you, you'll have to do it by yourself.'
3 'There's no point in writing it all out in longhand – it'd just be a waste of time.'

4 'I don't think you ought to feel too confident about your driving test, you know.'

5 'Why don't you phone him up and see if he's free tonight?'

6 'Make sure that you don't start giggling during the interview.'

7 'If you type this letter out for me, I'll buy you a drink, OK? Thanks!'

8 'You're the one who borrowed my dictionary, aren't you?'

9 'If you don't move your car, I'll call the police.'

10 'All right, if you want me to, I don't mind accompanying you.'

11 'I'm most awfully sorry, but I seem to have broken your fountain pen.'

12 'I don't really mind about your rudeness – I know you were in a bit of a state.'

⚠ When reporting something which was said in another place or a long time ago, other parts of the sentence may have to be changed, apart from the tense:

'I'll do it **tomorrow**.' – She told me that she would do it **the next day**.

'I was **here yesterday**.' – He said that he had been **there the day before**.

'Do I have do it **now**?' – I wondered if I had to do it **then/right away**.

'Look at **this** document.' – She wanted me to look at **the** document.

3.3 Who's talking?   Listening

A ▭ You're going to hear five different people talking. In each case it's not immediately obvious what they're talking about or even who they're talking to, so you'll have to pick up 'clues' to get the answers. You'll need to hear the recording more than once to get all of the clues and answers.

FIRST SPEAKER

1 How does the speaker feel and where is she?

2 Who is she talking to?

3 She says: '. . . they're all over the place . . .' – who or what are 'they'?

4 She says: '. . . it's almost time to pick them up . . .' – who or what are 'they'?

5 She says: '. . . don't look like that . . .' – how is the listener looking?

6 Why is the listener silent?

SECOND SPEAKER

7 Who is the speaker talking to?

8 Why has he started talking to her?

9 Who are all the people he refers to?

10 Why is the listener silent?

THIRD SPEAKER

11 Who is the speaker talking to?

12 She says: '. . . I told her not to include me . . .' – who is 'she'?

13 She says: '. . . I got all the stuff . . .' – what 'stuff' is she referring to?

14 She says: '. . . I got the bus all the way out there . . .' – what place is 'there'?

15 She says: '. . . they called it off . . .' – what is 'it'?

FOURTH SPEAKER

16 Who is the speaker?

17 Who is he speaking to?

18 He says: '. . . it couldn't have happened . . .' – what is 'it'?

19 He ends by saying: '. . . nor is there any likelihood in the future of . . .' – complete his sentence.

⋙→

FIFTH SPEAKER

20 What kind of person is the speaker?
21 Who is she talking to?
22 She says: '. . . you can't put them back . . .' – what are 'they'?
23 Why is the listener silent?
24 She says: '. . . Look, I'm sorry, I didn't mean . . .' – complete her sentence.

B Work in pairs. What kind of person do you imagine each of the speakers to be? Make notes of some words you could use to describe them. Then describe each person to another pair and ask them to guess which speaker you're describing.

C Write five short reports, giving the **gist** of what each speaker said in two or three sentences each. Rely on your memory and try to convey the essence of what they said, not a word-for-word report. Use suitable verbs from 3.2.

➡ Compare your paragraphs with another student when you've done this.

3.4 Women's rights   Reading & summary writing

A Work in groups. Read this passage and discuss your reactions to it with your partners. Could it equally well be a description of the situation in your country?

> We live in a man-made society. Man devised and built the framework of government that controls our daily lives. Our rulers, representatives and arbitrators have almost all been men. Male judges and justices of the peace compiled our system of common law. Men drafted and interpreted our statute laws. Men constructed a 5
> bureaucracy to administer the law. Men cultivated the jungle of red tape which often threatens to engulf us. Men outnumber women in Parliament by twenty-four to one. Over 80 per cent of local councillors are men. Two in three magistrates are men. Juries seldom include more than a couple of token women. Men have an 10
> overwhelming majority in the legal profession, in the police force, in the upper ranks of the civil service, and even among trade-union officials.

B Read the continuation of the text and then answer the questions that follow.

> The authority which men exercise over women is a major source of oppression in our society – as fundamental as class oppression. The 15
> fact that most of the nation's wealth is concentrated in the hands of a few means that the vast majority of women and men are deprived of their rights. But women are doubly deprived. At no level of society do they have equal rights with men.
>   At the beginning of the nineteenth century, women had virtually 20
> no rights at all. They were the chattels of their fathers and husbands. They were bought and sold in marriage. They could not vote. They could not sign contracts. When married, they could not own property. They had no rights over their children and no control over

their own bodies. Their husbands could rape and beat them without
fear of legal reprisals. When they were not confined to the home,
they were forced by growing industrialisation to join the lowest levels
of the labour force.

Since then, progress towards equal rights for women has been very
slow indeed. There have even been times when the tide seemed to
turn against them. The first law against abortion was passed in 1803.
It imposed a sentence of life imprisonment for termination within the
first fourteen weeks of pregnancy. In 1832 the first law was passed
which forbade women to vote in elections. In 1877 the first Trades
Union Congress upheld the tradition that woman's place was in the
home whilst man's duty was to protect and provide for her.

Nevertheless, the latter half of the nineteenth century saw the
gradual acceptance of women into the unions and the informal
adoption of resolutions on the need for equal pay. Between 1831 and
1872 the major Factory Acts were passed, which checked the
exploitation of women workers by placing restrictions on hours and
conditions of labour and by limiting their employment at night. In
1882 married women won the right to own property.

Wartime inevitably advanced the cause of women's rights –
women became indispensable as workers outside the home, as they
had to keep the factories and government machinery running while
the men went out to fight. They were allowed into new areas of
employment and were conceded new degrees of responsibility. In
1918 they got the vote. Again, during the Second World War, state
nurseries were built on a considerable scale to enable women to go
out to work. When peace came, however, women were unable to
hold on to their gains. Men reclaimed their jobs, and women were
forced back into the home and confined to their traditionally low-
paid, menial and supportive forms of work. The government closed
down most of the nurseries. Theories about maternal deprivation
emerged – women who had been told it was patriotic to go out to
work during the war were now told that their children would suffer
if they did not stay at home. Little progress was made for the next
two decades.

(from *Women's Rights: A Practical Guide* by Anna Coote and Tess Gill)

C Highlight these words and phrases in the passage, so that you can see
them in context (the line numbers are given in brackets).
Then match them to the words and phrases below which have similar meanings.

oppression (line 15)   *deprived* (line 17)   *doubly* (line 18)   *chattels* (line 21)
legal reprisals (line 26)   *confined* (line 26)   *upheld* (line 35)
provide for (line 36)   *resolutions* (line 39)   *indispensable* (line 45)
conceded (line 48)   *gains* (line 52)   *maternal deprivation* (line 55)
emerged (line 56)

children suffering through their mother's absence   decisions   essential
given unwillingly   in two different ways   possessions   punishment
restricted   robbed   supported   sustain/support   the rights they had won
tyranny   were revealed

D The passage describes several changes in the law affecting women. Complete each of the sentences below to explain *in your own words* what the legal position of women was before each of the changes.

> Before 1803 . . .
> Before 1832 . . .
> Before the 1831–72 Factory Acts . . .
> Before 1882 . . .
> Before 1918 . . .

E How did the attitude of the British government towards women change during and then after the two world wars? Write a short paragraph, using your own words where possible.

F When you've finished writing your answers to D and E, show your work to some other students and compare your work with theirs.

Then look at Activity 41 and compare your work with the model versions there.

3.5 Discrimination

A Work in pairs. Read these cases through and discuss which of them are permissible in your country, as far as you know.

1 A barman in a hotel bar refuses to serve drinks to a group of women.
2 A barman in a private golf club refuses to serve a woman a drink.
3 Jack and Jill are pupils in a mixed school: Jack is not allowed to join the cookery class that Jill goes to, and has to do carpentry instead.
4 Girl pupils in a mixed school are discouraged from doing maths and science.
5 A textbook on 'Famous Writers' describes no women writers at all.
6 Job advertisements:

   a) **ENTHUSIASTIC GIRL REQUIRED AS PERSONAL ASSISTANT**
   b) **MEN REQUIRED FOR WORK IN MIDDLE EAST**
   c) **EXCELSIOR HOTEL REQUIRES CHAMBERMAIDS FOR SUMMER SEASON**
   d) **WAITRESS REQUIRED TO SERVE IN SMALL FAMILY CAFÉ**

7 A woman is refused a manual job on a building site on the grounds that she is not muscular enough. A man gets the job later.
8 Four equally qualified people apply for the same job. The two male applicants are interviewed, but the women are not interviewed and no reason is given.
9 A female factory worker, who normally works a 40-hour week, is required to work 10 hours overtime during one week.
10 A factory manageress is required to start work at 6.30 a.m.

B Listen to the recording and put a cross (✗) beside the cases that represent actions which are illegal according to English law, and a tick (✓) beside the ones which are permissible in England.

➡ Discuss your reactions to the broadcast with a partner. How different are the laws affecting discrimination in your country?

C These days it's often considered undesirable to use words like *foreman* and *fireman* if neutral, non-sexist terms like *supervisor* and *firefighter* are available. Choose neutral words to replace each of these words and phrases:

bachelor & spinster   **unmarried person**
businessman & businesswoman   cameraman & camerawoman
chairman & chairwoman   headmistress & headmaster
policeman & policewoman   salesgirl/saleswoman & salesman
spokesman & spokeswoman   stateswoman & statesman
stewardess/air hostess & steward   cleaning lady/cleaning woman

NOTE: People who serve food are still called *waiters* and *waitresses*, and we do thank our *host* and *hostess* after a party and refer to the *hero* and *heroine* of a story.

D Here are some more male-orientated expressions. Can you think of non-sexist synonyms for these?

1 The man in the street   **The general public**
2 We must find the best man for the job.   5 There is a shortage of manpower.
3 Prehistoric men lived in caves.   6 Pollution is a problem for mankind.
4 Nylon is a man-made substance.   7 Her son has now reached manhood.

E Work in groups. Discuss these questions:
- What kind of discrimination is there in your country against old people (ageism) and members of ethnic minorities (racism)?
- To what extent do you agree with the principles underlying the laws explained in the broadcast?
- Should boys and girls be educated separately?
- What is the attitude of people in your country to feminism?

3.6 · Punctuation   Writing skills

A Write down the names of these punctuation marks, as in the example.

? **question mark**   ;   :   !   ...   -   —   " "   *   ( )   [ ]   /   '

B Add suitable punctuation and capital letters in the gaps in this text. Decide where to break the text into two paragraphs. When you've finished, **but not until then**, look at page 40.

> the authority which men exercise over women is a major source of oppression in our society   as fundamental as class oppression   the fact that most of the nation's wealth is concentrated in the hands of a few means that the vast majority of women and men are deprived of their rights   but women are doubly deprived   at no level of society do they have equal rights with men   at the beginning of the nineteenth century   women had virtually no rights at all   they were the chattels of their fathers and husbands   they were bought and sold in marriage   they could not vote   they could not sign contracts

⟫➤

> when married   they could not own property   they had no rights over their children and no control over their own bodies   their husbands could rape and beat them without fear of legal reprisals   when they were not confined to the home   they were forced by growing industrialisation to join the lowest levels of the labour force

C Correct the errors in these sentences and then comment on the rules of punctuation that have been broken in each:

1 Sitting on the beach we watched the windsurfers, falling into the water.
2 The aspect of punctuation, which is most tricky, is the use of commas.
3 Could you tell me, when to use a semi-colon?
4 Feeling completely baffled we tried to solve the problem, with which we were faced.
5 Although I was feeling under the weather I went to work this morning.
6 There were surprisingly no punctuation mistakes in his work.

D This job reference was typed by someone with good spelling, but poor punctuation. Proof-read it, correct the mistakes, and divide it into paragraphs.

```
I have known, Jan Smith both professionally and personally, for
several years, since 1992 when she first joined my department
she has been a reliable, resourceful and conscientious member of
my staff with a thoroughly professional attitude to her work;
she has cheerfully taken on extra responsibilities and can be
relied on, to take over when other staff are absent or
unavailable! She particularly enjoys dealing with members of the
public: and has a knack of putting people at their ease? She is
adept at defusing delicate situations — with an appropriate word
and a smile? As her portfolio shows she is also a very, creative
and talented person and her work shows great promise during her
time with us her attendance has been excellent ... She is an
intelligent thoughtful, and imaginative person, I have no
hesitation in recommending her for the post!!
```

E Write two short paragraphs describing two people that the rest of the class know, but without naming them or revealing their sex. Use *this person* and *they* instead of *he* or *she*.

Then, working in groups, show your paragraphs around the class and see if the other students can guess who is described, whether the descriptions are accurate – and whether the punctuation is correct.

★★ Clear punctuation helps the reader to follow your meaning. Commas, in particular, are useful for showing the reader where one phrase or clause ends, and the next one begins.
Always proof-read your own written work before handing it in.

A   Work in pairs. Discuss the difference in emphasis between these sentences:

1 At no level of society do women have equal rights with men.
   Women do not have equal rights with men at any level of society.

2 It occurred to me later that I had made a big mistake.
   Not until then did it occur to me that I had made a big mistake.

3 Rarely have I felt so upset about being criticised.
   I have rarely felt so upset about being criticised.

4 So lonely did he feel that he went round to see his ex-wife for a chat.
   He felt so lonely that he went round to see his ex-wife for a chat.

5 Little did they know that the sheriff was about to draw his revolver.
   They didn't know that the sheriff was about to draw his revolver.

6 At the top of the hill stood a solitary pine tree.
   A solitary pine tree stood at the top of the hill.

7 Bang went the door. In came Fred. On went all the lights. Out ran the cat.
   The door went bang. Fred came in. All the lights went on. The cat ran out.

B   Fill the gaps in these sentences with suitable words:

1 Little .... that she would win the competition.
2 Not only .... the piano brilliantly but she .... too.
3 Never in my life .... so humiliated!
4 Nowhere in the entire town .... able to find a room for the night.
5 No sooner .... the bath than the phone ....
6 So difficult .... the work that ....
7 Under no circumstances .... the fire doors ....
8 Not until .... finished .... allowed to leave the room.
9 Only after .... the police able to catch the thieves.
10 Not once during her entire .... in trouble with the law.
11 Not only .... rather naive but he also .... very sensitive.
12 No sooner .... our picnic than ....

C   Rewrite the sentences more dramatically, using structures from above:

1 We went out in our best clothes. The rain came down.
2 The umbrellas went up. We went home, wet through.
3 A tall dark stranger was sitting beside her in the train.
4 A fat tabby cat lay under the table, washing itself obliviously.
5 The edge of the cliff gave way and she fell down.
6 There was a ferocious dog behind the wall, barking furiously.
7 The thieves drove off, with the police in hot pursuit.
8 Then I realised that I had made the biggest mistake of my life.

★★   Inversion should be used sparingly as over-use can sound ridiculous. It can usually be avoided in conversation altogether. It does tend to come up regularly in the Use of English paper of the exam, though.

A Work in pairs. Complete these sentences with suitable words.

1 He isn't naive, he's ....
2 She isn't brave, she's ....
3 He wasn't sorry, he was ....
4 Instead of slowing down, he ....
5 She wasn't guilty, she was ....
6 They didn't help me, they ....

7 Instead of spending her money, she ....
8 Instead of pulling the door open, he ....
9 Instead of reassuring me, she ....
10 He didn't get angry, he ....
11 *Bad* isn't an antonym of *awful*, it's a ....
12 Instead of slamming the door, he ....

B Decide which of these words form their opposites with *in-* or with *un-*:

acceptable **unacceptable** *accessible* **inaccessible** *advisable appropriate aware bearable clearly competent considerate consistent conspicuous conventional convincing decided decisive desirable dignified discreet distinct efficient eventful expected explicable faithful foreseen forgettable frequent grateful gratitude imaginative manageable predictable rewarding sincere sincerity sociable sophisticated stability stable sufficient tolerant trustworthy visible wanted welcome*

C Decide which of these words form their opposites with *dis-* or *im-*, *il-* or *ir-*:

advantage **disadvantage** *legal* **illegal** *agreeable approve arm connect contented entangle legible legitimate logical loyal mature organised patient personal possible rational regular relevant respectful responsible satisfied similar*

D 🖊 Highlight twelve of the more difficult negative words from B and C. Then work in pairs and test your partner, by starting similar sentences to the ones in A:

YOU: 'It wasn't accessible . . .'   *YOUR PARTNER:* '. . . it was inaccessible.'

E Here are some slightly trickier ones. Think of a suitable opposite for these:

clumsy complimentary fearless neat rare restless tactful talkative thoughtless trivial
beauty knowledge noise praise pride promotion solitude success

F These adjectives are used pejoratively to describe someone's disposition or behaviour. Choose suitable opposites from among the words below.

bad-tempered **good-natured** conceited deceitful fussy lazy malicious mean narrow-minded neurotic pretentious secretive solitary sullen touchy

cheerful easygoing frank generous good-natured gregarious hard-working imaginative kindhearted laid back liberal modest nonchalant open perceptive sociable talkative trustworthy truthful unassuming

A 🔲 Before answering the questions, listen to the two poems read aloud.

Not Waving but Waving but Drowning

NOBODY heard him, the dead man,
But still he lay moaning:
I was much further out than you thought
And not waving but drowning.

Poor chap, he always loved larking   5
And now he's dead
It must have been too cold for him his heart gave way,
They said.

Oh, no no no, it was too cold always
(Still the dead one lay moaning)   10
I was much too far out all my life
And not waving but drowning.
                                              Stevie Smith

Epitaph

I AM old.
Nothing interests me now.
Moreover,
I am not very intelligent,
And my ideas   5
Have travelled no further
Than my feet.
You ask me:
What is the greatest happiness on earth?
Two things: 10
Changing my mind
As I change a penny for a shilling;
And,
Listening to the sound
Of a young girl   15
Singing down the road
After she has asked me the way.
                                         Christopher Logue

B Answer these questions about the poems:

  1 In the first poem, how did the man die?
  2 Which are the words spoken by the 'dead man'?
  3 Which are the words spoken by his friends?
  4 What does 'larking' mean in line 5?
  5 What was 'too cold' in line 7? What was 'too cold' in line 9?

≫➔

6   In what ways was he 'too far out' in line 11 and 'drowning' in line 12?
7   In what ways was he 'not waving' in line 12?

8   In the second poem, what was different for the poet when he was young?
9   How influential have his ideas been?
10 Why does he say that 'changing my mind' makes him happy?
11 Why does he feel happy at the 'sound of a young girl'?
12 Why is the poem entitled *Epitaph*?

C   Work in groups. Discuss these questions with your partners:
● What did you think of the two poems?
● What adjectives could you use to describe the people?
● Which one impressed you, or moved you or depressed you more?
● What are the similarities between the two poems?
● Who do you know who is like the drowning man or the old man in the poems?
● What is the effect of expressing the ideas in verse, rather than in prose without any line breaks?
● Are you fond of poetry? Give your reasons.

3.10   It takes all sorts . . .   Composition

A   Work in pairs. Note down five adjectives or phrases to describe each of these people. Try to avoid the most obvious or simple words, like *nice*, *young*, *kind*, etc.

Join another pair and follow these guidelines to describe the people in the photos:

- First impression of the person
- Appearance: clothes age hair
- Their character and the way they might behave

B *Write descriptions of TWO people whom you know well but who are quite different from each other – they could be two friends or relatives, for example, or someone you admire and someone you detest.* (about 150 words each)

1 First of all, make notes on the following points:

```
Appearance: age, clothes, complexion, eyes, hair
Personality/character
Family background
Past achievements
Occupation
Interests and hobbies
Why you like/dislike him/her
Examples of typical behaviour
```

2 Rearrange the notes in a suitable order. Decide which points should be left out because they are less interesting or less relevant.

3 Discuss your notes with a partner. Make any necessary amendments before writing your descriptions. Refer back to the 'golden rules' you wrote down in 1.9.

4 Show your completed descriptions to a partner, and ask for comments.

"Hey, listen, I don't really look like the kind of person who feeds pigeons, do I?"

4 Communication

A   Work in pairs. How would you describe these people's expressions? Imagine
they're about to talk to you. What are they going to say – and how will you reply?

B   In these sentences THREE of the alternatives can be used to complete the
sentence correctly and TWO are incorrect. The first is done as an example.

1 She's going to .... about gestures and body language.
   say   speak ✓   talk ✓   tell   give a lecture ✓
2 If you keep on .... I won't be able to understand what you're saying.
   grumbling   mumbling   muttering   nagging   whispering
3 During a lecture I try to .... down the main points that are made.
   doodle   jot   note   scribble   sketch
4 I'm afraid I've only had time to .... the articles you recommended.
   glance at   scan   skim   study   interpret
5 When he told me about his misadventures I couldn't help ....
   chuckling   grinning   sniggering   shrugging   stammering
6 He looked at me with a .... on his face when I told him what I had done.
   frown   gasp   gulp   scowl   sneer
7 On seeing the body hanging from the apple tree she started to ....
   murmur   scream   shriek   squeak   yell
8 She went on to .... that I wasn't working hard enough.
   implicate   imply   infer   intimate   suggest
9 And her .... made me feel guilty even though I'd done nothing wrong.
   attitude   dialect   expression   idiom   tone
10 She used a(n) .... which I couldn't quite follow.
   expression   clause   phrase   idiom   speech

A Work in pairs. Ask your partner these questions:
- Where can you hear the 'best English' spoken?
- Where can you hear the 'best accent' of your language spoken?

B Read these statements through and then read the first part of the passage. Decide whether the statements are true (T) or false (F), according to the text.

1 The writer admits that he is amused by his own prejudices about language.
2 It is bad to use American expressions in British English.
3 The 'popular lady columnist' writes a column about language.
4 'I guess' is an expression imported from the USA into Britain.
5 The writer uses capital letters in 'the British Way of Life' because he considers it to be superior to other cultures.
6 The writer ridicules people who despise foreign languages.
7 The writer believes that German is an ugly language.

Anthony Burgess

A language is a system of communication used within a particular social group. Inevitably, the emotions created by group loyalty get in the way of objective judgements about language. When we think we are making such a judgement, we are often merely making a statement about our prejudices. It is highly instructive to examine these occasionally. I myself have very powerful prejudices about what I call Americanisms. I see red whenever I read a certain popular woman columnist in a certain popular daily paper. I wait with a kind of fascinated horror for her to use the locution 'I guess', as in 'I guess he really loves you after all' or 'I guess you'd better get yourself a new boy-friend'. I see in this form the essence of Americanism, a threat to the British Way of Life. But this is obviously nonsense, and I know it. I know that 'I guess' is at least as old as Chaucer, pure British English, something sent over in the *Mayflower*. But, like most of us, I do not really like submitting to reason; I much prefer blind prejudice. And so I stoutly condemn 'I guess' as an American importation and its use by a British writer as a betrayal of the traditions of my national group.

Such condemnation can seem virtuous, because patriotism – which means loyalty to the national group – is a noble word. While virtue burns in the mind, adrenalin courses round the body and makes us feel good. Reason never has this exhilarating chemical effect. And so patriotic euphoria justifies our contempt of foreign languages and makes us unwilling to learn them properly. Chinese is still regarded in the West as a huge joke – despite what T.S. Eliot calls its 'great intellectual dignity' – and radio comedians can even raise a snigger by speaking mock-Chinese. Russian is, of course, nothing more than a deep vodka-rich rumble bristling with 'vitch' and 'ski'. As for German – that is an ugly language, aggressively guttural. We rarely admit that it seems ugly because of two painful wars, that it is all a matter of association. Sometimes our automatic sneers at foreign languages are mitigated by pleasant memories – warm holidays abroad, trips to the opera. Italian can then seem beautiful, full of blue skies, *vino*, sexy tenors. Trippers to Paris, on the other hand, furtively visiting the *Folies Bergère*, project their own guilt on to the French language and see it as 'naughty', even 'immoral'.

C Now read the second part of the passage and answer these true/false questions.

1 Although a rural accent may sound attractive, it may also be looked down on.
2 The writer believes that a Cockney (London) accent doesn't sound as attractive as a BBC announcer's accent.
3 Languages shouldn't be described as either 'beautiful' or 'ugly'.
4 Prunes are associated with death in English poetry.
5 British people's accents may not just tell a listener what region they come from, but also the social class they belong to.
6 East Midland English was once a regional dialect used by the élite in England.
7 People who use Standard English may have more power than people who use regional dialects.

Within the national group, our prejudices tend to be very mixed and, because they operate mainly on an unconscious level, not easily recognisable. We can be natives of great cities and still find a town dialect less pleasant than a country one. And yet, hearing prettiness and quaintness in a Dorset or Devon twang, we can also despise it, because we associate it with rural stupidity or backwardness. The ugly tones of Manchester or Birmingham will, because of their great civic associations, be at the same time somehow admirable. The whole business of ugliness and beauty works strangely. A BBC announcer says 'pay day'; a Cockney says 'pie die'. The former is thought to be beautiful, the latter ugly, and yet the announcer can use the Cockney sounds in a statement like 'Eat that pie and you will die' without anybody's face turning sour. In fact, terms like 'ugly' and 'beautiful' cannot really apply to languages at all. Poets can make beautiful patterns out of words, but there are no standards we can use to formulate aesthetic judgements on the words themselves. We all have our pet hates and loves among words, but these always have to be referred to associations. A person who dislikes beetroot as a vegetable is not likely to love 'beetroot' as a word. A poet who, in childhood, had a panful of hot stewed prunes spilled on him is, if he is a rather stupid poet, quite capable of writing 'And death, terrible as prunes'. We have to watch associations carefully, remembering that language is a public, not a private, medium, and that questions of word-hatred and word-love had best be tackled very coldly and rationally.

We are normally quick to observe regional variations in the use of the national language, but we feel less strongly about these than we do about class divisions in speech. If we speak with a Lancashire accent*, we will often be good-humoured and only slightly derisive when we hear the accent of Wolverhampton or Tyneside. Sometimes we will even express a strong admiration of alien forms of English – the speech of the Scottish Highlands, for instance, or Canadian as opposed to American. But we feel very differently about English speech when it seems to be a badge or banner of class. The dialect known variously as the Queen's English or BBC English or Standard English was, originally, a pure regional form – so-called East Midland English, with no claim to any special intrinsic merit. But it was spoken in an area that was, and still is, socially and economically pre-eminent – the area which contains London, Oxford and Cambridge. Thus it gained a special glamour as the language of the Court and the language of learning. It has ever since – often falsely – been associated with wealth, position, and education – the supra-regional dialect of the masters, while the regional dialects remain the property of the men. In certain industrial areas it can still excite resentment, despite the fact that it no longer necessarily goes along with power or privilege.

4

* An *accent* is a set of sounds peculiar to a region, as opposed to a *dialect*, which covers, in addition to peculiarities of sound, peculiarities of grammar and vocabulary.

(from *Language Made Plain* by Anthony Burgess)

D   Highlight these words in the passage and match them with the words with similar meanings below:

¶ 1 *objective   prejudice   instructive*
¶ 2 *exhilarating   euphoria   mitigated*
¶ 3 *associations   formulate   aesthetic   pet*
¶ 4 *derisive   badge   intrinsic   the men   excite*

arouse   artistic   bias   connotations   contemptuous   devise   emblem favourite   happiness   impartial   inherent   moderated   revealing stimulating   workers

E   Work in groups and discuss your reactions to the passage:
- Compare the author's comments on British attitudes with the attitudes of people in your own country to other languages. Do they share similar prejudices?
- Which of his comments on British attitudes to accents and dialects are comparable to the attitudes of people in your own country?

A   Work in pairs. Discuss the difference in meaning between these sentences.
Then decide how each one might continue, as in the example.

Example: They went on running . . . **even though they were tired.**
             They went on to run . . . **five more miles**.

1   We stopped to take photos, but . . .   We stopped taking photos, but . . .
2   Did you remember to send the fax or . . . ?   Do you remember sending the fax or . . . ?
3   I can't help you to feel better, but . . .   I can't help feeling better, but . . .
4   I'm not used to using a typewriter, but . . . I used to use a typewriter, but . . .
5   I heard her scream, but . . .   I heard her screaming, but . . .

B   Match up the verbs and phrases below to make suitable collocations.

to answer	to a letter
to call	a letter / the phone
to contact	someone a letter
to drop	someone a line
to get	someone on the phone
to give	someone by phone / by post
to keep	someone a ring
to reply	someone a story
to tell	through to someone on the phone
to write	in touch with someone

Now use the collocations above to complete each of these sentences. Add a
suitable preposition if necessary. In some cases more than one version is
possible.

1   I'm sorry ...**not to have kept**... in touch with you.
    or ...**for not having kept**...   *or* ...**that I didn't keep**...
2   Is there any point .... by post?
3   I'm not looking forward .... all these letters.
4   Don't forget .... a thank-you letter for your birthday present.
5   Have you heard her .... about the penguin and the polar bear?
6   I strongly advise you .... his letter by return of post.
7   He never writes letters because he's so used .... on the phone.
8   Her number was engaged all day but I finally succeeded .... in the evening.
9   Don't forget .... a line to let me know how you are.
10 It may be worth .... a ring if you ever need any advice.

C   Complete each sentence with your own ideas, using *-ing* or *to* ___ :

1   To get from the airport to the city centre I don't recommend ....
2   I've never been to America but I hope ....
3   After a heavy meal I can't face ....
4   The night before an important exam it's unwise to risk ....
5   After struggling to follow the first paragraph I gave up ....
6   Some people enjoy .... to Beethoven but I prefer ....
7   The first chapter was so exciting that I kept on ....

C Discuss these questions in groups:

- If you owned the Interpreter, when might you use it?
- Have you ever used a phrasebook when visiting a foreign country? What was your experience?
- Do you always assume people in another country will speak English or do you make an effort to learn some of the language before going there?
- What are the ten most useful phrases you'd try to learn if you were visiting another country for the very first time?
- Which do you use more often: an English-to-English dictionary or a bilingual one? Give your reasons.

D Work in groups of three. In this dictionary comparison activity Student A should look at Activity 25, student B at 30 and C at 39.

Each Activity contains definitions of some of these words. Together you should pool your information and discuss which dictionary seems most helpful and clear.

You shouldn't read your entries out loud (that would take a very long time) but you may wish to read out *brief* quotations.

irony sarcasm collocation
cliché platitude proverb slogan jargon

➡ Now compare the dictionary entries in all three Activities. Suppose you didn't know any of the words above: which of the entries would be most helpful?

4.7 Paragraphs – 1 Writing skills

A Paragraphs in books tend to be longer than in an essay, a report or an article in the press. Look again at the reading passages you've studied so far in this book. How many paragraphs are there in these passages?

    1.6 *Long's winding road to the top*
    2.1 *Eight feet in the Andes*
    3.4 *Women's rights*
    4.2 *Attitudes to language*

B There are no hard-and-fast rules for paragraphs, but here are some guidelines.

Highlight any points that are new to you, or which you want to remember.

- A new paragraph signifies a new theme, or a change of direction.
- Paragraphs help the reader to follow your thought processes.
- Short paragraphs are easier to read than long ones.
- When there is dialogue, each speaker usually requires a new paragraph.
- A new paragraph gives prominence to the first sentence, which sets the tone for the rest of the paragraph. A strong opening sentence for each paragraph keeps the reader's attention.
- The last sentence of a paragraph is given prominence: it is often the pay-off line before a new theme begins.

➤➤➤

C Look at *The great escape*, which you read in 3.1. Go through the first twenty or so paragraphs of the article, noting the reasons why the writer chose to start and end each paragraph at the place she does. The first six are done as examples:

First sentence plunges the reader into the story:
¶ 1 Looking around . . . right in front of the cabin.
Still the same event as first paragraph, but new speaker:
¶ 2 "Hi, I'm Lise," she shouted . . . here on your own!"
End of what Lise said. Back to narrator's feelings:
¶ 3 I'd stopped thinking that days ago.
Flashback to start of chain of events:
¶ 4 "I want to be alone," I had declared . . . like a bear in the middle of nowhere.
More precise description – new paragraph gives prominence to first sentence:
¶ 5 Everything seemed perfect. A friend . . . right down to the water's edge.
New paragraph gives prominence to next sentence:
¶ 6 I knew I could be entirely alone here. No roads . . . "No one wants to be that alone."

D This is the end of the same article, printed without paragraphs. Decide where to begin each new paragraph. Don't refer back to the passage until you've finished.

A few days later, a strange boat anchored in front of the house and three men made their way to shore. They were from the Department of Fisheries, monitoring the herring run. "Liz told us you were out here on your own. How's it going? Aren't you lonely?" "Liz?" I thought, and, "Lonely?" as I put the coffee pot on. That day I ran out of coffee and learned more about herring. I had visitors on 14 of my 21 days of solitude. I learned a lot, not just about herring and trees and whales, but about solitude and loneliness. In such a remote landscape, people are very aware of each other. The presence of a person – any person – matters. People are assumed to be interesting creatures, and important. In the exhausting bustle of Central London, that doesn't always seem to be the case. I have been lonely in the rush hour at Oxford Circus. I was never lonely in my days of solitude on the far coast of Canada. Next year I've been asked to go back to that coast, to house-sit once again in that green, silent place. I'll go, of course. And I'll know, next time, to take more coffee.

★★ A 350–word essay should contain at least three paragraphs, probably more. When planning an essay, decide where each new paragraph will begin. Note down a strong opening sentence for each paragraph before you start writing.
Try to put these ideas into practice in your next composition in 4.9.

"Dear Diary, how are you? I am fine. Cold enough for you? Isn't this snow something? I mean have you ever seen anything like it?..."

A What you should do is study these examples before doing the exercises:

What annoys me is intolerance.   Intolerance is **what** annoys me.
What I need is a friend to lend a helping hand.
All I need is a friend to lend a helping hand.

It doesn't really matter **whether** he gets here in time or not.
Whether or not he gets here in time doesn't really matter.

Whatever she does seems to be successful.
Wherever she goes she makes friends easily.
Whoever she meets, they take a liking to her.

B Work in pairs. Use your own ideas to complete each sentence. Then exchange
sentences with another pair. Rewrite their sentences using different structures.

1 What I hate is ...*people being rude to me.*
2 One thing I like is ....
3 What I feel like doing................
4 There's nothing I enjoy more than ....
5 Something that often surprises me is ....

6 All I want is ....
7 What we need now ....
8 I just don't want ....
9 What I want to do right now is ....

C Match the sentences that mean the same as each other.

1 Say what you like. —————— Speak to whoever you want.
   Talk to anyone you want to. ———— Say whatever you want to.

2 Whatever you do, don't tell everyone.   Tell anyone anything you like.
   Make sure you don't tell everyone.   Tell anyone whatever you want.

3 Whoever did you give it to?   Who in the world did you give it to?
   To whom did you give it?   Who did you give it to?

4 Why ever don't you phone her?   Why do you never phone her?
   Why don't you ever phone her?   Why on earth don't you phone her?

5 Whenever I mention it he takes offence.   When I mention it he loses his temper.
   He reacts badly every time I mention it.   Each time I mention it he gets angry.

D Rewrite these sentences without changing the meaning:

1 He takes a phrasebook with him everywhere.   Wherever ....
2 It doesn't matter when you arrive.   You can ....
3 I only stuck out my tongue at her.   All ....
4 You did something that was very rude.   What ....
5 She just needs someone to tell her troubles to. All ....
6 You can put it anywhere you like.   I don't mind ....
7 You can write or phone – as you like.   Whether ....
8 I don't know what time you'll arrive, but get in touch. Whenever ....
9 He made a very impressive speech.   What ....
10 I was astonished by her confidence.   What ....

A 🔲 You'll hear an American, an Irishwoman and an Englishman discussing accents. Listen to the recording and decide whether the following statements are true (T) or false (F), according to what the speakers say:

1 There is more uniformity of accents in the USA than in Britain.
2 American people have a good ear for different accents.
3 Americans seem to think that British and Australian people speak alike.
4 British people can distinguish various American accents.
5 There are more regional accents in the USA and Canada than in Britain.
6 Hardly any people in Britain speak with a standard RP accent.
7 Americans often dislike hearing a British accent.
8 People in some regions of Britain are suspicious of someone with an RP accent.
9 Pupils in schools in England were once encouraged to lose their accents.
10 In the USA, Southerners used to make fun of someone with a Northern accent.
11 According to the Englishman, a regional accent won't prevent you getting a job.
12 Mike and Jackie both agree with the Englishman's views on this.

B Work in pairs and discuss these questions about your language.

1 How many people speak your language? Which countries do they live in?

2 How many different languages are spoken in your country? Is there a single 'official language'?

3 What language (and which dialect or variety of it) is used in schools? Do the children in your area speak the same language or dialect when they are at home?

4 Do you use a different variety of your language (or a different dialect) when talking with friends or family to the one which you use with strangers or people from other parts of the country? Is there a 'high' and 'low' variety of your language? What situations are the different varieties used in? What are some of the differences in vocabulary and grammar? Can you give any interesting examples?

5 What are the main regional accents and dialects that most people in your country can recognise? Do people in the capital regard the speakers of any of these as 'funny' or 'uneducated'?

6 Do the people in the regions where different languages or dialects are used feel they have less power than the people in the capital? Do they have TV and radio programmes in their own language or dialect?

7 Do middle-class people talk differently to working-class people? Are there any regional accents which are considered to be less 'educated' or less socially acceptable than others? What is claimed to be the 'best accent' in your language?

8 Are there any other points not covered by the questions above that you think would help to give a clearer picture about your country and language?

➡ Make notes on your answers to the questions which are most relevant to your language and the questions which were thought-provoking.

C Rearrange the notes you've made (perhaps using arrows, lines or different colours) to make the sequence of ideas and information as coherent as possible, in preparation for writing a composition on this topic:

> *'Write a short report about the different languages, dialects and accents in your country.'* (about 350 words)

D Work in pairs or small groups. Explain to your partner(s) what you're going to write. Add any further points to your notes that now seem necessary.

E Remembering the work on paragraphs that you did in 4.7, decide which points each paragraph of your report will contain.

Write down the first sentence of each paragraph. Compare your sentences with a partner's.

F Write your report. Include a sketch map or diagram if you wish.

Before handing your written report to your teacher, show it to the same student(s) you talked to earlier and ask for comments.

"Funny how you soon forget his regional accent."

A   Which of the following would you MAKE and which would you DO?

> an agreement with someone   an appointment with someone
> an arrangement   an attempt   your best   business with someone
> certain about something   a comment about something   your duty
> an excuse   a good impression   someone a favour   friends with someone
> harm to someone   a lot of money   love   a mistake   a profit or a loss
> progress   a reservation   sure   someone a good turn   the washing-up
> wrong or right   your own thing

B   Find synonyms for the phrases in italics, or explain their meaning. Use a
dictionary if necessary.

1   I've read the report through twice, but I can't *make out* what he's getting at.
2   Someone was coming down the hill, but I couldn't *make out* who it was.
3   It's so unfair, he's always *doing me down* in front of my friends.
4   Adrift alone in the ocean, they knew that they were *done for*.
5   I don't see what this *has to do with* you!
6   It was a three-seater sofa, but they refused to *make room* for me.
7   None of it is true – I *made* it all *up*!
8   I'm sorry you had to do all the work for me, I'll *make* it *up* to you, I promise.
9   They were finding it increasingly difficult to *make both ends meet*.
10   How can I ever *make amends* for what I've done?
11   It's not very important really, you're *making a mountain out of a molehill*.
12   Shh, don't *make a scene* – we can talk about it when we get home.
13   It's a terrible portrait, it really doesn't *do justice to him*.
14   It's a shame we were held up, but now we can *make up for lost time*.
15   I can't put a letter in with the parcel now that it's been *done up*.

C   Fill the gaps in these sentences with suitable phrases from the list below. You
may need to change the form of the verbs.

1   I left my bike outside the shop and someone has .... it!
2   You've .... this room .... since my last visit. What pretty wallpaper!
3   We went out for a meal together to .... our disappointment.
4   I can't .... coffee in the morning – it helps to wake me up.
5   We collected £18 for her leaving present, so I .... it .... to a round
    £20.
6   Your shoes need ...., otherwise you'll trip over the laces.
7   Do you agree that all examinations should be ....?
8   You're heading in the wrong direction if you're .... the station.
9   If too many new staff are taken on, some of us older ones will be .... our
    jobs.
10   He threw everything on the floor, and then .... without another word.

> *do away with   do out of   do up   do up   do without*
> *make for   make off   make off with   make up   make up for*

5 Food and drink

A   Work in groups.

1   Think of the area you live in, or the place you're studying in. Decide what is the best place locally to get the following things, and give your reasons:
   fresh fruit   bread and cakes   a quick snack   a good inexpensive meal
   a good cup of coffee   a slap-up meal   a refreshing drink   a sandwich

2   Find out your partners' reactions to these photos:

B   Work in pairs. Write down three examples of each of these types of food. Try to think of some unusual examples, using a dictionary if necessary.

Appetisers (hors d'oeuvre)   **melon   avocado   prawn cocktail   paté** *Fish and shellfish* *Poultry* *Game* *Herbs* *Spices* *Dairy products* *Nuts* *Desserts* *Cakes and buns*

C   Work in pairs and discuss these questions:
- Which are your favourite foods in each category above?
- Imagine it's your birthday – write a menu, including all your favourite foods.
- What are the specialities of your region or country? What are the ingredients required and how are they made?

A Work in groups and discuss these questions:

Susan and Stephen Hill

- What do you think are the pros and cons of running a restaurant? Would *you* like to run a restaurant? Give your reasons.
- If you were going to run a restaurant or café near where you live, what kind of food would you serve? What kind of atmosphere would you try to create?
- From a restaurateur's point of view, what are the attributes of an ideal customer?
- From a customer's point of view, what are the qualities of a good restaurant?

B [cassette] You'll hear an interview with two restaurateurs. Listen to the recording and answer these questions.

1 Why did Stephen and Susan Hill decide to specialise in pancakes?
2 Which of these pictures best illustrates Stephen's dessert speciality?

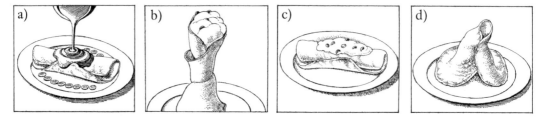

3 Tick the following attributes of an ideal customer which Stephen mentions. According to him, the ideal customer is someone who...

appreciates fresh ingredients	doesn't complain
doesn't mind spending money	eats out regularly
enjoys eating out	gives generous tips
is very knowledgeable about cooking	takes an interest in food
communicates their wishes to the restaurant staff	

4 What is important when running a small restaurant?
5 Which of these tasks are done by Susan and which are done by Stephen?

cooking pancakes	making desserts
making ice cream	making soups
preparing pancake fillings	preparing salad dressings
taking orders	welcoming customers

6 What do they enjoy about running a restaurant?

C Work in groups. Ask your partners these questions:

In an average week...
- How often do you eat lunch out? How often do you eat dinner out?
- How many meals do you prepare or help to prepare?
- How many times do you lay the table and do the washing-up?
- How often do you go shopping for food items?

➡ How do your habits compare with those of a 'typical person' from your country?

A Read the article and then answer the questions below.

Feel free to protest

HOBSON'S CHOICE has taken on an added meaning at Berni Restaurants, the chain of more than 230 steak houses owned by Grand Metropolitan.

Nowadays if you don't like what is provided in your meal you don't pay. And that covers the service too.

Slow waitresses, soup-spilling waitresses, surly waitresses, and "please make up your mind" waitresses are out.

Under what Berni call a customer service guarantee, diners who complain about either the meal or the service have their bill torn up. One of the intentions is to get round the traditional British habit of not complaining, but not going back either.

A poll conducted by Berni found that 60 per cent of dissatisfied customers said they wouldn't go back to an offending restaurant. To break down this reserve, the scheme was initiated by a group of Berni managers and tried out in the north of England, where results were sufficiently encouraging to spread the scheme to the rest of Britain.

Armed with this knowledge and thinking that it didn't seem too difficult to get a free meal, I descended on the Berni Inn at Wimbledon, where my waitress was Martha, who failed to provide me with any opportunity to use the repertoire of "Waiter, there's a fly in my soup" jokes I had rehearsed beforehand. The food proved a match for the service. Simon Smith, the manager, told me he had been pleasantly pleased at a lack of unscrupulous diners trying to take advantage of the scheme. Complaints had generally been justified.

In fact some people who did complain had to be persuaded to leave the bill to him. Many had not even realised the scheme was operating.

"We're finding that those who complained and had their bill torn up are returning and bringing others with them. In the first five weeks we lost £1,000 in unpaid bills, but we're getting a lot of favourable publicity by word of mouth.

"I am sure we'll keep more customers longer this way."

James Allen

Decide whether these statements are true (T) or false (F), according to the passage.

1 The scheme was the brainchild of Berni's marketing department.
2 The scheme was introduced because Berni were losing a lot of customers.
3 The scheme was introduced because British people don't like to complain.
4 Berni wanted customers to complain if they were dissatisfied.
5 A lot of customers who complained didn't know their bill would be torn up.
6 The quality of the food at Wimbledon was even better than the service.
7 The manager in Wimbledon approved of the scheme.
8 The scheme had to be abandoned because it was being abused.

B Work in groups and discuss these questions:
- Could such a scheme operate in restaurants in your country?
- Have you ever complained (or been with someone who complained) in a restaurant? What happened?
- What other situations have you actually been in where you made a complaint?
- What are the qualities of a good restaurant? Describe a good restaurant you have been to and a bad restaurant you remember going to.

A   Work in pairs. Discuss the differences in emphasis between these sentences – in some cases there is no difference:

1   I'm afraid all the cakes have been eaten.   I'm afraid I've eaten all the cakes.

2   Arsenal beat Chelsea in the final.   Spurs were beaten in the semi-finals.
    Manchester United were beaten in the quarter-finals by Southampton.

3   He thinks people are plotting against him.   He thinks he's being plotted against.

4   The dough was rolled out and then cut into teddybear shapes.
    We rolled out the dough and then we cut it into teddybear shapes.

5   She doesn't think that she is being paid enough.
    She doesn't think that her employer is paying her enough.

6   There was nothing to do.   There was nothing to be done.

7   My wallet has been stolen!   Someone has stolen my wallet!
    That man stole my wallet!   I've had my wallet stolen!

B   Highlight all the passive verbs and passive participles in the reading text in 5.3. Why has the passive, rather than the active, been used in each case?

If each example is rewritten using an active verb, what difference does this make to the tone, style or emphasis?

C   Rewrite these sentences using the passive: the subject can be omitted where it seems irrelevant or misleading. Your rewritten sentences should be compared with a partner's.

1   Someone told us that the bill would include service.   *understand*
    We were given to understand that service would be included.
2   A friend told me that the college has awarded you a scholarship.
3   The crash badly damaged both cars but it didn't cause the injury of anyone.
4   After the lifeguard had rescued the bather, an ambulance took him to hospital.
5   Someone has seen an escaped prisoner, whom the police believe to be dangerous.
6   After the surgeon had operated on him, she told him to stay in bed for a week.
7   Shops all over the world sell Tabasco sauce.
8   Nottingham Forest held Liverpool to a draw.
9   Thousands of demonstrators may crowd into the square tonight.
10 We expected the plane to land at noon, but something has delayed it.   *schedule*
11 The rain brought about the cancellation of the tennis match.   *rain off*
12 They had masses of requests for free samples of the new product.   *flood*

➡ For more advanced uses of the passive, see 12.7.

A   Work in groups. Before you listen to the recording, read this paragraph and discuss its implications:

> Today the Earth's finite resources are unequally shared by 5,300 million people, increasing by three people each second. The UN's lowest estimate of world population in the year 2100 is 7,500 million. This figure is unrealistically optimistic; the true figure is more likely to be between 11,000 and 14,200 million. The vast majority of these people would live in developing countries, facing crippling shortages of land, food, and water. There would also be a far greater number of older people for the working population to support.

(from *Save the Earth* by Jonathon Porritt)

B   You'll hear part of an interview with Fiona Bristow, who talks about the effects of food shortages on people in developing countries. Here are some key points from the interview. Fill the gaps with suitable phrases or words.

Fiona Bristow

1   If you are undernourished you are more .... to diseases and find it harder to .... from them than people in the West.
2   When sharing out food, women in developing countries put themselves at the .... of the .... within the family, and the ' .... ' isn't large enough to feed the whole family.
3   Education makes a woman more .... She learns how to improve the .... of her children's .... She knows how to demand .... and she has more ....
4   According to the speaker, the key to improving the quality of life in the Third World lies in an .... approach, by providing ...., ..., ..., ... and ....

C   Work in groups and discuss these questions:
- To what extent do you share the speaker's views?
- What further problems were not mentioned in the interview?
- How much help for developing countries should be provided by government agencies rather than charities like Oxfam, Population Concern, Caritas, etc.?
- What are the responsibilities of people in developed countries to the Third World?

A   Work in pairs. Decide which of the alternatives fit into the gaps – in most cases more than one alternative can be used.

1   It's important that she .... told the truth.
     is   be   should be   will be   is going to be
2   I'm sorry that you .... upset about this.
     feel   do feel   will feel   should feel   ought to feel
3   This is a big problem – what do you think I ....?
     do   shall do   should do   ought to do   can do
4   We were all sitting watching TV when who .... but Billy.
     arrived   could arrive   would arrive   should arrive   did arrive
5   I insist that I .... my money back after such a terrible meal.
     am given   be given   was given   am being given   should be given

B   Study these examples before doing C below.

Reactions   When expressing reactions, using *should* is more formal, and sounds rather less direct than a present tense:

*I'm very sorry that you **should feel** upset.*
*It's a pity that she **should not be** on speaking terms with him.*
*It has always worried me that he **should feel** lonely.*
*It's disgraceful that we **should have to pay** extra for service.*
*It's interesting that they **should want** to visit us.*

Suggestions and recommendations   When making suggestions and recommendations, using *should* tends to sound less bossy and more formal than a present tense. *Be* + past participle can also be used with the same effect.

*I recommend that he **should take up** cooking as a career.*
*I suggest that she **should be asked** to make a speech on our behalf.*
*I propose that she **be given** everything she needs.*

C   Complete these sentences, using *should* or *be* + past participle:

1   It is very important that you .... before you start writing.
2   It is absolutely essential that he .... his work on time.
3   I insist that the washing-up .... before you go to bed.
4   It's wrong that the government .... tax on petrol.
5   It's a nuisance that we .... so much homework at the weekend.
6   It's necessary that ....
7   I'm disappointed that ....
8   It's awfully sad that ....
9   It bothers me that ....
10 I propose that Jill .... president of the society.

➡   See 13.7 for the use of *should* in conditional sentences like these:
     If you should meet Tim, give him my regards.
     Should the doors be locked, the key may be obtained from the caretaker.

A Read this piece and then look at the notes that follow.

LUTHERAN PIE

ONE FALL DAY I went to the kitchen and got out a bag of flour and made the first apple pie I made in my life. Made it from scratch, including mixing butter with flour to make a great crust, and loaded it with sour apples and brown sugar and nutmeg, baked it to a T, and of course it was delicious. My guests for dinner were a couple who seemed to be coasting from a bad fight. We ate the pie and sat in a daze of pleasure afterward, during which the wife said that it reminded her of pies she ate when she was a little Norwegian Lutheran girl in Normania Township on the western Minnesota prairie. "We had love, good health, and faith in God, all things that money can't buy," she said, glancing at her husband, apropos of something. "This time of year, we were always broke, but somehow we made it. We'd fix equipment, feed the animals, and sleep. My mother made apple pie. One year she made thirty in one day. My dad was sick and thirty of our neighbors came in with fourteen combines and harvested his three hundred acres of soybeans. It took them half a day to do it, at a time when they were racing to get their own soybeans in, but out there, if your car broke down in the country, the next car by would stop. My mother baked thirty pies and gave one to everybody who helped us." Naturally I was pleased – until it occurred to me that I would never bake another one as good, having hit a home run on my first try. (They are still married by the way.)

Garrison Keillor

B Imagine that these notes were made by the writer *before he wrote the passage*. Decide which style of notes might be most helpful for *you* if you were going to write a similar composition.

 List the advantages and disadvantages of each note-making technique and compare your list with a partner.

1 FIRST APPLE PIE
Ingredients: flour & butter
   sour apples & brown sugar & nutmeg
– Turned out perfect!
Guests: couple who had recently had a row
Wife reminded of:
– pies eaten when a girl in Minnesota
– times of hard work and no money
– helpful and friendly people

Illness of father
– neighbours came to harvest beans
– mother made 30 pies
Conclusion
Realised next pie would not be as good
as the first

2 Apple pie: flour, butter, sour apples, brown sugar, nutmeg
Guests: couple (recent row)
Wife: childhood in Minnesota – hard work, no money, helpful people
Father ill: neighbours helped with harvest – mother 30 pies
Next pie not so good

3

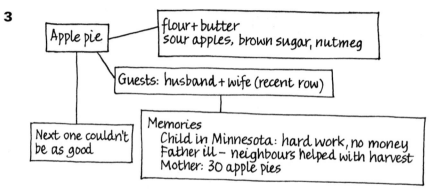

```
Apple pie ─── flour + butter
               sour apples, brown sugar, nutmeg

         └── Guests: husband + wife (recent row)

Next one couldn't     Memories
be as good            Child in Minnesota: hard work, no money
                      Father ill – neighbours helped with harvest
                      Mother: 30 apple pies
```

C Try out a note-making technique you haven't used before with this passage, as if you were going to write your own composition on the same subject. Compare your completed notes with a partner's.

Hot time in the old town tonight

TABASCO, the fiery pepper sauce without which a Bloody Mary would be just another yucky tomato juice, and many casseroles would be
5 bland stews, is made on a single family-owned plantation close to the bayou swamplands of southern Louisiana.

The sultry climate is ideal for
10 growing red peppers, and the Avery Island plantation, complete with a colonial-style mansion straight out of *Gone With the Wind*, rests on top of a huge salt dome, which
15 provides the second key ingredient.

A mash of ripe peppers is mixed with salt in white oak barrels, which are sealed with perforated wooden lids beneath salt caps and left for three
20 years while the mixture ferments.

There is no cooking involved, but during the hottest weather gases and juices escape through the salt layer.

The company claims that each barrel
25 is inspected by a member of the McIlhenny family when it is opened.

But while they check for odour, texture and colour, no actual tasting is done – nobody could undertake that job and last longer than a 30 week.

The seeds and skins are strained off, and the residue mixed with vinegar in 2,000 gallon vats, then stirred for four weeks prior to 35 bottling.

The eye-stinging atmosphere in the low-roofed shed containing row upon row of vats of pepper sauce is every bit as unpleasant as you would 40 imagine.

The family has been in the business for over 150 years and sells Tabasco in over 100 countries. There are many competing brands made nearby, but 45 none is sold widely outside Louisiana, nor possesses anything like the same international reputation, which the McIlhennys put down to the care they take aging the raw mash of peppers 50 and salt.

Tom Rowland

[Tabasco is a registered trade mark of the McIlhenny Company.]

D What dish have you cooked that you were most pleased with or proud of? Tell your partner about it.

Make notes on the process, trying out a different note-making technique. Then write one or two paragraphs explaining what you did and why you were so pleased or proud. Show both your paragraphs *and* your notes to a partner.

A Work in pairs. Before you listen to the recording, look at these diagrams, which show the process of margarine manufacture. As you can see, they are in the wrong order. Using a pencil, number the steps in what looks like the right order. The first and last steps are numbered already.

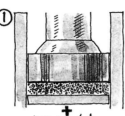
① Heat and crush plant seeds

Add lecithin & monoglyceride

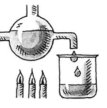
Deodorise by heating to melting point

React oil with hydrogen to produce hardened oils

Add skimmed milk, water & salt

Add fuller's earth to bleach oil

Add caustic soda to remove any waste as soap

Add artificial flavour, colour & vitamins

RESULT: still contaminated with gums and resins

RESULT: refined oil

RESULT: unemulsified ingredients

RESULT: blended oils

Mix with fish & animal oils

Neutralise, bleach and filter to remove waste products

⑮ Extrude into plastic tub ... and put a lid on it

B 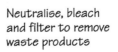 Listen to the recording and number the diagrams to show the correct sequence of the manufacturing process.

⟫➔

C  Work in groups of four. Students A and B look at Activity 5, C and D look at 23. Each pair has different information about the processes of brewing beer and making wine.

1 Study the information and make notes on the main points of the process, or highlight the important information.
2 Student A should join C and B should join D to form new pairs. Tell your new partner what you found out. Discuss what the two processes have in common, and how they are different.

D **EITHER**:

Write an article on wine or beer production (see Activities 5 and 23) in a similar style to the one in 5.9 C. Do this by making your own notes, and without quoting verbatim from the Activity. (about 300 words)

OR:

Make notes on another culinary or non-culinary process, and write a description of the process. You may need to do some research on this.

"Make up your minds! It's only food."

6 Travel and transport

A   Work in groups. Discuss these questions with your partners:
- Which five countries in the world would you like to visit one day?
- And which five countries have you no desire to visit ever?
  – Give your reasons for your choices.

B   Fill the gaps in this description of the map, using the words on the right:

Seatown is a small fishing ......**port**...... lying at the centre of a sheltered
........................, which forms a natural .... The town lies in the south-
east corner of a fertile .... separated from the north coast by a
.... On the north coast, to the east of the ...., is a freshwater
.... enclosed by a .... and surrounded by .... To the
east is an impressive .... with high .... where seabirds nest.
The River Trent, at whose .... Seatown lies, is fed by many small
.... which rise in the hills to the north, but its .... is over 100
miles to the west. To the south of the town across the river the ....
is rocky and it is possible to walk across to an offshore island at ....,
though at .... the crossing should not be attempted as there are
strong .... For those who enjoy coastal .... it is well worth
climbing to the .... of the hill to the north of Seatown: there is a
breathtaking .... from there when the .... is good.

      Seatown is a popular holiday .... : it has a particularly mild
.... and is renowned for the quality of its fresh ....

bay   cliffs
climate   coastline
currents   harbour
headland   high tide
lake   low tide
marshes   mouth
plain   port ✓
range of hills
resort   sandbank
scenery   seafood
source   streams
summit   view
visibility   woodland

C Choose THREE words or phrases for each sentence that make sense in the gaps.

1 The Vatican in Rome is visited every year by millions of ....
   commuters   holidaymakers   passengers   pilgrims   vagrants   travellers
2 I enjoy visiting places abroad where the people are ....
   churlish   courteous   easygoing   hospitable   morose   sulky   sullen
3 Not liking crowds, I prefer going on holiday to somewhere that's ....
   abandoned   backward   derelict   dull   godforsaken   off the beaten track   out of
   the way   secluded
4 The .... takes up to four hours on the motorway, but it's quicker by train.
   crossing   drive   flight   journey   passage   travel   trip   voyage   way
5 I'm going overseas next week and I'll be .... for the rest of the month.
   abroad   absent-minded   away from home   missing   offshore   on the run   out in
   the country   out of the country

D Note down five countries that you have visited, or might visit one day.

- What do you call a citizen of each country?
- What languages do they all speak?
- What are the principal cities called – and how are they pronounced?
- Which nationalities are the most frequent visitors to your country, and what are the
  attractions of your country to them?

6.2 Learning the language   Reading

A Read this text and then answer the questions below.

I studied my Turkish phrasebook, and learned a few of
the most useful ones by heart. One was about how I did
not understand Turkish well, which I copied into my
notebook and carried about with me. Many Turks can't
understand that anyone really does not know Turkish;
they think that if they say it often enough and loud
enough it will register. They did this whenever I said this
phrase; it seemed to start them off asking what seemed
to be questions, but I only said my piece again, and after
a time they gave it up. Sometimes they said "Yorum,
yorum, yorum?" as if they were asking something, but I did not know
what this word meant, and I thought they were mimicking what they
thought I had said.

This was all that happened about it for a few days, then one day
when I said my piece to the porter he nodded, and went to the   15
telephone and rang someone up, and presently a man came downstairs
and bowed to me as I stood in the hall and said something to me in
Turkish. I had better explain here that there was a misunderstanding
which was my fault, for I discovered some time afterwards that I had
copied the phrase in the book which was just below the one which   20

meant "I do not understand Turkish," and the one I had copied and learnt and had been saying to everyone for days meant "Please to phone at once to Mr Yorum," though this seems a silly phrase to print in a book for the use of people who do not know Mr Yorum at all and never would want to telephone to him. But one day this Mr Yorum turned up at the hotel to stay, and the porter saw then what I wanted him to do, and he rang Mr Yorum in his room and asked him to come down. But I did not know then about my mistake, and when Mr Yorum spoke to me I said again that I did not understand Turkish, and he bowed and pointed to himself. I thought he must be offering to interpret for me, but when I tried English on him he shook his head and said, "Yok, yok," and I could see he knew none. So I looked up the Turkish for "What can I have the pleasure of doing for you?" and said it, but of course I did not understand his answer, and that is the worst of foreign languages, you understand what you say in them yourself, because you have looked it up before saying it, but very seldom what the foreigners say to you, because you have not looked up that at all. So I looked through the book till I found "Who are you, sir?" and he said in reply, "Yorum, Yorum, Yorum." I saw there was some confusion somewhere, but there is always so much confusion in Turkey that I let it go, and ordered drinks for both of us, and we drank them, then he went away, quite pleased that I had telephoned to him to come and have a drink.

(from *The Towers of Trebizond* by Rose Macaulay)

Find the answers to these questions in the passage and underline (or highlight) the relevant information there. Then write down your answers, using your own words.

1 What did many Turks do when they encountered a non-Turkish speaker?
2 Why was the author confused at the reaction to her 'useful phrase'?
3 Why was the hotel porter the first to understand her?
4 Why did Mr Yorum point to himself when they first met?
5 Why did the narrator think he was pointing to himself?
6 Why didn't the writer try to resolve the confusion with Mr Yorum?

B   Work in pairs. Discuss these questions:

● Have you had any similar experiences with English or other foreign languages?
● How much of your language does a tourist in your country need to know?
● Which parts of the passage did you find amusing?
● What do you think happened next in the story?

C   Work in pairs. One of you should look at Activity 4, the other at 19. These Activities contain the next paragraphs of the story. Find out what happened when Mr Yorum was called down to the hotel lobby yet again. Then tell your partner about it in your own words.

A Work in pairs. Discuss the differences in meaning, if any, between these sentences.

1 I'll phone him after work.   I'm phoning him after work.
   I'm going to phone him after work.   I'll be phoning him after work.

2 It's still raining in Scotland.   It's still going to rain in Scotland.
   It will still be raining in Scotland.   It still rains in Scotland.

3 I think I'm going to scream.   I think I'll scream.

4 When are we having lunch?   When do we have lunch?
   When are we going to have lunch?   When shall we have lunch?

5 I'll work hard tonight.   I'll be working hard tonight.

6 Will you be going shopping today?   Are you going to go shopping today?
   Are you going shopping today?   Will you go shopping today?
   Do you go shopping today?

B These sentences all refer to the future. Fill the gaps with suitable words. In some cases various answers are possible.

1 I think I .... sneeze. .... you give me a tissue, please?
2 .... able to make people understand when you .... Turkey?
3 Have you decided how to get there? .... by car or .... a bus?
4 Supposing your car .... on the way there, what .... do?
5 Our flight is due .... at 9.30, but I'm afraid it .... delayed.
6 By the time the plane ...., we .... waiting for four hours.
7 I'm looking forward .... the book, when you .... finished with it.
8 In the next century tourism .... more and more highly developed.
9 While you .... holiday, I .... in the office. I hope you .... a postcard.
10 I've no idea when I .... finished my work.
11 As soon as I .... the results, I .... you a ring to let you know.
12 It's time we .... what we .... this weekend.
13 I hope nobody .... me at 8 o'clock because I .... still .... dinner then.
14 What .... happen at the frontier if I .... my passport at home?
15 What .... you .... while I .... across the Atlantic to New York?
16 No one knows for sure what the future .... us.

➡ Compare your answers with a partner.

C Work in groups and discuss these questions about the future:

• What are the most interesting things you're going to do during the coming month? Which are you looking forward to most?
• Looking ahead ten years or so, how will your life then be different from now?
• How will the world be different ten years from now?

➡ Write two paragraphs summarising the main points of your discussion. Compare your paragraphs with a partner's.

A 🔲 You'll hear three people describing journeys they remember. Listen to the stories and decide which of these pictures accurately illustrate the events described. More than one picture may be correct for each story.

B In these quotations from the recording, what do the words in italics mean?

the thing was *making very heavy weather of it*
Knut up front was getting more and more *agitated*
it had got stuck *teetering* on the edge
lo and behold
from the sublime to the ridiculous
I was rather *bleary-eyed*
I found this very *rickety* old ladder
I quickly *extricated* myself

C Work in groups. Tell your partners about your personal experience of a memorable journey you have had, either close to home or travelling further afield.

D Write the first paragraph of your story, or maybe one of your partners' stories.

A Work in pairs. Decide which of these sentences sound right and which don't.

1 We dreadfully enjoyed our holiday.   We particularly enjoyed our holiday.
 We quite enjoyed our holiday.   We remarkably enjoyed our holiday.
 We slightly enjoyed our holiday.   We very much enjoyed our holiday.

2 The weather was bitterly cold.   The weather was deeply cold.
 The weather was extraordinarily cold. The weather was greatly cold.
 The weather was rather cold.   The weather was utterly cold.
 The weather was quite cold.   The weather was absolutely cold.

3 The food was absolutely perfect.   The food was fairly perfect.
 The food was almost perfect.   The food was extremely perfect.
 The food was highly perfect.   The food was awfully perfect.
 The food was quite perfect.   The food was very perfect.

➡ What are the differences in meaning between the sentences that do sound right?

B Work in pairs. Fill the gaps with adverbs from the list below. Use a *different* adverb in each gap. Later, join another pair and compare answers.

1 I .... agree with what you just said.
2 She .... resented my interference.
3 I .... adore Chinese food.
4 We .... regretted what we had done.
5 It was .... dark and I was .... alone.
6 We .... prefer travelling by car.
7 I've .... forgotten what I was going to say.
8 I .... appreciate what you have done.
9 You really have been .... kind.
10 Are you sure that you .... understood what they meant?

*absolutely altogether awfully bitterly completely deeply dreadfully
entirely especially extraordinarily extremely fully greatly highly
incredibly particularly perfectly quite* (= absolutely) *really remarkably
simply strikingly terribly thoroughly totally utterly very much*

C Now fill these gaps with adverbs from the list above, again using a different adverb in each sentence.

1 I was .... sorry for what I had done.
2 We decided to approach the problem .... differently.
3 This work has been done .... well.
4 She is a(n) .... nice person, but he is a(n) .... nasty character.
5 It was a(n) .... unusual restaurant.
6 Have you .... finished?
7 He was driving .... dangerously.
8 It was a(n) .... interesting story.
9 I was .... certain I had met them before.
10 We were .... disappointed when the show was called off.

➡ Which of these qualifying adverbs could you use in each of the sentences above?
almost   nearly   pretty   quite (= somewhat) *rather   slightly   somewhat*

D Adjectives with 'absolute' meanings like these aren't normally intensified with *very* or *extremely*. But we can emphasise them with *absolutely*, *really* and *quite* (= absolutely):

> *absurd appalling awful brilliant delightful enormous essential*
> *excellent furious hopeless huge impossible marvellous perfect*
> *splendid terrible vital wonderful*

Fill the gaps in these sentences with suitable adjectives and emphasising adverbs.

1 It sounds as though you had a(n) .... time on holiday.
2 We stayed in a(n) .... hotel.
3 We had a(n) .... journey.
4 It was .... to change our holiday booking at the last minute.
5 She is a(n) .... musician, but she's terribly temperamental.
6 Her performance was ....

E Work in groups. Tell your partners about some holidays, day trips and journeys you remember, using some of the vocabulary you've practised in this section.

6.6 The friendly sky

A Work in groups and discuss these questions:

- Have you ever flown? If so, how often? What was it like?
- Are you afraid of flying? If so, why?
- What would you say to a friend who refuses to travel by plane?

B In this passage the writer, Jonathan Raban, is waiting at an airport in the United States for a flight to Seattle. First read the passage – and enjoy it.

Jonathan Raban

I spend a lot of time anxiously listening to the announcements over the loudspeaker system. In almost all respects, these summonses and bulletins are enunciated with extreme clarity by women speaking in the painfully slow and fulsomely stressed tones of infant teachers in a school for special-need children. It is only when they reach the flight number of the plane concerned or the name of the passenger who must immediately report to the United Airlines information desk that their voices go into misty soft focus. I keep on hearing that I am urgently wanted, but sit tight, fearing paranoia. They don't want me. They can't want me. They want Josephine Rubin, or John A.T. Horobin, or Sean O'Riordain, or Jennifer Raymond, or Jonah the Rabbi or Rogers and Braybourne.   10

When I first arrived here, I fed some coins into a newspaper-dispenser and took out a copy of the local broadsheet – the *Post-Dispatch*, the *Courant*, the *Plain Dealer*, the *Tribune*, the *Herald*, or whatever it was. It was an unhappy diversion. It spoke too eloquently of the world one had left behind by coming here – that   15
interesting world of School Board Split, City Cop on Take, Teamsters Boss To Quit, Highways Commission Probe – Official. It made me feel homesick for reality: the only news that interested me now was the depressing stuff on the V.D.U.s. *Cancelled. Delayed.* Did the controllers ever get to write *Crashed, Missing, Hijacked* on these screens?   20

What puzzles me is that I seem to be entirely alone in my frustration and distress. Almost every flight is going out late, and there must be several thousand people in this airport, switching their departure gates, phoning home, putting another Scotch-and-soda down on their tab in the cocktail lounge. The men's neckties are loosened, their vests unbuttoned. They sit with open briefcases, papers spread in front of them as if this place was a comfortable home-from-home. I watch one man near me. He's got a can of beer, a basket of popcorn, and he's two thirds of the way through a sci-fi thriller by Arthur C. Clarke. The bastard hasn't got a care in the world. His eyes never drift up to the V.D.U.; he never cocks his head anxiously when Teacher starts talking through the overhead speakers. He's on a domestic flight. He's a domestic flier.

An hour and a half later it is still raining, but we're getting somewhere here – at least I thought so 50 minutes ago when I buckled in to seat 38F and began looking out through the lozenge of scratched, multiplex plastic at the men in earmuffs and storm-gear on the ground below. Since then we haven't budged. We've suffered faint, pastiche imitations of Scott Joplin, Count Basie and Glen Miller on the muzak system. My neighbour in 38E, who is careless of the usual rules of body space, has worked her way slowly through four pages of the *National Enquirer*, moving her lips as she reads. In the seats ahead, there has been a good deal of folding and refolding of copies of *Business Week* and the *Wall Street Journal*. Still no one seems much disconcerted except me. The inside of the plane is hot and getting hotter. The stewards, flirting routinely among themselves, are proof against any damn-fool questions from me.

The muzak clicks off. A voice clicks on.

"Hi!" – and that seems to be it for a good long time. Then, "I'm, uh, Billy Whitman, and I'm going to be your pilot on this flight here to . . . " I think I can hear Mr Whitman consulting his clipboard. " . . . uh, Seattle this morning. Well – it was meant to be morning, but it looks to me now to be getting pretty damn close to afternoon . . . "

He's putting on the entire cowlicked, gum-shifting country boy performance.

"I guess some of you folks back there may be getting a little antsy 'bout this delay we're having now in getting airborne . . . Well, we did run into a bit of a glitch with Control up there, getting our flight-plan sorted . . . "

We haven't got a flight-plan? Is Mr Whitman waiting for someone to bring him a *map*?

"But they got that fixed pretty good now, and in, uh, oh, a couple or three minutes, we should be closing the doors, and I'm planning on getting up into the sky round about ten minutes after that. So if you all sit tight now, we'll be getting this show right on the road. Looks pretty nice up there today . . . no weather problems that I can see so far . . . at least, once we get atop this little local overcast . . . and I'm looking for a real easy trip today. Have a good one, now, and I'll be right back to you just as soon as we go past something worth looking out the window for. Okay?"

Click.

After the video and the stewards' dumbshow about what to do in "the unlikely event" of our landing on water (where? The Mississippi?), Captain Whitman takes us on a slow ramble round the perimeter of the airport. We appear to be returning to the main terminal again when the jet takes a sudden deep breath, lets out a bull roar, and charges down the runway, its huge frame shuddering fit to bust. Its wings are actually flapping now, trying to tear themselves out at their roots in the effort to achieve lift-off. It bumps and grinds. The plastic bulkheads are shivering like gongs. Rain streams past the window, in shreds, at 200 miles an hour.

This is the bit I hate. We're not going fast enough. We're far too heavy to bring off this trick. We're breaking up. To take this flight was tempting fate one time too many. We're definitely goners this time.

But the domestic fliers remain stupidly oblivious to our date with death. They go on reading. They're lost in the stock market prices. They're learning that Elvis Presley never died and has been living as a recluse in Dayton, Ohio. These things engage them. These guys are – bored. The fact, clear enough to me, that they are at this moment rocketing into eternity is an insufficiently diverting one to make them even raise their eyes from their columns of idiot print.

Somehow (and this Captain Whitman must know a thing or two) we manage to unpeel ourselves from the obstinate earth, which suddenly begins to tilt upwards in the glass. An industrial outskirt of the city shows as an exposed tangle of plumbing; there's a gridlock of cars on a freeway interchange, their headlamps shining feebly through the drizzle. The airport beneath us is marked out like a schoolbook geometrical puzzle. Then, suddenly, we're into a viewless infernal region of thick smoke, with the plane skidding and wobbling on the bumpy air. It's rattling like an old bus on a dirt road. In 38E we're deep in the miracle of Oprah Winfrey's diet. In 38F we're beginning to suspect that we might conceivably survive.

My ears are popping badly. The noise of the engines changes from a racetrack snarl to the even threshing sound of a spin-dryer. On an even keel now, we plough up steadily through the last drifts and rags of storm cloud and the whole cabin fills with sudden brilliant sunshine. We're in the clear and in the blue; aloft, at long last, over America.

75

80

85

90

(from *Hunting Mr Heartbreak* by Jonathan Raban)

C   Decide whether the following statements are true (T) or false (F), according to the text. Justify your answers to a partner.

1   The writer can easily understand every word of the airport announcements.
2   Reading the local newspaper fails to cheer him up.
3   He feels angry with the other passengers for not being scared, like him.
4   He observes that the men seem to feel less at ease than the women at the airport.
5   The woman sitting beside him is well-educated.
6   The *National Enquirer* is a business newspaper.
7   The pilot seems tense.
8   The flight is going to take them across the ocean.
9   He is reassured by the pilot's announcement.
10   They take off after taxiing all round the airfield.
11   He doesn't usually feel frightened during take-off.
12   He realises that he is not the only person aboard who is terrified.
13   As the plane takes off there is a wonderful view of the city below.

D   Highlight THREE parts of the passage that amused you. Point them out to a partner, and compare each other's reactions.

Look again at the discussion questions in A – what would be the writer's own answers to the questions, do you think?

E   Go through the passage highlighting the vocabulary you want to remember. But that doesn't mean every word you didn't know. For example, you probably didn't know the American slang words *antsy* or *glitch*, but you can guess their meanings from the context.

Rewrite each sentence using the words on the right, but without altering the word in any way.

1   Why on earth didn't you tell me before?   **ever**
    Why ever didn't you tell me before?
2   It is fortunate that our tickets arrived in time.   **luckily**
3   We went on waiting until midnight for the plane to take off.   **still**
4   Someone told me my flight was cancelled when I got to the airport.   **arriving**
5   I had never flown before which was why I was very nervous.   **having**
6   I only want to spend the rest of my life with you.   **what**
7   They go on holiday in the winter and in the summer too.   **not only**
8   We didn't realise that our hotel was right beside the airport.   **little**
9   I propose that we should send him a letter explaining the situation.   **be sent**
10 We were amazed about his feelings of shyness.   **feel**
11 She always gets the right answers.   **never**
12 We wrote several letters of complaint before we got our money back.   **only**

★★   When doing this kind of exercise, first identify the structure that is required, then rewrite the sentence. Concentrate on conveying the meaning as well as getting the grammar right. Don't change more than you have to.

A   Read this article through and then answer the questions below.

The naked truth about road safety

VICTIMS of what a BBC television documentary last year called The Greatest Epidemic of Our Time are mostly male, mostly in the prime of life,
5 number some 6,000 a year in Britain, 50,000 in the USA, and worldwide more than quarter of a million. And it's not Aids but road accidents.
   Some 10 million people have been
10 killed on the roads this century. We're talking about something comparable only with natural disasters, famines, disease and war. As far as the citizens of the United States are concerned, cars
15 have killed far more people than wars. Since 1913 nearly 3 million of them have been killed on the roads. This is three times as many as the number killed in all wars that the USA has ever fought,
20 including two World Wars, Korea and Vietnam.
   Recent aircraft disasters have concentrated our minds on air safety.

Yet the daily slaughter on the roads is largely ignored.
   Our society contemplates road

deaths with a remarkable equanimity which is only disturbed when a great many happen spectacularly in the same place at the same time, as when on Monday 13 people died in the motorway crash on the M6. Horrifying though that figure is, it is less than the average of 16 people in Britain (136 in the USA) whose deaths *every day* have no memorial.

Another spectacular accident occurred the previous Monday when 120 vehicles piled up on the M1. This took place in thick fog, whereas the M6 crash was in what were described as near perfect driving conditions. Since nobody was killed in the fog crash, and 13 were killed in the other one, it is reasonable to ask what is meant by perfect weather conditions.

Common sense tells us that driving is more difficult when there is less daylight and more fog, and when there is less friction between the tyres and the surface of the road. Common sense also tells us to drive more carefully in such conditions, and therefore more safely. When people drive more slowly, collisions are less damaging. Even if there are more accidents, they are less serious.

This is confirmed by a ten-year study of traffic accidents in Ontario. The number of injuries was lowest in February, highest in August. The difference in fatalities was even more pronounced: just over 80 in February, nearly 200 in August. Statistics in Sweden tell a similar story. John Adams, a lecturer at University College London, speculates that "if all roads were to be paved with a substance having the same coefficient of friction as ice, the number of people killed on the roads would be substantially reduced."

If this proposal sounds a little over the top, it is far from the only one to be found in Dr Adams's recently published study of road safety regulations, *Risk and Freedom*. Here are some more of his thought-provoking statements, solidly documented and backed by abundant statistics.

As traffic increases, road accident deaths drop dramatically. Small cars are involved in fewer accidents than big cars. Bermuda, with a speed limit of 20 mph, has a worse road accident record than Britain.

The same is true of the United States, which not only has lower speed limits than ours but also better roads. There is no convincing evidence that motorcycle helmet laws or the compulsory wearing of seat belts have saved lives.

It is this last statement that Dr Adams's critics, and they are many, have found most contentious. Some of them misrepresent his views in a way which, if it is not wilful, must come from an inability to read. Adams does not deny, as some of them appear to think, that an individual in a car crash has a better chance of survival with some form of constraint (a car occupant's seat belt) or protection (a motor cyclist's crash helmet). What he queries is whether *compulsory* seat belts, crash helmets and other safety regulations reduce the overall accident and fatality rate.

He finds that though there have been reductions in fatalities in some countries in which seat belt laws have been passed, they have not been as great as the reductions that have occurred in the same period in countries in which seat belt laws have not been passed.

The argument centres on what is called risk-compensation. Prevent people from taking one risk and they'll substitute another.

Adams makes the point by asking motorcyclists to imagine two sets of circumstances. In one the rider wears helmet and visor, leather jacket and trousers, gauntlets and heavy duty boots. In the other he has no helmet and is wearing a T-shirt, shorts and sandals. Anyone who has ridden a motorbike would agree with Adams's respondents, that they would drive much more carefully in the less protected state. The Swedish safety poster showing two motorcyclists who are naked other than for their crash helmets unintentionally makes the same point. They would drive very carefully indeed, and not because of the crash helmets.

RICHARD BOSTON

B Highlight the following words and phrases in the passage and explain their meanings:

in the prime of life (line 4) *equanimity* (line 27) *friction* (line 50)
pronounced (line 63) *thought-provoking* (line 77) *abundant* (line 78) *contentious* (line 94) *misrepresent* (line 95) *wilful* (line 96)

C Discuss your answers to these questions with a partner. Highlight the relevant sentence(s) in the passage, then write your answers to the questions, using your own words and without quoting directly from the passage.

1 What has been the effect of recent aircraft crashes?
2 What was the difference between the M1 crash and the M6 crash?
3 How does common sense lead to improved road safety?
4 What were the results of the traffic survey in Ontario?
5 How have some of Dr Adams's critics been unfair?

D Write a summary of the points made by Dr Adams in about 80 words.

6.9 Avoiding repetition

A Repetition of words in a composition can distract your reader's attention from what you're trying to say, and make your work look boring or unimaginative – unless it is deliberate and the repetition is meant to catch the reader's attention. Compare these two passages. Which do you prefer – and why?

> Greece receives eight million foreign visitors a year. These foreign visitors spend two billion dollars a year. Greek visitors to other countries spend half a billion dollars a year. Each foreign visitor to Greece spends about $300.
>
> Switzerland receives eleven million foreign visitors a year. These foreign visitors spend five billion dollars a year. Swiss visitors to other countries spend four billion dollars a year. Each foreign visitor to Switzerland spends about $450.

> Eight million people a year visit Greece, while eleven million go to Switzerland. These visitors spend about $300 and $450 per head, making a contribution of two billion and five billion dollars to the Greek and Swiss national incomes. This is counterbalanced by the money spent by Greek and Swiss visitors to other countries of half a billion and four billion dollars respectively.

B Work in pairs. Look at the example before starting the exercise:

1 Each sentence below contains some statistics about travel and tourism. Rewrite each sentence below, using opposites, synonyms, pronouns or different grammatical structures to make each sentence less repetitive. Compare each of your rewritten sentences with each of another pair's rewritten sentences.

> *Each sentence below contains some statistics about travel and tourism. Rewrite the sentences, using opposites, synonyms, pronouns or different grammatical structures to make them less repetitive. Compare your rewritten sentences with another pair's.*

2 35% of British tourists take a package holiday, less than 10% of German tourists take a package holiday.
3 British people spend £500 per head when on holiday, Spanish people spend over £700 per head when on holiday.
4 68% of Swedish people take an annual holiday, 64% of British people take an annual holiday, 59% of German people take an annual holiday.

DO ADVERTISEMENTS SOMETIMES DISTORT THE TRUTH?

The short answer is yes, some do.

Every week hundreds of thousands of advertisements appear for the very first time.

Nearly all of them play fair with the people they are addressed to.

A handful do not. They misrepresent the products they are advertising.

As the Advertising Standards Authority it is our job to make sure these ads are identified, and stopped.

WHAT MAKES AN ADVERTISEMENT MISLEADING?

If a training course had turned a 7 stone weakling into Mr Universe the fact could be advertised because it had been proved.

But a promise to build 'you' into a 15 stone he-man would have us flexing our muscles because the promise could not always be kept.

'Makes you look younger' might be a reasonable claim for a cosmetic.

But pledging to 'take years off your life' would be an overclaim akin to a promise of eternal youth.

A garden centre's claim that its seedlings would produce a 'riot of colour in just a few days' might be quite contrary to the reality.

Such flowery prose would deserve to be pulled out by the roots.

If a brochure advertised a hotel as being '5 minutes walk to the beach', it must not require an Olympic athlete to do it in the time.

As for estate agents, if the phrase 'overlooking the river' translated to 'backing onto a ditch', there would be nothing for it but to show their ad the door.

HOW DO WE JUDGE THE ADS WE LOOK INTO?

Our yardstick is The British Code of Advertising Practice.

Its 500 rules give advertisers precise practical guidance on what they can and cannot say. The rules are also a gauge for media owners to assess the acceptability of any advertising they are asked to publish.

The Code covers magazines, newspapers, cinema commercials, brochures, leaflets, posters, circulars posted to you, and now commercials on video tapes.

The ASA is not responsible for TV and radio advertising. Though the rules are very similar they are administered by the Independent Broadcasting Authority.

WHY IT'S A TWO-WAY PROCESS

Unfortunately some advertisers are unaware of the code, and breach the rules unwittingly. Others forget, bend or deliberately ignore the rules.

That is why we keep a continuous check on advertising. But because of the sheer volume, we cannot monitor every advertiser all the time.

So we encourage the public to help by telling us about any advertisements they think ought not to have appeared. Last year over 7,500 people wrote to us.

WHAT DO WE DO TO ADVERTISERS WHO DECEIVE THE PUBLIC?

Our first step is to ask advertisers who we or the public challenge to back up their claims with solid evidence.

If they cannot, or refuse to, we ask them to either amend the ads or withdraw them completely.

Nearly all agree without any further argument.

In any case we inform the publishers, who will not knowingly accept any ad which we have decided contravenes the Code.

If the advertiser refuses to withdraw the advertisement he will find it hard if not impossible to have it published.

WHOSE INTERESTS DO WE REALLY REFLECT?

The Advertising Standards Authority was not created by law and has no legal powers.

Not unnaturally some people are sceptical about its effectiveness.

In fact the Advertising Standards Authority was set up by the advertising business to make sure the system of self control worked in the public interest.

For this to be credible, the ASA has to be totally independent of the business.

Neither the chairman nor the majority of ASA council members is allowed to have any involvement in advertising.

Though administrative costs are met by a levy on the business, no advertiser has any influence over ASA decisions.

Advertisers are aware it is as much in their own interests as it is in the public's that honesty should be seen to prevail.

If you would like to know more about the ASA and the rules it seeks to enforce you can write to us at the address below for an abridged copy of the Code.

The Advertising Standards Authority. ✔

If an advertisement is wrong, we're here to put it right.

ASA Ltd, Dept. T, Brook House, Torrington Place, London WC1E 7HN.

A Highlight these words in the passage and then write an explanation of what they mean:

a handful (line 7)   *weakling* (line 16)   *pledging* (line 28)   *akin* (line 31)
ditch (line 50)   *yardstick* (line 55)   *breach* (line 84)   *unwittingly* (line 85)
monitor (line 89)   *sceptical* (line 120)   *levy* (line 133)

B Explain who or what is referred to by the words encircled in the quotations below. You'll need to refer back to the passage to do this.

Nearly all of (them) play fair with the people (they) are addressed to (line 5)
(They) misrepresent the products (line 7)
would have (us) flexing our muscles (line 20)
(it) must not require an Olympic athlete to do (it) in the time (line 46)
what (they) can and cannot say (line 59)
any advertising (they) are asked to publish (line 62)
any advertisements (they) think ought not to have appeared (line 93)
If (they) cannot (line 101)
or withdraw (them) completely (line 103)
sceptical about (its) effectiveness (line 120)
For (this) to be credible (line 125)

C Write your answers to these questions:

1 What examples of misrepresentative advertisements are given?
2 How does the ASA act on complaints made by members of the public?
3 How does the ASA maintain its independent status?

D In about 80 words, describe the role of the ASA and how it operates. Make notes before you start writing.

7.7 Further uses of -ing Advanced grammar

A Fill the gaps in the sentences in this revision exercise:

1 When .... a complaint, I prefer to be friendly and polite, instead of ....
aggressive or rude.
2 I found out what ingredients the product contained by .... the label. On
.... that it contained artificial flavouring, I decided against .... it.
3 It's no use .... him, he won't take any notice of you.
4 There's no point in .... the book in translation if it's available in English.
5 It's impossible to sneeze without .... your eyes.
6 In addition to .... this course, she spends a lot of time at home .... things
like .... novels in English and .... with friends by .... letters.
7 I've heard so much about you, I've really been looking forward .... you.
8 I felt depressed because I'm not used .... alone.

B Study these examples before filling the gaps in the exercise below:

I very much appreciated their / them coming to see me.
We were puzzled about everyone's / everyone feeling ill after the meal.
Janet / Her arriving on time for a change was quite a surprise.

The possessive (*their, everyone's, her*) in the examples sounds more formal than a straightforward pronoun or noun (*them, everyone, Janet*).

A possessive is not normally used when several words are involved:

I very much appreciated Janet and Maurice coming to see me.

⟫➔

A possessive cannot be used after verbs like *see*, *hear*, *feel*, *notice*, *watch* and *smell*:

> *Can you smell something burning?*
> *I didn't hear you calling me.*

1 Their father doesn't approve of .... home late. And he doesn't approve of .... television either. In fact, he insists on .... home before 11 and says that .... books will improve their minds.
2 We were all delighted to hear about Bill .... so well in the interview. His success is due to .... such a good impression on the interviewer.
3 They both smoke like chimneys, and I can't get used to .... during meals, and .... me for a light is particularly irritating.
4 I'll never forget that time we went for a walk with Tony and Jane. Do you remember .... into the river and then .... to save him?

C Finish the incomplete sentences in such a way that each one means the same as the complete sentence before it.

1 I don't advise you to travel to London to do your shopping. It isn't worth ...
2 It was inconsiderate of you not to consult me beforehand. Your ...
3 We were upset that he forgot to inform us. We were upset about his ...
4 It might be a better idea to save your money, not spend it. Instead of ...
5 She is a champion athlete and speaks four languages fluently. Besides ...
6 He has a job in an office and works in a shop at weekends. As well as ...
7 You won't find out if they're open if you don't phone them. Without ...
8 As I opened the door, I heard a strange noise. While ...
9 He has been in love with her from the moment he first saw her. Ever since ...
10 Let's do something exciting: for example, we could take up windsurfing. Shall we do something exciting, like ...?

| **7.8** **Sequencing ideas** | Writing skills |

⚠ The sequence in which points are made in an essay changes their impact on the reader. Some points have to be arranged in a logical order, and related ideas are often grouped together; some points can be arranged in different ways to provide different kinds of emphasis. The first point often 'sets the scene' for the rest of the essay, while the final point is usually perceived as the conclusion.

A Work in pairs. Decide on a suitable sequence for these ideas about 'The Green Consumer'. Discuss what difference rearranging the points in various ways makes to the strength of the argument.

Compare your sequence of points with the sequence used in the passage in Activity 44. Your sequence may turn out to be different from the original.

1 We must mobilise consumer power to defend not only our own health but the health of the planet
2 More and more consumers want to buy responsible products
3 Advertising creates false 'plastic' needs, often forcing out real needs
4 Concern about effects on environment: locally & globally
5 Concern about effects on our own health
6 Concern about effects on Third World

7 People increasingly concerned about what they consume
8 Green Consumers demanding more information about environmental performance of products & animal testing & implications for Third World
9 People want to know what additives their food & drink contains

B Now write a summary of these points from *The Green Consumer Guide* in your own words, arranging them into a suitable order. (about 60 words)

KEY ISSUES FOR THE GREEN CONSUMER

In general, the Green Consumer avoids products which are likely to
- adversely affect other countries, particularly in the Third World
- cause significant damage to the environment during manufacture, use or disposal
- use materials derived from threatened species or from threatened environments
- cause unnecessary waste, either because of over-packaging or because of an unduly short useful life
- consume a disproportionate amount of energy during manufacture, use or disposal
- endanger the health of the consumer or of others
- involve the unnecessary use of – or cruelty to – animals, whether this be for toxicity testing or for other purposes

---

7.9 Knowing your rights

A Listen to the interview in which an expert outlines a customer's rights in law when buying goods. Fill in the gaps and answer the questions below.

1 Whenever a purchase is made, the buyer and seller enter into a ....

2 The trader has three main obligations:
 a) that the goods are 'of .... quality' (this includes .... goods) – e.g. a pair of shoes that .... after two weeks don't meet this obligation.
 b) that the goods are 'fit for any particular .... made known to the ....'
 – e.g. wrong advice given by salesman fails to meet this obligation.
 c) that the goods are 'as ....' by the seller or on the packet – e.g. frozen prawns illustrated as .... and .... (but which are in fact ....) don't fulfil this obligation.

3 What should you do if goods are faulty? Tick what the speaker recommends.
 a) Take the item back to the shop ☐
 b) Ask the retailer to collect the item ☐
 c) Accept a cash refund ☐
 d) Accept a credit note ☐
 e) Accept a replacement ☐
 f) Agree to the item being repaired ☐
 g) Return the item to the manufacturer ☐

4 A trader is not legally obliged to give a refund . . .
    – if you examined the goods before purchase and didn't notice any ....
    – if you were told of any specific .... at the time of purchase
    – if you .... the seller's advice on the .... of the product
    – if you .... the seller's claim that he wasn't .... enough to offer advice
    – if you .... about wanting the goods
    – if you .... the item as a ....

5 When can a shopkeeper refuse to sell you something?
6 Why is it advisable to keep your receipt in a safe place?
7 If a trader refuses to give you a cash refund, you should go to your local
    C............ A............ B............ or to the T............ S............ Office.
8 Why is it unusual for a dissatisfied customer to take a seller to court?

B Work in groups and discuss your reactions to the recording:

• What are a customer's rights in your country? How do they compare with the rights of a customer in England?
• Have you ever had to take something back to a shop? What happened?
• What advice would you give to a dissatisfied customer about returning goods?

7.10 Prepositions

Fill the gaps in this newspaper article with suitable prepositions.

VOLVO, renowned ......1...... its solid and reliable, if somewhat dull cars, is about to discover how well its estate cars can withstand getting run over ......2...... a monster truck.

The Swedish car company ......3...... a reputation ......4...... integrity recently ran television commercials filmed ......5...... Texas which showed a row of cars being flattened ......6...... "Bearfoot", a giant truck ......7...... 500 kg tyres. Only a Volvo stood up ......8...... the cruel and unusual punishment.

The advertisement depicts the contest ......9...... a real event, but some residents ......10...... Austin, Texas, who participated ......11...... extras ......12...... what was actually a dramatisation, smelt something fishy and contacted the Attorney-General's office ......13...... the filming to pass on their doubts.

This week Volvo's American subsidiary was forced to admit ......14...... newspaper advertisements that the commercial was phoney because modifications were made ......15...... the vehicles. The Volvos used ......16...... the filming had been reinforced ......17...... timber and steel, and some ......18...... the audience said they saw the roof supports ......19...... other cars being sawn off.

Volvo's public grovelling should have been the end ......20...... the matter, but not ......21...... the Hot Rod Association, which produces car-crushing events starring powerful trucks driving ......22...... mud and towing 25,000 kg sleds. Now it plans to recreate the Volvo ad, again using Bearfoot but this time the Volvo 240 estate car will be an ordinary road model.

"Bearfoot is out ......23...... revenge because it was duped," says Steve Greenberg ......24...... the HRA.

Volvo officials have resigned themselves ......25...... humiliation. "We realise this is a logical extension ......26...... our ads," concedes a Volvo official.

➡ Before the lesson, collect some advertisements from magazines or newspapers.

A Work in groups. Read this article and discuss your reactions to it. Then look at each other's ads and discuss how effective they are.

CENSORED

A POSTER of a blood-spattered new-born baby emblazoned across hoardings all over Bournemouth and Poole may be banned.

⁵ Complaints have flooded into the Advertising Standards Authority and to hoarding companies and at least two local posters have already been covered up.

¹⁰ United Colours of Benetton, the fashion firm advertised, was warned against its display by the ASA.

  "We advised them against using ¹⁵ it because we felt it likely it would cause considerable offence," said ASA official Caroline Crawford. "We were very surprised to find they have been displaying it."

²⁰ The Authority has had hundreds of phone calls and letters from around the country – some from areas where it was on show outside maternity departments and even ²⁵ an abortion clinic.

  Locally, the poster is on show at several sites: in Bournemouth and Poole, including a hoarding near Poole Quay, close to Tower Park and at The Triangle. ³⁰

  One hoarding company accepting the poster, Maiden Ltd, has already blanked out two of its sites in Holdenhurst Road ³⁵ following complaints – but one still remains near Bournemouth Station.

  One has been covered up near ASDA superstore after customer complaints and one outside Nigel ⁴⁰ Newbery's butcher shop next door to the Dolphin pub in Holdenhurst Road.

  As the hoarding was being blanked out by a workman, 32-year- ⁴⁵ old Mr Newbery explained: "I complained to the hoarding company after customers kept coming in complaining.

  "Personally I find it very ⁵⁰ offensive. My own ten-year-old daughter Amanda said it was horrible and even my seven-year old Nicola said it was 'gross'.

⫸➡

55 "I know that's what new-born children look like and it's different if you're looking at your own – but what's it got to do with clothes and fashion?"

60 Round the corner in Victoria Place, 53-year-old mother of five, Sandra Gray phoned up to protest.

"It's horrible. All the people I work with agree all that blood and 65 gore is not something you want on a giant poster. It could disturb a mother-to-be."

A Benetton press officer said: "At first we had a negative response, 70 but recently the calls were equally divided between those upset and those congratulating us on its reality. We don't come into the world as pink fluffy bundles. Many 75 want copies and say they wish they'd photographed their children at such an exhilarating and profound moment," she added.

She continued: "Earlier, we emphasised the unity of life by 80 showing children of different colours. This poster focuses on the unity of humanity by showing that we all enter the world the same way. 85

The ASA has no legal powers to censor poster displays but as hoarding companies must abide by its recommendations, the poster looks doomed. 90

● Smaller versions of the poster sent to Benetton's own shop in Old Christchurch Road are not being displayed because they might upset people. 95

David Haith

B Look at the notes below and decide which points you would include in a 300-word essay on this topic, bearing in mind that the points must all be relevant:

Outline the harmful and the beneficial effects of advertising.

- Need created for totally unnecessary products (e.g. kitchen gadgets)
- Plethora of brands of goods, different only in name (e.g. detergents)
- Goods more expensive due to costly advertising budgets
- Young people may be harmed by certain advertisements (e.g. alcoholic drink)
- Ads stimulate envy among the less well-off; may lead to rise in crime rate (e.g. thefts of expensive cars)
- Commercials on TV interrupt programmes – very annoying
- Ads create desire for more and more material possessions
- Ads lead to dissatisfaction with one's standard of living – may lead to people trying to live beyond their means
- Many commercials on TV have insidious tunes that linger in the brain
- Many ads are amusing and informative – often more amusing than the programmes on TV or articles in a magazine
- Ads stimulate competition between companies, thus keeping prices down
- Ads create consumer awareness, giving information about a range of products
- Ads in newspapers and magazines keep their cost down – many couldn't survive without advertisements
- The world would be dull and drab without amusing and colourful ads

➡ Add any further points you want to make to the notes above.
Decide on the sequence of the points in your composition.

C Write your composition. Include examples of particular advertisements that seem to support your arguments.

8 The press

THE TIMES   **THE Sun**

The Economist   *The***Guardian**

THE INDEPENDENT

DAILY Mirror   **Daily Mail**

A   Work in groups and discuss these questions:

- Which newspapers do you read regularly? Which do you prefer and why?
- Which English-language newspapers have you read? What were they like?
- Is there a local English-language newspaper in your country? What's it like?
- What current affairs programmes do you watch or listen to on the TV or radio?
- Which newspaper would you recommend if you were asked? Give your reasons.

B   Match these words and phrases to their synonyms below:

> *article circulation editorial issue magazines main story newsreader*
> *the papers reporter reviewer*
>
> critic the dailies journalist lead story leader monthlies & weeklies
> newscaster number number of copies sold report

C   Here are some typical newspaper headlines. Each is explained in everyday language, with some words missing. Fill the gaps.

1 **Quake toll rises**
   The number of .... of the .... has risen.

2 **'Tories set to win poll'**
   Someone says that the .... party is .... to win the forthcoming by-election.

3 **Premier backs peace moves in docks**
   The .... says that (s)he .... the .... to reconcile both sides in the port workers' dispute.

4 **Police name Mr Big**
   The police have revealed the .... of the .... of the robberies.

5 **Jobless total tops 3m – PM to face critics in Commons**
   .... 3 million people are now .... The Opposition will be asking the .... some difficult questions in ....

⟫➔

6 **Key MP held on bribes charge**
A prominent .... has been .... because he is alleged to have ....
bribes.

7 **Washington ups arms spending**
The .... government have .... their defence budget.

8 **£3m drugs haul at Heathrow**
Customs officers at Heathrow Airport have .... drugs .... £3 million.

9 **HEADS UP IN ARMS OVER CUTS – TEACHERS TO BE AXED**
.... teachers are .... because spending on schools is to be ....
Some teachers are going to lose ....

10 **Fish talks in Brussels**
.... between EC .... ministers are to be .... in Brussels.

A Work in groups and discuss these questions:
- What do you remember about the woman below?
- What do you know about her fall from power in November 1990?

Now read these extracts from *The Economist's* BRITAIN THIS WEEK column:

Michael Heseltine   Geoffrey Howe   Douglas Hurd   John Major

Out in the cold

The Tories found themselves in crisis over their policy towards Europe. A week that began with ominous rumbles at the European Community's Rome summit produced fireworks in the Commons on Tuesday, as Mrs Thatcher asserted her opposition to economic and political union – and closed with high drama at Westminster when **Sir Geoffrey Howe resigned** as deputy prime minister and leader of the Commons on Thursday. After a half hour meeting between them in the early evening, Downing Street said Mrs Thatcher had accepted his resignation "more in sorrow than in anger".

NOVEMBER 3 1990

Tory torments

The prime minister took an **unrepentant stand** over Europe in her first big speech in the Commons since Sir Geoffrey Howe's resignation. She also told Saddam Hussein "either he gets out of Kuwait soon or we and our allies will remove him by force . . . he has been warned".

After criticising Mrs Thatcher's style and stance on Europe, **Michael Heseltine** retreated to his old position that he would not challenge her for the leadership. Party managers brought forward the deadline for any challenger to appear by, earnestly hoping for none.

NOVEMBER 10 1990

The race is on

After tantalising the Tories for months, Michael Heseltine finally challenged Margaret Thatcher for the **Tory leadership**. He had said he would not do this in any foreseeable circumstances; but no one foresaw this week. His platform: anti-poll tax, pro-listening to colleagues, lots of Eurovision – and better odds for Tory MPs at the next election.

Having arrived at the Lord Mayor's banquet dressed in regal gown and train, the prime minister figuratively donned cricket pads and boots for her after dinner speech. "There will be **no ducking the bouncers**. . . the bowling's going to get hit all round the ground. That's my style," she said, anticipating the challenge to come.

In his resignation speech to the Commons, Sir Geoffrey Howe became the sheep that roared. MPs gasped as he laid into Mrs Thatcher's attitude to Europe. She sees a continent "teeming with ill-intentioned people", he said – and risks leaving Britain "once again scrambling to join the club. . . after the rules have been set."

Uncertainty over the Tory party's leadership knocked the **pound** for six. It fell almost to DM 2.88, leaving it looking the weakest currency in the ERM. Unemployment recorded its largest monthly increase for four years.

NOVEMBER 17 1990

End of an era

Margaret Thatcher resigned after 11½ years as prime minister. In the first ballot for the **Conservative leadership** she got 204 votes, while her challenger Mr Michael Heseltine won only 152; but the margin was less than the 15% lead needed for victory. At first she said she would fight on. But her cabinet colleagues persuaded her to stand down. The pound and shares soared.

Mrs Thatcher told the Queen of her intention to resign but agreed to continue as prime minister until a new leader was chosen. Two **new candidates** joined the race: Mr Douglas Hurd, the foreign secretary, and Mr John Major, the chancellor. Sir Geoffrey Howe, the man who precipitated the challenge, said he would not stand.

The **Labour party** could hardly contain its delight at the Tories' disarray. Mr Neil Kinnock proposed a motion of no confidence in the government.

NOVEMBER 24 1990

A fresh start

Mr John Major, aged 47, was elected as the Tory leader and on November 28th was appointed Britain's **new prime minister** – the youngest this century. With 185 votes in the second ballot of the Tories' leadership contest, he was two short of an absolute majority. But Mr Michael Heseltine (131 votes) and Mr Douglas Hurd (56 votes) both withdrew from the race.

Mrs Margaret Thatcher answered her last question – her 7,450th – as prime minister in the Commons. Hours later, she said she was "thrilled and delighted" at the triumph of her protégé, Mr Major. After a visit to the Queen next day to hand in **her resignation**, she set off with Denis and the removal van from Downing Street to Dulwich.

Remembering a rash quip from Mrs Thatcher, before his election, about her future as a backseat driver, and derided as Son of Thatcher by Labour, Mr Major quickly asserted his authority in shuffling names for his **new cabinet**. Mr Heseltine was made environment secretary, to tackle the poll tax; Norman Lamont became chancellor; and Chris Patten took on the party chairmanship, in place of Kenneth Baker, who became Home Secretary.

DECEMBER 1 1990

B Arrange these events into the correct sequence:

...... The first ballot of Tory MPs was held.
...... A second ballot of Tory MPs was held.
...... Geoffrey Howe made a public attack on the party leader.
...... Messrs Hurd and Major decided to stand against Mr Heseltine.
...... Mr Heseltine announced that he would stand for election as party leader.
...... Mr Heseltine became environment secretary in the cabinet.
...... Mr Heseltine denied that he would stand for election as party leader.
...... Mr Major became PM when Messrs Hurd and Heseltine stood down.
...... The deputy prime minister resigned.
...... The ex-PM announced that she was standing behind the new PM.
...... The PM announced her intention to stand again.
...... The PM announced her intention to stand her ground.
...... The PM announced that she would stand down.
...... The PM defended her stand on her European policy.
...... The PM got more votes than Mr Heseltine, who was standing against her.

C Now read this article, which appeared on 28 November 1990. Note down your answers to the questions that follow.

To Margaret and the Tory party: a son and heir

Andrew Rawnsley

AFTER a prolonged and painful labour, the Conservative Party last night announced that it had given birth to a new Prime Minister – a baby boy called John.

His mother, Margaret, was reported to be "thrilled". It was the son and heir she had always wanted.

When the new-born leader emerged in Downing Street to utter his first words, he blinked at first, unaccustomed to the glare of the photographers' flashlights. By his side, First Lady Norma clutched his hand.

The Prime Minister-elect was excited by his victory. Not that his famously grey exterior expressed much excitement. We only knew he had felt a bit of a thrill because he told us so.

"It is a very exciting thing to be leader of the Conservative Party," he said in such a flat voice that he might have just come first in the school egg-and-spoon race.

When they heard the result in committee room 14, Tory backbenchers banged their desks, and then flooded into the lobbies and corridors of Westminster calling his name. "Major! *Major!*, MAJOR!", they shouted, the traditional cry that declares the party is

3

4

5

6

1

2

114

now as totally united behind its new leader as it was behind the last one, and will remain so until the time comes to knife him in the back.

Tory backbenchers reeled with astonishment that they had elected somebody so unknown and untested, replacing the longest-serving Prime Minister this century with the youngest.

They had chosen as their leader somebody who grew up in a family of circus entertainers and then, at the age of 16, ran away to join a firm of accountants.

It will take some getting used to one particularly amazing fact about the new Prime Minister. She is a man. Though so little is known about John Major, everybody will have to take that, as so much else, on trust.

Posterity will want to record the words used by the new Prime Minister on his day of triumph.

In an effort to prove that his greyness is only skin deep, sources close to Mr Major had earlier revealed that, at breakfast, the Boy Prime Minister had cracked his first joke. History will remember that the successor to Pitt, Gladstone, Disraeli, and Churchill told the world: "I had two shredded wheat this morning, and I hope to have three tomorrow."

By lunchtime, that appeared to have exhausted Mr Major's humour reserves. "I am patient," he said, when asked how he thought the vote was going. "We will have to wait and see." That use of the Royal We so soon confirmed him as the natural successor to Mrs Thatcher.

Both his rivals put a brave face on it. Michael Heseltine gamely offered his "congratulations" and confirmed that he was taking his hairdrier out of the ring. Douglas Hurd also made a graceful withdrawal having been exposed, true to Foreign Office tradition, as the Third Man.

In Downing Street last night, Mrs Thatcher was seen with her boy inside No 11, no doubt handing over the front door keys to Number Ten.

And almost certainly reminding him of her declared intention to be "a very good backseat driver".

Mr Major can expect to hear a familiar voice shouting directions over his shoulder: "Right! Right! Right! No U-turns!"

There's this consolation for the new Prime Minister – he doesn't have very far to move. But once inside Number Ten, Mr Major will have to prove that the Conservative Party has not sent a boy to do a woman's job.

1 How did the new PM show his excitement at being elected?
2 How did he show he had a sense of humour?
3 How loyal are the party members likely to be to the new PM?
4 What was the delayed reaction of the MPs who had elected him?
5 What kind of family background did he come from?
6 What profession did he first take up?
7 What colour does the writer use to describe the new PM?
8 How would you describe the tone of the article and the writer's motive?

⟫➔

D　　Highlight these words and phrases in the article on pages 114–15 and then fill the gaps in the definitions below.

> labour ¶ 1　son and heir ¶ 2　First Lady ¶ 3　clutched ¶ 3
> knife him in the back ¶ 6　ran away to join ¶ 8　take . . . on trust ¶ 9
> posterity ¶ 10　put a brave face on it ¶ 13　gamely ¶ 13
> backseat driver ¶ 15　consolation ¶ 17

1 Normally, a *son and heir* is a male child who will ....
2 *Labour* is normally associated with ....
3 The *First Lady* normally refers to the wife of ....
4 A .... normally *clutches* the hand of a ....
5 When you *knife someone in the back* you ....
6 In traditional stories, young people *run away from home to join* ....
7 If you *take something on trust* you believe it without seeing any ....
8 *Posterity* is ....
9 We *put a brave face on it* when ....
10 *Gamely* means the same as ....
11 A *backseat driver* normally refers to someone who ....
12 A *consolation* is ....

E　Work in groups. Discuss these questions:

- How have other political leaders ended their careers?
- How is the President or Prime Minister of your country chosen?
- How important is it for a country to have a charismatic leader?

"Actually, it surprises me that a man like you doesn't hold political office."

A Work in pairs. Discuss the differences in meaning (if any) between these sentences:

1 Could you finish the article?   Were you able to finish the article?
2 Can you carry this box?   Can you help me to carry this box?
3 You can't leave yet.   You needn't leave yet.
4 I don't need to read the paper today.   I needn't read the paper today.
  I don't have to read the paper today.   I mustn't read the paper today.
  I haven't to read the paper today.   I shouldn't read the paper today.
  I haven't read the paper today.   I haven't got to read the paper today.
5 There could be an election this year.   There has to be an election this year.
  There should be an election this year.   There will be an election this year.
6 That could be Tony at the door.   That must be Tony at the door.
  That will be Tony at the door.   That can't be Tony at the door.
  That might be Tony at the door.   That should be Tony at the door.

B Report each sentence in two ways: once using a modal verb and once using a longer phrase, as in the example.

1 'You must do it now.' She said that . . .   *She said that we had to do it.*
  She said that we were obliged to do it. or She said that it was necessary for us to do it.
2 'Maybe we can help you.' She said that ....
3 'You can't use a dictionary in the exam.' He told me that ....
4 'Must you be leaving so soon?' She asked me if ....
5 'You mustn't believe everything you read in the newspapers.' He told us that ....
6 'I daren't dive into the swimming pool.' She told us that ....
7 'You need to book a table.' He told us that ....
8 'What time must I arrive there?' She wondered ....

C Rewrite each headline as a full sentence.

1 **Left set to win election**
2 **Ban on smoking in cinemas**
3 Seat belts to be worn in rear seats
4 **70 mph speed limit to be lifted**
5 1000s forced to flee after quake
6 **Recession looms again**
7 'Non-swimmers on the up' says sports minister
8 Rail strike stops commuters getting home

D Work in pairs. Imagine that you're giving advice to a British person who is about to visit your country for the first time. What advice would you give about social customs, rules of behaviour and laws, using these modal verbs?

can/can't   have to/don't have to   need to/don't need to/needn't
must/mustn't   should/shouldn't

➡ Write eight sentences, giving the most important pieces of advice.

Lisa Wood

FINANCIAL TIMES
EUROPE'S BUSINESS NEWSPAPER

A [cassette] Lisa Wood is a journalist on the *Financial Times*. Imagine that you are interviewing her, and note down the main points she makes below:

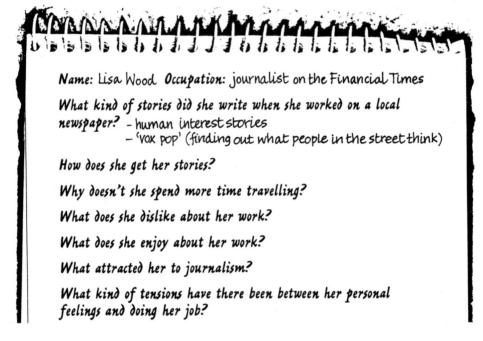

Name: Lisa Wood Occupation: journalist on the Financial Times

What kind of stories did she write when she worked on a local newspaper? – human interest stories
– 'vox pop' (finding out what people in the street think)

How does she get her stories?

Why doesn't she spend more time travelling?

What does she dislike about her work?

What does she enjoy about her work?

What attracted her to journalism?

What kind of tensions have there been between her personal feelings and doing her job?

B Work in groups. Discuss your reactions to the interview:

- What would you *not* enjoy about doing Lisa's job?
- What kind of personality and skills do you need to be a good reporter?
- Do newspapers in your country invade people's privacy after a tragic event? What are your views on this?

Choose the word or phrase which best completes each sentence:

1 The vice-chancellor's speech .... the writer.
   amused   failed to convince   frightened   terrified
2 The lad from Oldham's time at university was .... than the writer's.
   less successful   more fun   more intellectual   more strenuous
3 While he was in the university library the writer . . .
   couldn't concentrate   dozed off   read books from cover to cover   worked hard
4 Towards the end of his time at university the writer . . .
   gave up hope   organised himself better   worked harder
   wrote a long dissertation
5 The writer recommends . . .
   studying for a short time every day   finishing one task before starting another
   studying only when you are alert   deciding when each kind of task is best done
6 'Circling round a self-monitoring loop' (¶ 11) means . . .
   approaching your studies in circuitous way   continuing to study for a long time
   planning your study methods   evaluating the success of your study methods

B ![icon] Highlight these words and phrases in the passage, and use a dictionary to
look up the meanings of any you are unsure of. Make sure you look at the
examples given as well as the definitions. Then look again at the words in
context.

bluffing ¶ 2   *assiduously* ¶ 3   *blotted out* ¶ 3   *at sea* ¶ 5
segments ¶ 5   *strategically* ¶ 5   *dribble away* ¶ 5   *dipping into* ¶ 7
glazed over ¶ 7   *prime* ¶ 10   *swamp* ¶ 12

C ![icon] Work in pairs. Highlight FOUR phrases in the passage which you consider
to be key phrases. Then compare your ideas with another pair and discuss these
questions:

- Which of the advice given in the passage do you agree with?
- Which do you already follow? Which ought you to follow?
- How does life at a British university, as described in the passage, differ from
  university life in your country?

*"Frankly, Mr and Mrs Rumbelow, I'm a little worried
about your William – I don't know who he is!"*

A   Work in pairs. Discuss any differences in meaning or emphasis between the sentences:

    1   She said, 'I'll be arriving tomorrow.'
        She told me that she was arriving tomorrow.
        She told me that she was arriving the next day.

    2   She said to me, 'You really should spend more time reading, shouldn't you?'
        She advised me to spend more time reading.
        She urged me to spend more time reading.

    3   Everyone said, 'That's just nonsense!'
        No one agreed with my idea.
        Everyone dismissed my idea as unrealistic.

    4   We doubted whether the scheme would succeed.
        We didn't know whether the scheme would succeed.
        We had no doubt that the scheme would fail.

    5   He said, 'If you phoned us from the airport, we could come and pick you up.'
        He said they could come and pick me up if I rang them from the airport.
        He said they could have come to collect me if I'd called them from the airport.

B   Use these verbs to report what the people said in as few words as possible. Then compare your sentences with a partner's.

> *assure   claim   congratulate   deny* ✓ *disagree   insist   promise   regret*
> *remind   reproach   suggest   warn*

    1   'No, it wasn't me. I didn't borrow your bike.'   **She denied borrowing my bike.**
    2   'I'll let you know as soon as they get here. OK?'
    3   'Don't forget: you've got to hand in your work this evening.'
    4   'It's a shame you couldn't make it to the party last night.'
    5   'Well done! I always thought you'd pass.'
    6   'Don't worry, as long as you keep your head, you'll manage all right.'
    7   'You really must come and visit us next weekend!'
    8   'I don't really think that what you said makes sense.'
    9   'If you park on this double yellow line, you'll get a ticket.'
   10   'You shouldn't have behaved like that. You should be ashamed of yourself.'
   11   'If I had more time, I'd help you with your work.'
   12   'Might it be a good idea if we all organised our time more efficiently?'

C   🔲 You'll hear the same words spoken in five different ways, each conveying a different attitude or mood. Select ONE adjective to describe each attitude:

> *amazed   angry   depressed   diffident   disappointed   half-hearted*
> *heart-broken   hysterical   impressed   sarcastic   shocked*

1		4	
2		5	
3			

Write five sentences summarising what each speaker said, imagining that you were the person addressed. For example:

> **The first speaker complained that my work hadn't improved and compared it**
> **unfavourably with everyone else's.**

10 Nature and the environment

Arthur J. Elsey: 'A tempting bait', 1906

A   Work in groups and discuss these questions:
  • What are your reactions to this painting?
  • What are the implied attitudes to animals, nature and the countryside?
  • Do you have any pets at home – or do any of your relations have them?
  • What are your views on keeping pets in cities?
  • Would you describe yourself as an animal-lover ?
  • How 'environmentally aware' do you think you are?

➡ Note down TEN vocabulary items connected with the topic of this unit that were used in your discussion. Compare your list with members of another group.

B   Work in pairs and choose the word that best completes each of the sentences.

  1 Many species of animals and plants today are ....
      dangerous   endangered   precarious   risky   under danger
  2 The indiscriminate use of pesticides has .... many rare species.
      abolished   cancelled   devastated   postponed   vanished   wiped out

➡➔

145

3 Modern farm animals and crops are the result of centuries of selective ....
     breeding   cultivation   education   mating   reproduction

4 It took a long time for the theory of evolution to be ....
     absorbed   accepted   acknowledged   tolerated

5 Much of our knowledge about evolution comes from the study of ....
     artefacts   fossils   relics   ruins   tracks

6 My friend is a keen amateur ....
     natural historian   naturalist   naturist   nationalist

7 He gets very .... about experiments being carried out on live animals.
     worked down   worked out   worked over   worked up

8 One of the effects of acid rain is that it causes plants to ....
     contract   flourish   shrink   thrive   wither

9 Waste paper can be .... instead of being burnt.
     decomposed   incinerated   recycled   revamped

10 There are over 850,000 named .... of insects on this planet.
     colonies   families   species   styles   varieties

11 Rabbits and mice are ....
     amphibians   carnivores   marsupials   rodents

12 Crocodiles and alligators are ....
     crustaceans   herbivores   mammals   reptiles

13 The oak and the beech are ....
     bushes   coniferous trees   deciduous trees   shrubs

14 Crows and vultures are ...., living on carrion.
     parasites   predators   scavengers   scroungers

15 The lioness lay in wait for her ....
     game   lunch   prey   target   victim

16 Rats, mice and cockroaches are usually considered to be ....
     cuddly   mischievous   pets   vermin   weeds

17 Cattle and chickens are .... animals.
     domestic   domesticated   house-broken   obedient   tame   wild

18 Your cat has scratched me with its ....
     claws   fangs   hoofs   nails   paws   pincers   whiskers

19 We all admired the parrot's beautiful ....
     bark   coat   fleece   fur   hide   plumage

20 Many insects, such as wasps and ants, use their .... to touch objects.
     aerials   antlers   feelers   horns   whiskers

21 A .... hatches from an egg laid by a butterfly.
     caterpillar   chrysalis   maggot   moth   snake   worm

22 We saw a huge .... of birds through our binoculars.
     crowd   flock   herd   pack   shoal   swarm

23 The .... that we've gathered in the woods will taste delicious fried in butter.
     champions   leaves   lichen   mushrooms   toadstools

24 Squirrels and rabbits are .... little creatures.
     amiable   courteous   delicious   elegant   endearing   extravagant   fierce

➡ Look again at the words that you didn't use in the gaps. Do you know why each is wrong in the context? Highlight any of them that you want to remember.

Ray Gambell

A You'll hear an interview with Ray Gambell, a leading expert on whales. Before you listen to the recording, discuss with your partner what you already know about whales and about campaigns to save them from extinction.

B 📼 The first part of the interview is about research methods. Decide whether these statements are true (T) or false (F), according to the speaker.

1 Whales are not being caught commercially at present.
2 Individual hump-backed whales can be recognised by the colour of their tails.
3 Thousands of samples have been taken from the tails of hump-backed whales.
4 Hump-backed whales breed in the Arctic and feed in the Caribbean.
5 In the past, research involved examining large numbers of dead whales.
6 Using current research methods, information can be gathered much more quickly than it used to.

C 📼 In the second part of the interview you'll hear about different people's attitudes to 'saving the whales'. Answer these multiple-choice questions.

1 The Inuit peoples (Eskimos) of the Arctic . . .
  a) hunt whales together for enjoyment
  b) would die out if they didn't hunt whales
  c) depend on whale meat and products for their survival
2 When Ray watched Eskimos hunting whales he found the experience . . .
  a) sickening   b) fascinating   c) shocking
3 To Western people today the whale represents the idea of . . .
  a) beauty   b) freedom   c) pleasure
4 For Western people, the whale is no longer thought of as a source of . . .
  a) meat   b) oil   c) raw materials
5 Nowadays Western people view commercial whale hunters as . . .
  a) brutal   b) primitive   c) distasteful

⟫➤

D In the last part of the interview, Ray talks about why he thinks whales are exciting animals. Put a tick beside the reasons he gives:

He feels an inexplicable affinity with them   Their brains are large
They have feelings like human beings   All whales are enormous
They can move in breathtakingly spectacular ways
They can perform tricks   They can communicate with each other
They may be on the verge of extinction   Some whales are impressively large
They are perfectly suited to living in the sea

E Work in groups and discuss your reactions to the recording:

What species do you know about which are endangered?
Why is it important that endangered animals and plants don't become extinct?
How can endangered species be saved?

10.3 Conditional sentences – 1

A Work in pairs. Discuss any differences in meaning or emphasis between these sentences:

1 If you don't leave now, you'll be late.   If you leave now, you won't be late.
   If you left now, you wouldn't be late.   If you didn't leave now, you'd be late.
   Unless you leave now, you'll be late.

2 When I have time, I'll feed the cat.   If I have time, I'll feed the goldfish.
   If I had time, I'd feed the ducks.   If I had time, I'd have fed the birds.
   If I'd had time, I'd have fed the dog.   When I had time, I'd feed the rabbits.

3 I feel upset when I think about the destruction of the rainforests.
   I'd feel upset when I thought about people destroying the rainforests.
   I'd feel upset if I thought about the rainforests being destroyed.
   I feel upset if I think about the destruction of tropical rainforests.
   I felt upset when I thought about jungles being destroyed.

4 If you're interested I'll tell you about my dream.
   If you were interested I'd tell you about my dream.

B Rewrite each sentence, beginning each new sentence with *If . . .* , keeping the meaning as close as possible to the original sentence.

1 Don't go too close to that dog in case it bites you.
2 I didn't give you a hand because I didn't realise that you needed help.
3 The amount of carbon dioxide in the atmosphere must be reduced, otherwise the ozone layer will be permanently damaged.
4 Forests once covered most of Europe, before they were cut down.
5 Pollution is caused because people are ignorant about its effects on the environment.
6 Animals can't speak in their own defence, so we must speak up for them.
7 Everyone should drive more slowly so that there is less pollution.
8 Without acid rain these lakes would still have fish in them.

C Complete each sentence with your own ideas, as in the example.

1 Would you feel sick if ...**you had to eat raw fish?**
2 If he hadn't been so generous, ...

3 If you aren't careful, ...

4 If she doesn't phone me by Friday, ...

5 If everyone cared more about the environment, ...

6 If any species becomes extinct, ...

7 If human beings became extinct, ...

8 Unless the governments of the world cooperate, ...

D Work in groups and discuss these questions. Then write a paragraph summarising your discussion. Compare your summary with another group.

- What might happen if global warming continues?
- What might happen if everyone voted for the Green Party?
- What might happen if everyone stopped eating meat and fish?
- What might have happened if the world's population hadn't grown so large?

10.4 Changing the climate

A Read this passage and then answer the questions on the next page.

ANTONIO Ibañez is under siege. Since a Spanish TV crew visited his laboratory outside Barcelona last year, he has fielded inquiries from all over the world. Libya,
1 Morocco, Algeria, Mauritania, Brazil, Peru, India, Australia and Saudi Arabia are all interested in what could prove to be a way of turning tracts of desert into cultivatable land. They want to try Ibañez's plastic palm tree.

The spark for Ibañez's invention was hearing of widespread frosts in desert areas at night. How, he wanted to know, could
2 that water be prevented from evaporating rapidly when the sun rose. He decided to look for a natural solution – and copy it.

His plastic palm tree is a passive device, designed to be planted on a grand scale – thousands of them – and left to get on with it. "Basically, the trees do two things," says
3 Ibañez. "They lower the temperature and raise humidity." Cooler air tends to encourage clouds to move in, increasing moisture and lowering temperatures.

Tiny capillaries in the trees' trunks and leaves absorb water, while polyurethane layers of differing densities in the trunk retain water and release it slowly during
4 the day. The temperature-sensitive foam leaves open to increase water absorption at night and close to reduce evaporation during daylight.

The roots are pumped into the ground in liquid form to a depth of 25 metres, where the non-toxic polyurethane quickly sets. The roots then absorb water from the soil

and anchor the tree against the violent winds that can sweep desert zones. In an 5 artificial plantation, the trees' height varies from eight metres in the centre to five metres at the edge, to force wind to blow harmlessly over any life growing in the gaps between the trees.

It is under the canopies and between trees that a new microclimate will start to form, Ibañez believes. It will be a cooler, humid zone with a daytime high of 22°C, 6 rather than the hostile 70°C of before. At night, rather than temperatures of about –5°C, the air could be a life-supporting +5°C.

Once a stable microclimate has been reached, says Ibañez, very gradually the plastic trees can be replaced by natural ones – and the synthetic frontline moved on. 7 "In this way we can win back kilometres of desert," he says. It is not just desert areas that could benefit, he suggests, but rainforests too.

Somewhere in Libya, his theory is being put to the test. Packed into a couple of hectares of desert are 30,000 of Ibañez's trees. The plantation is "working," he has 8 been told, but the details are "top secret". Plantations are also planned for Morocco and the Canary Islands.

But sceptics remain. Jorge Wagensberg, director of Spain's Museum of Science, doesn't believe the trees will work at all. 9 "The designer ignores the distance between an idea and its practical application." To hope to change the climate with a few trees, he says, is wildly optimistic.

Ibañez agrees his idea won't work on a small scale. "To change an area with one tree is impossible, but with thousands it can be done."

10

His palm trees, if they prove effective, could make him a rich man. All he wants, though, he says, is money to build a centre for scientific investigation. "It's sad, but the government isn't interested in funding it."

11

Rupert Widdecombe

Choose the word or phrase which best completes each sentence.

1 Ibañez's idea was inspired by the . . .
   a) climate in desert regions b) demand from many desert countries
   c) knowledge that moisture is present in deserts
   d) way in which desert peoples find water
2 The plastic leaves . . .
   a) open at night and close during the day b) are always closed
   c) are always open d) close at night and open during the day
3 The roots of the plastic trees are . . .
   a) thin b) thick c) short d) porous
4 Which illustration represents a plantation of plastic trees?

5 Trees in desert regions are vulnerable to . . .
   a) damage caused by grazing animals b) thunderstorms
   c) high winds d) sand storms
6 Eventually the plastic trees will . . .
   a) be planted elsewhere b) disintegrate
   c) no longer be needed d) replace real trees
7 Ibañez's scheme is currently being tried out but . . .
   a) he doubts whether it will be successful
   b) he doesn't know for certain if it is successful
   c) further tests are needed to discover if it is successful
   d) he will not reveal whether it is successful
8 Ibañez's ultimate aim is to . . .
   a) become a wealthy man b) influence the climate of desert areas
   c) set up a research centre
   d) persuade the government to set up a research centre

B Find words in the passage with similar meanings to these words and phrases:
   deal with ¶ 1   *large area* ¶ 1   *secure* ¶ 5   *unvarying* ¶ 7   *use* ¶ 9
   excessively ¶ 9

★★ When answering multiple-choice questions like the ones above, it's sometimes easier to eliminate (and cross out) the wrong answers first, and *then* decide what the right answers might be.

Be careful though: sometimes it's the *least* likely-looking answer that is actually right – especially if the writer holds unconventional views, or if you're reading about an unfamiliar topic!

A   How would you describe the style of each of these sentences: formal, colloquial or neutral (i.e. neither stiffly formal nor very colloquial)?

I do like little kittens and puppies – they're ever so sweet, aren't they?
I consider young kittens and puppies to be the most endearing creatures.
Small kittens and puppies are delightful, I think.
Ibañez agrees that his idea will not function satisfactorily on a small scale.
Ibañez agrees that his idea won't work on a small scale.
He doesn't think his idea's going to work – not on a small scale at any rate.

Look at the article about plastic palm trees in 10.4 and highlight some examples of **neutral style**.

B   Rewrite these colloquial sentences in a more neutral (i.e. more formal but not stiffly formal) style:

1   It's a lot better to use renewable energy – not fossil fuels like coal, gas and oil.
    Renewable energy resources are preferable to fossil fuels, such as coal, gas and oil.
2   How's your dad? Is he OK again yet?
3   Well, she hit the roof when they broke it to her that she'd got the sack.
4   To grow organic fruit and vegetables they don't use artificial fertiliser, you know.
5   We were ever so scared when this huge great dog came bounding up to us.
6   For pity's sake, mind what you're doing with that knife!
7   There's no point in testing cosmetics and shampoo on animals – and it's cruel too.
8   Why on earth didn't you turn the light off when you left the room?
9   Hey, it looks as if it's going to rain pretty soon.
10 Don't throw litter in the street – put it in a bin or something, for goodness sake.

C   Rewrite these formal sentences in a more neutral, less formal style:

1   It is unwise to bathe here due to possible contamination of the water.
    It's not advisable to go swimming here because the water may be polluted.
2   Meteorologists maintain that the rate of increase in the global warming process is accelerating.
3   It is conceivable that a slight rise in temperature would have a dramatic effect on the ice in polar regions.
4   Discarding cans and bottles leads to excessive consumption of energy and materials. It is preferable to recycle them.
5   The service of luncheon commences at noon.
6   Passengers are requested to exercise caution when alighting from the train.
7   To whom was the recommendation submitted?
8   We regret that the playing of personal stereos and musical instruments is not permitted on the premises.
9   Whilst all vegetarians eschew meat, vegans consume neither fish nor dairy products.
10 It is regrettable that the government is not willing to provide financial support for scientific investigation.

⟫→

D Work in pairs. Write a paragraph giving your views about being economical with energy (turning off lights, driving slowly, etc.) in the style you'd use in an informal letter to a friend.

Pass your paragraph to another pair, who should rewrite it in a more neutral style.

★★ When writing a composition in the exam it's best to aim for a fairly neutral style, rather than a style that is over-colloquial or stiffly formal. However, a personal letter should be written in a friendly, colloquial style.

Contractions (*isn't*, *it's*, etc.) are often used in a neutral style. In the exam you wouldn't be penalised for using them, but it may be safer to stick to full forms. In academic essays or job applications contractions should not be used,

10.6 Charles Darwin

Reading & summarising

A Read the passage and write your answers to the questions that follow. Do this on your own, without using a dictionary. Remember to highlight the relevant parts of the passage, and make notes before you start writing anything.

➡ Time how long it takes you to do this exercise.

Charles Darwin
1809-82

In 1832 a young Englishman, Charles Darwin, twenty-four years old and naturalist on HMS *Beagle*, a brig sent by the Admiralty of London on a surveying voyage round the world, came to a forest outside Rio de Janeiro. In one day, in one small area, he collected sixty-eight different species of small beetle. That $_5$ there should be such a variety of species of one kind of creature astounded him. He had not been searching specially for them so that, as he wrote in his journal, 'It is sufficient to disturb the composure of an entomologist's mind to look forward to the future dimensions of a complete catalogue'. The conventional view of his time was that all species were immutable and that $_{10}$ each had been individually and separately created by God. Darwin was far from being an atheist – he had, after all, taken a degree in divinity in Cambridge – but he was deeply puzzled by this enormous multiplicity of forms.

During the next three years, the *Beagle* sailed down the east coast of South $_{15}$ America, rounded Cape Horn and came north again up the coast of Chile. The expedition then sailed out into the Pacific until, 600 miles from the mainland, they came to the lonely archipelago of the Galapagos. Here Darwin's questions about the creation of species recurred, for in these islands he found fresh variety. He was fascinated to discover that the Galapagos animals bore a general resemblance to those he had seen on the mainland, but different from them in detail.

The English Vice-Governor of the Galapagos told Darwin that even within the archipelago, there was variety: the tortoises on each island were slightly different, so that it was possible to tell which island they came from. Those that lived on relatively well-watered islands where there was ground vegetation to be cropped, had a gently curving front edge to their shells just above the neck. But those that came from arid islands and had to crane their necks in order to reach branches of cactus or leaves of trees, had much longer necks and a high peak to the front of their shells that enabled them to stretch their necks almost vertically upwards.

The suspicion grew in Darwin's mind that species were not fixed for ever. Perhaps one could change into another. Maybe, thousands of years ago, birds and reptiles from continental South America had reached the Galapagos, ferried on the rafts of vegetation that float down the rivers and out to sea. Once there, they had changed, as generation succeeded generation, to suit their new homes until they became their present species.

The differences between them and their mainland cousins were only small, but if such changes had taken place, was it not possible that over many millions of years, the cumulative effects on a dynasty of animals could be so great that they could bring about major transformations? Maybe fish had developed muscular fins and crawled on to land to become amphibians; maybe amphibians in their turn had developed water-tight skins and become reptiles; maybe, even, some ape-like creatures had stood upright and become the ancestors of man.

In truth the idea was not a wholly new one. Many others before Darwin had suggested that all life on earth was interrelated. Darwin's revolutionary insight was to perceive the mechanism that brought these changes about. By doing so he replaced a philosophical speculation with a detailed description of a process, supported by an abundance of evidence, that could be tested and verified; and the reality of evolution could no longer be denied.

Put briefly, his argument was this. All individuals of the same species are not identical. In one clutch of eggs from, for example, a giant tortoise, there will be some hatchlings which, because of their genetic constitution, will develop longer necks than others. In times of drought they will be able to reach leaves and so survive. Their brothers and sisters, with shorter necks, will starve and die. So those best fitted to their surroundings will be selected and be able to transmit their characteristics to their offspring. After a great number of generations, tortoises on the arid islands will have longer necks than those on the watered islands. And so one species will have given rise to another.

This concept did not become clear in Darwin's mind until long after he had left the Galapagos. For twenty-five years he painstakingly amassed evidence to support it. Not until 1859, when he was forty-eight years old, did he publish it and even then he was driven to do so only because another younger naturalist,

Alfred Wallace, working in South East Asia, had formulated the same idea. He called the book in which he set out his theory in detail, *The Origin of Species by Means of Natural Selection or the Preservation of Favoured Races in the Struggle for Life*. 65

Since that time, the theory of natural selection has been debated and tested, refined, qualified and elaborated. Later discoveries about genetics, molecular biology, population dynamics and behaviour have given it new dimensions. It remains the key to our understanding of the natural world and it enables us to recognise that life has a long and continuous history during which organisms, both plant and animal, have changed, generation by generation, as they colonised all parts of the world. 70

75

(from *Life on Earth* by David Attenborough)

1   How did the primary purpose of the HMS *Beagle*'s voyage differ from Darwin's?
2   What astonished Darwin in Brazil?
3   What is the meaning of 'immutable' in line 10?
4   What is meant by 'Darwin was far from being an atheist' in line 11?
5   What first intrigued Darwin about the Galapagos animals?
6   What is meant by 'recurred' in line 19?
7   How did the tortoises on each Galapagos island differ?
8   How did Darwin suggest the animals had found their way to the Galapagos?
9   What is the meaning of 'insight' in line 48?
10   What was revolutionary about Darwin's ideas?
11   What are 'hatchlings' (line 54)?
12   How quickly did Darwin publish his theory?
13   What made him publish his book when he did?
14   How have modern discoveries changed ideas on natural selection?

15   Summarise Darwin's innovative description of the process of natural selection. (70–100 words)

B   After you have compared your answers with a partner, work in groups or as a class and discuss these questions:

- How long did it take you to do this section?
- What did you find most difficult about doing the exercise while timing yourself?
- What did you do when you didn't know (or couldn't find) an answer?
- In an exam do you read the questions through *before* you read the passage? Or is it better to read the passage through first (to get the gist) and then read it more carefully, searching for the answers? Give your reasons.

★★   Although this passage is about twice the length of the one you'll have to read in the exam, the amount of writing you'll have to do is about the same. In the exam you should aim to do the Questions and Summary in Paper 3 in about 50 minutes. This time includes reading the passage through, making notes, and checking your work through for mistakes at the end. If this exercise took you much more than an hour, you should try to speed up your performance.

A   Work in pairs. Discuss the differences in meaning (if any) between these
sentences:

1   I wish that dog would stop barking.   I wish that dog had stopped barking.
     I wish that dog didn't bark.   I want that dog to stop barking.
2   It's time for you to do the washing-up.   It's time you did the washing-up.
3   If only it were Friday!   If it were only Friday . . .
     Only if it was Friday . . .   If it's only Friday . . .
4   Would you rather I didn't help you?   Would you rather not help me?
     Would you prefer it if I didn't help you?   Would you prefer me not to help you?
5   I was going to phone her tonight.   I intended to phone her tonight.
     I am going to phone her tonight.   I was to have phoned her tonight.
6   I wish I knew the answer.   I wish to know the answer.

B   Fill each gap with suitable words or phrases:

1   I do wish you .... me when I'm trying to study.
2   It's high time something .... industry from polluting the environment.
3   You're very late! I'd prefer .... a little earlier next time.
4   If only people .... the dangers of global warming 20 years ago!
5   I wish .... ride a horse.
6   I wish there .... to save the whales.
7   We .... and see you on Sunday but there wasn't enough time.
8   What a noise you're making! I'd rather .... a bit more quietly.
9   Well, it's 9.30, do you think it's .... yet?
10   Isn't it time the cat .... ? It looks very hungry.

MºLACHLAN

A The writer of this passage (a zoologist who runs a zoo himself) wants to convince the reader of his views on zoos and safari parks.

Work in pairs. Read the passage and highlight the words and phrases that show the writer's feelings, attitude and passionately-held opinions.

I must agree with you (if you are anti-zoo), that not all zoos are perfect. Of the 500 or so zoological collections in the world, a few are excellent, some are inferior and the rest are appalling. Given the premises that zoos can and should be of value scientifically, educationally and from a conservation point of view (thus serving both us and other animal life), then I feel very strongly 5 that one should strive to make them better. I have had, ironically enough, a great many rabid opponents of zoos tell me that they would like all zoos closed down, yet the same people accept with equanimity the proliferation of safari parks, where, by and large, animals are far worse off than in the average zoo. An animal can be just as unhappy, just as ill-treated, in a vast 10 area as in a small one, but the rolling vistas, the ancient trees, obliterate criticism, for this is the only thing that these critics think the animals want.

It is odd how comforted people feel by seeing an animal in a ten-acre field. Safari parks were invented purely to make money. No thought of science or conservation sullied their primary conception. Like a rather 15 unpleasant fungus, they have spread now throughout the world. In the main, their treatment of animals is disgraceful and the casualties (generally carefully concealed) appalling. I will not mention the motives, or the qualifications of the men who created them, for they are sufficiently obvious, but I would like to stress that I know it to be totally impossible to run these 20 vast concerns with a knowledgeable and experienced staff, since that number of knowledgeable and experienced staff does not exist. I know, because I am always on the look-out for such rare beasts myself.

I am not against the conception of safari parks. I am against the way that they are at present run. In their present form, they represent a bigger hazard 25 and a bigger drain on wild stocks of animals than any zoo ever has done. Safari parks, properly controlled and scientifically run, could be of immense conservation value for such things as antelope, deer and the larger carnivores. But they have a long way to go before they can be considered anything other than animal abattoirs in a sylvan setting. 30

I feel, therefore, that one should strive to make zoos and safari parks better, not simply clamour for their dissolution. If Florence Nightingale's sole contribution, when she discovered the appalling conditions in the hospitals of the last century, had been to advocate that they should all be closed down, few people in later years would have praised her for her 35 acumen and far-sightedness.

My plan, then, is that all of us, zoo opponents and zoo lovers alike, should endeavour to make them perfect; should make sure that they are a help to animal species and not an additional burden on creatures already too hard pressed by our unbeatable competition. This can be done by being much more critical of zoos and other animal collections, thus making them more critical of themselves, so that even the few good ones will strive to be better. | 40

(from *The Stationary Ark* by Gerald Durrell)

B Here are more examples of words and phrases which show a writer's attitude. Highlight the ones that you would like to remember.

1 It is .... that animals are kept in captivity.
   appalling   disgraceful   dreadful   frightful   shocking   terrible
   absurd   incomprehensible   odd   ridiculous   strange   ironic

2 Some zoos are .... but most of them are ....
   admirable   excellent   fine   praiseworthy
   appalling   atrocious   disgraceful   dreadful   frightful   shocking

3 .... something must be done as soon as possible.
   Clearly   Obviously   Quite frankly   There is no doubt that
   Undoubtedly   Without a shadow of doubt

   As far as I'm concerned   I feel very strongly that
   I would like to stress that   It seems to me that   Personally
   My view is that   You must agree that   It is generally agreed that

4 ...., there is a straightforward solution to this problem.
   Ironically enough   Strangely enough   Oddly enough   Actually   In fact
   In spite of this   Mind you   Nevertheless   Still

5 I .... good zoos but I .... bad ones.
   am all in favour of   advocate   applaud   approve of   favour   support
   am against   condemn   strongly disapprove of   object to
   reject the idea of

C Fill these gaps with words or phrases you highlighted above.

1 It is .... that most safari parks are simply money-making enterprises.
2 .... there are some zoos which are run to make a profit, but not all.
3 ...., some zoos are absolutely ....
4 I .... zoos as such – .... I enjoy a day at the zoo.
5 .... hunting animals is a(n) .... leisure activity.
6 .... there is nothing wrong with people having pets, ... keeping a large dog in a city apartment is ....

D Write a couple of paragraphs, giving your own views on any one of these topics which you feel strongly about:
   • Using animals in laboratories for testing cosmetics
   • Shooting animals for 'sport'
   • Keeping large, fierce dogs as 'pets'
   • The destruction of the rainforests
   • Training animals to perform in circuses
   • Eating meat

A Work in groups. Look at the ideas on these pages and discuss your reactions.

According to the experts:

- Between 1990 and 2000 10% of the estimated 30 million species of plants and animals will be lost forever. By 2030 another 20% are likely to be lost. The extinction of one plant species can cause the loss of 30 dependent organisms.
- By 1990 half the world's rainforests had already been destroyed. Of the remaining half, one third will disappear between 1990 and 2000 and another third by 2030.
- Between 1990 and 2000 the average temperature will rise by 1° C. By 2100 it will rise by 3° C to 5° C. This will have unpredictable effects on local weather patterns. The sea level is likely to rise between 10 cm and 2 m.
- There were 600 million motor vehicles in 1990. By 2000 there will be 750 million, and by 2030 1,100 million.
- The total world population in 1990 was 5,300 million. By 2000 there will be 6,000 million, and by 2030 there may be 8,000 to 10,000 million mouths to feed and by 2100 11,000 to 14,000.

(information from *Save the Earth* by Jonathon Porritt)

'This is what you should do: love the Earth and sun and the animals, despise riches, give alms to everyone that asks, stand up for the stupid and crazy, devote your income and labour to others, hate tyrants, argue not concerning God, have patience and indulgence towards the people, take off your hat to nothing known or unknown or to any man or number of men . . . re-examine all you have been told at school or church or in any book, dismiss what insults your own soul, and your very flesh shall be a great poem.'

Walt Whitman

If the Earth were only a few feet in diameter, floating a few feet above a field somewhere, people would come from everywhere to marvel at it. People would walk around it marvelling at its big pools of water, its little pools and the water flowing between. People would marvel at the bumps on it and the holes in it. They would marvel at the very thin layer of gas surrounding it and the water suspended in the gas. The people would marvel at all the creatures walking around the surface of the ball and at the creatures in the water. The people would declare it as sacred because it was the only one, and they would protect it so that it would not be hurt. The ball would be the greatest wonder known, and people would come to pray to it, to be healed, to gain knowledge, to know beauty and to wonder how it could be. People would love it, and defend it with their lives because they would somehow know that their lives could be nothing without it. If the Earth were only a few feet in diameter.

Joe Miller

B *Write an essay giving your views on some of the issues you discussed.* (about 350 words)

A First, read this 'fill the gaps' passage through, just to get the gist.

It is not ......1...... to ......2...... an unknown animal. Spend a day in the tropical forests of South America, turning over logs, looking beneath bark, sifting through the moist litter of leaves, followed by an evening ......3...... a mercury lamp on a white screen, and one way and another you will ......4...... hundreds of different kinds of small creatures. Moths, caterpillars, spiders, long-nosed bugs, luminous beetles, harmless butterflies ......5...... as wasps, wasps shaped like ants, sticks that walk, leaves that open wings and fly – the variety will be ......6...... and one of these ......7...... will almost certainly be undescribed by science. The difficulty will be to find ......8...... who know enough about the groups ......9...... to be able to single out the new one.

No one can say ......10...... how many species of animals there are in these greenhouse-humid dimly lit jungles. They contain the ......11...... and the most varied assemblage of animal and plant life to be found anywhere on earth. Not only are there many categories of creatures – monkeys, rodents, spiders, hummingbirds, butterflies, but most of those types ......12...... in many different ......13...... . There are over forty different species of parrot, over seventy different monkeys, three hundred hummingbirds and tens of thousands of butterflies. If you are not ......14...... , you can even be ......15...... by a hundred different kinds of mosquito.

B Work in pairs. Decide which words are most suitable to fit in each of the numbered gaps – some are grammatically or stylistically unsuitable.

1 difficult ✓ hard ✓ problematic ✗ strenuous ✗ tricky ✗
2 come across discover find identify meet
3 lighting pointing reflecting shining
4 collect discover gather glimpse identify pick up
5 disguised dressed masquerading posing
6 ample big enormous huge immense
7 animals creatures insects things types
8 experts friends guys people specialists
9 characteristics concerned themselves there
10 almost exactly just nearly precisely quite sincerely
11 best biggest deepest richest strangest thickest wildest
12 are become exist happen remain survive
13 forms manners types ways zones
14 asleep awake careful cunning fortunate unlucky
15 attacked bitten poisoned stung threatened

➡ Where you ticked more than one answer, which is the one you feel is the best?

★★ When doing an exercise like A in the exam (without B to help you!), you should bear in mind the context, the sense of the passage, and its style. In the exam some of the gaps will require grammatical words: prepositions, articles, conjunctions, etc.

A Which of the following would be preceded by PUT and which by SET?

pressure on someone   a trap for someone   your teeth on edge
two and two together   someone at their ease   a question to someone
a stop to something   a good example   someone in the picture
fire to something   your watch   pen to paper   the scene

B Find synonyms for the phrases in italics, or explain their meaning. Use a
dictionary if necessary.

1 I think I *put my foot in it* when I asked her what the matter was.
2 Having the car fixed *set* me *back* £250! That's *put paid* to my holiday plans.
3 Keep your options open: don't *put all your eggs in one basket*.
4 If you take a flash photo while he's playing the violin you may *put* him *off*.
5 Her bad performance in her flute exam can be *put down to* nerves. Let's hope it
   doesn't *put* her *off* playing altogether.
6 You've let her get away with being late too often: it's time you *put your foot down*.
7 The bad weather has *set* the building programme *back* by several weeks.
8 When they *set up* the scheme they *set out* to make it as innovative as possible.
9 You're always *putting* me *down*! *Put yourself in my shoes* and imagine what it feels
   like. Don't you realise that it *puts* both of us *in a bad light*?
10 I *wouldn't put it past* him to have made the whole story up.

C Fill the gaps in these sentences with suitable phrases from the list below. You
may need to change the form of the verbs.

1 It wasn't her idea – someone else must have .... her .... it.
2 They were going out together for five years before they .... house together.
3 He has tremendous ideas but he's not very good at .... them ....
4 I don't want to .... you ...., but I've got nowhere to stay. Can you
   .... me .... for the night?
5 It doesn't take much encouragement .... him .... gossiping.
6 If you don't like the situation, you'll just have to .... it, I'm afraid.
7 You can't stand in the way of progress: you can't .... the clock ....
8 The room was in such a mess that he immediately .... tidying everything up.
9 Holidays are expensive: you can save up by .... a little money each month.
10 They won't turn on the central heating until the really cold weather ....
11 5,000 words! You must have .... a lot of hours on this work.
12 In her book she .... to examine the wide variety of species in the world.

put across / over   put aside / put away / set aside
put back   put in   put out   put up
put up to   put up with   set about
set in   set off   set out   set up

11 A good read

A   [cassette icon] You'll hear three people talking about reading and why they enjoy it. Tick the boxes beside the TRUE statements, according to what they say.

1 **Christine**'s mother used to take her to the library every week. ☐
2 She likes stories where you want to know what happens next. ☐
3 It once took her three months to read a P.D. James novel. ☐
4 She and her father are avid readers. ☐
5 **Jilly** is interested in the style of the books she reads. ☐
6 She enjoyed *A Year in Provence* by Peter Mayle more than *Cider With Rosie* or *As I Walked Out One Midsummer Morning* by Laurie Lee. ☐
7 **Vince** likes humorous fiction. ☐
8 Both David Lodge and Malcolm Bradbury write about similar topics. ☐
9 He has laughed out loud while reading Malcolm Bradbury. ☐
10 Garrison Keillor writes about city life in the USA. ☐
11 **Vince** believes that reading stimulates your imagination. ☐
12 **Christine** vicariously shares other people's feelings by reading novels. ☐
13 She often wants to read on to find out how a conflict or problem is resolved. ☐
14 She forgets the real world when she is reading. ☐
15 At New Year she resolved to read more and has found time to do so. ☐

B   Work in groups and discuss these questions:
- Which of the people interviewed do you identify with most?
- What enjoyment do you get from reading for pleasure?
- What kinds of books and magazines would you like to read if you had more time?
- Name one fiction or non-fiction book you've enjoyed. What did you particularly enjoy about it?
- About how many books do you read in English during a year, and how many in your own language?

C   In these sentences THREE of the alternatives are correct and the rest are wrong.

1 As I prefer fiction to non-fiction I often read ....
   best-sellers   biographies   memoirs   thrillers   whodunits
2 Before buying a book it's a good idea to read the ....
   bibliography   blurb   contents   dustjacket   sleeve
3 The opening page of a book often has a(n) ....
   appendix   dedication   foreword   index   preface
4 I've just read the reviews of a newly-published .... of poetry.
   album   anthology   book   collection   gathering
5 The plot of a popular romantic novel is not usually very ....
   complex   intricate   involved   mixed   multiple
6 It was a very long book and it took me ages to .... through it.
   flip   get   struggle   thumb   wade

A   These are the opening paragraphs of the first chapter of three well-known novels. Read them through before you answer the questions in B on the next page.

1

To the red country and part of the grey country of Oklahoma the last rains came gently, and they did not cut the scarred earth. The ploughs crossed and recrossed the rivulet marks. The last rains lifted the corn quickly and scattered weed colonies and grass along the sides of the roads so that the grey country and the dark red country began to disappear under a green cover. In the last part of May the sky grew pale and the clouds that had hung in high puffs for so long in the spring were dissipated. The sun flared down on the growing corn day after day until a line of brown spread along the edge of each green bayonet. The clouds appeared, and went away, and in a while they did not try any more. The weeds grew darker green to protect themselves, and they did not spread any more. The surface of the earth crusted, a thin hard crust, and as the sky became pale, so the earth became pale, pink in the red country and white in the grey country.

In the water-cut gullies the earth dusted down in dry little streams. Gophers and ant lions started small avalanches. And as the sharp sun struck day after day, the leaves of the young corn became less stiff and erect; they bent in a curve at first, and then, as the central ribs of strength grew weak, each leaf tilted downward. Then it was June, and the sun shone more fiercely. The brown lines on the corn leaves widened and moved in on the central ribs. The weeds frayed and edged back toward their roots. The air was thin and the sky more pale; and every day the earth paled.

In the roads where the teams moved, where the wheels milled the . . .

2

We drove past Tiny Polski's mansion house to the main road, and then the five miles into Northampton, Father talking the whole way about savages and the awfulness of America – how it got turned into a dope-taking, door-locking, ulcerated danger-zone of rabid scavengers and criminal millionaires and moral sneaks. And look at the schools. And look at the politicians. And there wasn't a Harvard graduate who could change a flat tyre or do ten push-ups. And there were people in New York City who lived on pet food, who would kill you for a little loose change. Was that normal? If not, why did anyone put up with it?

'I don't know,' he said, replying to himself. 'I'm just thinking out loud.' Before leaving Hatfield, he had parked the pick-up truck on a rise in the road, and pointed south.

'Here come the savages,' he said, and up they came, tracking across the fields from a sickle of trees through the gummy drizzling heat-outlines of Polski's barns. They were dark and their clothes were rags and some had rags on their heads and others wide-brimmed hats. They were men and boys, a few no older than me, all of them carrying long knives.

Father's finger scared me more than the men did. He was still pointing. The end of his forefinger was missing to the big knuckle, so the finger stump, blunted by stitched skin folds and horribly scarred, could only approximate the right direction.

'Why do they bother to come here?' he said. 'Money? But how . . .

3

In the late summer of that year we lived in a house in a village that looked across the river and the plain to the mountains. In the bed of the river there were pebbles and boulders, dry and white in the sun, and the water was clear and swiftly moving and blue in the channels. Troops went by the house and down the road and the dust they raised powdered the leaves of the trees. The trunks of the trees too were dusty and the leaves fell early that year and we saw the troops marching along the road and the dust rising and leaves, stirred by the breeze, falling and the soldiers marching and afterwards the road bare and white except for the leaves. 5

The plain was rich with crops; there were many orchards of fruit trees and beyond the plain the mountains were brown and bare. There was fighting in the mountains and at night we could see the flashes from the artillery. In the dark it was like summer lightning, but the nights were cool and there was not the feeling of a storm coming. 10

Sometimes in the dark we heard the troops marching under the window and guns going past pulled by motor-tractors. There was much traffic at night and many mules on the roads with boxes of ammunition on each side of their pack-saddles and grey motor-trucks that carried men, and other trucks with loads covered with . . . 15

B You'll need to refer back to the three extracts to answer these questions. Work in pairs or groups – or discuss your answers in pairs later.

1 Which extract conveys an impression of time passing?
2 Which extract conveys an impression of movement?
3 Which extract conveys an impression of a degenerating, violent world?
4 How are these impressions conveyed? What stylistic devices are used to create the impressions?
5 Which extract uses the fewest modifying adjectives?
6 Which extract uses the simplest grammatical structures?
7 Which extract uses the style of spoken conversational English?
8 Which extract uses repetition to achieve its effect?
9 What do you think might be the theme of the book each extract comes from ? What might come next in the story?
10 Which of these books do you think the extracts come from?

1981   1929   1926   1939

172

A Work in pairs. Discuss the differences in emphasis between these sentences.

1 Did Jane Austen write *Emma*?   Was *Emma* written by Jane Austen?
   Was it Jane Austen who wrote *Emma*?   Was it *Emma* that Jane Austen wrote?
   Was Jane Austen the author who wrote *Emma*?
   Was Jane Austen the author of *Emma*?

2 What I enjoy reading is thrillers.   I enjoy reading thrillers.
   Thrillers are what I enjoy reading.   It's thrillers that I enjoy reading.

3 It was me who borrowed your book.   I borrowed your book.
   I was the one who borrowed your book.   It was I who borrowed your book.

B Fill these gaps with suitable words or phrases.

1 It was .... that they managed to .... of the mountain.
2 Is it Valentina or Lorenza who .... Venice?
3 It's .... that you .... me about the danger.
4 It's not because he ...., it's because he .... that he can't make friends.
5 It wasn't .... before we .... what a big mistake ....
6 Why .... that my friends are so unpunctual and .... on time?
7 If you call the office I expect it .... John .... the phone.
8 It used .... my sister .... the great reader in our family, but now it .... the most books.

C Rewrite these sentences using an *It* ... construction to emphasise the words in italics.

1 I went to bed early *because I was feeling worn out*.   It was because ....
2 *A strange noise* woke me up in the early hours.   It ....
3 I heard the noise *at half past four in the morning*.   It ....
4 I realised what had happened *when I looked out of the window*.   It ....
5 *Then* I found I couldn't get back to sleep.   It ....
6 I finally did get to sleep *at about eight o'clock*.   It ....
7 I didn't wake up *until lunchtime*.   It wasn't ....
8 She finished reading the book *only yesterday*.   It ....
9 Do you enjoy the *humour* of her stories?   Is it ....
10 Did you read *'Emma' or 'Persuasion'* recently?   Was it ....

Verbs and adverbs of manner can't be used with *It's ... that ...*:
✗ It's fall over that he did.   ✗ It was fast that he ran   ✗ It was well that she did.

★★ In the exam, if one of your compositions is too short you'll lose marks. And if one of your compositions is too long, it'll probably contain more mistakes – and writing the extra words will take up more of your time.
     Do you know how many lines of your handwriting are equivalent to 100 words? And how many lines are equivalent to 350 words?
     To check how long a composition is: count the words in 10 lines, divide by 10 (to get the average number of words per line) and then multiply the answer by the total number of lines.

Abdulrazak Gurnah

A   Before you listen to the interview with the novelist Abdulrazak Gurnah, discuss
how, as a professional writer, he may have answered these questions:

- How do you go about writing a book?
  Do you wait until the inspiration comes? Do you set yourself targets?
- What do you enjoy about writing?
- What motivates you as a writer?

B   Decide if these statements are true (T) or false (F), according to the
speaker:

1 *Memory of Departure* is about a journey from Africa to England.
2 The protagonist of *Pilgrim's Way* is overwhelmed by his difficulties.
3 *Pilgrim's Way* is about Africa as well as England.
4 Some of the characters in *Memory of Departure* are people he actually knows.
5 Events that really happened form the basis of *Memory of Departure*.
6 Only a person who has had a lot of experiences can become a good writer.
7 The process of writing involves a lot of painstaking and dull work.
8 It is impossible to say what the practical purpose of writing a book is.
9 He believes that his writing has a purpose, but he can't explain what it is.
10 It becomes increasingly difficult for him to get ideas for new books.
11 Before embarking on a new project he makes very detailed plans.
12 His principal pleasure comes from expressing his ideas effectively in writing.
13 Reading a good novel combines the pleasures of getting involved in ideas,
    language and a well-told story.

C   Work in groups and discuss these questions:

- What do you think you might enjoy/not enjoy about Abdulrazak's novels?
- Who is the most famous living writer in your country? What do you know about
  her/his life and works?
- What is the most famous classic book written in your language? Describe it.
- Who is your favourite British and who is your favourite American writer? What do
  you know about their lives and works?

★★   Exam questions focus on some, but not all, of the information given. If you study the
questions first, you'll know what to listen out for.

➡ If you're preparing one of the prescribed texts for the exam, start with the questions in section A. If not, start with section B. Imagine that one of you is the 'examiner' and the other the 'candidate', changing roles halfway.

A   Work in pairs and discuss these questions:
- What is your impression so far of the prescribed book you're reading? What do you find appealing about it? What do you find difficult about it?
- Is it the kind of book you'd normally read for pleasure? Is it a book that you 'can't put down', or is it heavy going?
- How relevant does it seem to your own tastes, experiences and concerns?
- What are your reactions to its style? And to its plot? And to its characters?
- Can you give some examples of things you've found particularly interesting, moving or amusing? Read out an extract to illustrate this, if possible.

➡ If there's still time, look at B and discuss the more general points there.

B   Work in pairs and discuss these questions:
- How much reading do you do? How much time do you spend each week reading books, and how much time reading newspapers or magazines? How much do you read in English, rather than in your own language?
- What kinds of books do you enjoy reading? Do you choose different sorts of books for different occasions (journeys, holidays, reading in bed, etc.)?
- If you could choose between reading a book or seeing the same story as a film, on video or on TV, which would you prefer?
- Who are your favourite authors? Describe the kinds of books they write.
- Describe one book you have particularly enjoyed reading recently. What did you like about it? What were its faults?
- Are there any books you'd like to re-read one day (or have re-read)? What are the qualities of such a book?
- Is there any particular book you'd recommend to your partners? What do you think they'd enjoy about it?

C   Work in pairs. Make notes in preparation for a composition of about 350 words on ONE of these topics:

Either: *Describe a book you have particularly enjoyed reading, making it sound as appealing as possible.*

or: *Explain what you find particularly striking or moving about the prescribed book you are reading.*

➡ Try to cover the following aspects of the book:

Theme   Plot   Characters   Style   Message   Relevance to your life

D   Show your completed composition to a partner and ask for comments.

12 How things work

A   Work in pairs and discuss what each photograph shows.

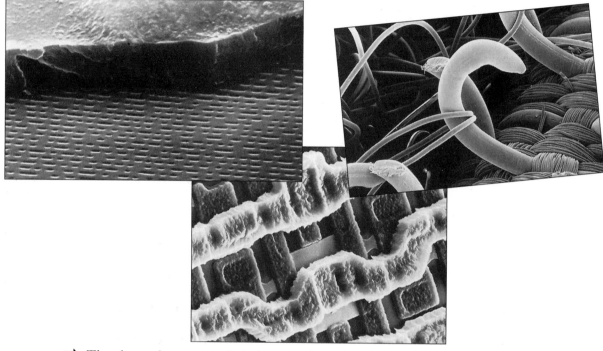

➡ The photos show some relatively recent inventions. What other 20th century inventions or scientific breakthroughs have changed our lives as much, or even more than the inventions shown?

B   Work in pairs. Choose ONE answer to complete each sentence.

1 Technology deals with the .... of science.
   apparatus   application   empiricism   practicability
2 .... is one of the physical sciences.
   anatomy   botany   meteorology   sociology
3 .... is one of the life sciences.
   archaeology   astronomy   astrology   zoology
4 .... is one of the social sciences.
   anthropology   chemistry   geology   physics
5 Many solutions to technical problems are discovered by ....
   experience   hit and miss   rule of thumb   trial and error
6 Albert Einstein was the most brilliant mathematician of his ....
   class   country   generation   year
7 The highest academic degree that a scientist can be awarded is a(n) ....
   BSc   DP   MSc   PhD

8 A scientific hypothesis is tested in a series of .... experiments.
   controlled   limited   supervised   theoretical

9 The success of her research can be attributed to 10% .... and 90% hard work.
   common sense   effort   greed   inspiration

10 The government is spending $3.5m on .... a new research laboratory.
   setting in   setting out   setting over   setting up

11 The budget for R & D has been .... by the company's board.
   elevated   lifted   raised   risen

12 His ideas are invariably criticised as .... by fellow scientists.
   imaginative   impractical   ingenious   theoretical

13 A food processor has become an indispensable piece of .... in the home.
   contraption   device   equipment   gadget

14 The designer has applied for a .... for her new invention.
   copyright   patent   royalty   trade mark

15 It must have taken a genius to .... this complicated apparatus.
   think of   think out   think through   think up

16 Water is a chemical .... made up of hydrogen and oxygen.
   compound   element   mixture   solution

17 A substance that causes a chemical reaction is a(n) ....
   addition   additive   catalyst   enzyme

18 This appliance has to be plugged into a(n) .... to make it work.
   cable   inlet   plug   socket

19 An electrical circuit is protected from overloading by a(n) ....
   adaptor   flex   fuse   transformer

20 All the information required to operate the machine is stored in a tiny ....
   console   control panel   dashboard   microchip

21 If the warning light should come on, turn the red .... to OFF.
   button   dial   knob   lever

22 The amount of fuel remaining in the tank is shown on the petrol ....
   gauge   indicator   pump   signal

23 Most motor vehicles have a pressed steel body mounted on a rigid steel ....
   axle   base   chassis   undercarriage

24 The person in charge of this construction site is a qualified civil ....
   builder   engineer   mechanic   servant

25 You've got to .... – it's a brilliant piece of design!
   give it to her   hand it to her   take it to her   take it from her

Tar-rahhh!!

Time to crack that timer

Tim Hunkin

1 YOU ARE not alone if the Luddite in you is roused by wrestling with the complexities of the timing system on your video recorder. A survey by an American company revealed in 1987 that 70 per cent of people admitted defeat when confronted by their video timer's buttons.

2 Tomorrow, a new six-part series of The Secret Life of Machines on Channel 4 tries to bridge this and other infuriating gaps between man and his understanding of modern machines. Presented by cartoonist and engineer Tim Hunkin, the programme sets out to demystify the workings of everyday objects, from cars to watches.

3 Hunkin believes that a short-trousered enthusiasm for taking machines apart to see how they work has been lost because of their increasing dependence on electronics. Rather than being put off by inscrutable layers of circuitry, however, the programme encourages viewers to mend their own machines.

4 "Electronics is just a veneer," he says. "Most of the objects in the series have their roots in a time before electronics was invented."

5 By conducting experiments, such as constructing a simple radio receiver from a 5p piece, Hunkin illustrates the basics on which they work and, in the process, tries to make modern machines less intimidating.

6 Although "technophobia" is not a recognised clinical condition, like fear of insects, the inability to come to grips with everyday pieces of technology can cause anxiety.

7 The greatest modern "techno-fear" is the computer, which increasing numbers of people have to get to grips with in their jobs. "What you call 'technophobia' often stems from peer group pressure," says Dr John Hall, a consultant adviser in clinical psychology to the Chief Medical Officer. "People feel that if they fail to grasp a technical task, then they're no good."

8 Japanese technology has been quick to help consumers suffering from "button fatigue" – that inability to set a video or operate a word processor. Home products are now marketed on the strength of "fuzzy logic", a computer control system which makes the difficult decisions for you.

9 Instead of battling with the switches of domestic technology, a washing machine with fuzzy logic will gauge the dirtiness and weight of a clothes load and set the wash programme itself.

10 Although psychologists have encountered few cases of true "technophobia" – that is, people who are paralysed with anxiety when confronted with new technology – Dr Neil Cossins of London's Science Museum believes the malaise exists in the milder form of an instinctive disregard for and distrust of innovation.

11 "There is a deep-seated cultural antipathy to industry and its scientists, technologists and engineers," he says. Indeed, in a Daily Telegraph survey last summer 28 per cent thought that the overall influence of science and technology on everyday life over the past 50 years was negligible, positively harmful or even disastrous.

12 Hunkin hopes the series will help to assuage fear or ignorance of technology by looking at the frustration of ownership and the human stories of the inventors.

Andrew Marshall

A Find words and phrases in the passage which mean the same as the following:

someone who hates or fears machines   give up   make less mysterious   puzzling
facade   medical   learn how to use   derives from
their friends' opinions   understand   come across   faced with
lack of interest   suspicion   antagonism   alleviate

B   Choose the word or phrase which best completes each sentence:

1   Tim Hunkin believes people are mystified by machines because they . . .
   a) are basically very complicated
   b) contain so many electronic components
   c) have never taken them apart
   d) haven't been trained as engineers
2   'Fuzzy logic' is used in domestic appliances to . . .
   a) encourage people to scrap their old appliances
   b) help humans to make decisions
   c) make advertisements for them more appealing
   d) take decision-making away from humans
3   At work, someone who can't understand computers or technology . . .
   a) is embarrassed to admit it
   b) is made to feel inadequate by their colleagues
   c) is unwilling to ask their colleagues for help
   d) may become mentally ill
4   Dr Cossins says that many people are .... when faced with new technology.
   a) depressed   b) resentful   c) terrified   d) uneasy
5   Which of these features will Tim Hunkin's TV series contain?
   a demonstration of how to programme a video recorder   ☐
   demonstrations of how various machines work   ☐
   explanations of the basic principles underlying each machine   ☐
   information about inventors' lives   ☐
   information about new technology from Japan   ☐
   interviews with inventors   ☐   interviews with psychologists   ☐
   showing the kind of problems people have with machines   ☐
   simple experiments   ☐

C   🗣🗣 Work in pairs. One of you should look at Activity 9, the other at 26. You'll each have some information by Tim Hunkin about the workings of a refrigerator and a vacuum cleaner.

12.3   Verbs + prepositions   Grammar review

⚠   These are the only prepositions used with the verbs in A, B and C:

   about   for   from   in   on   out of   to   with   (and *by* in passives only)

A   Some verbs are normally always followed by a preposition:

   *Who does that white coat **belong to**?*
   *You must be **confusing** me **with** someone else.*
   *Where do you come **from**?*

Fill in the missing prepositions in this list:

   combine something ....   compare something ....   concern yourself ....
   contrast something ....   deal ....   depend ....   dispense ....
   engage ....   impose something ....   invest ....   lean ....
   mistake it/them ....   part ....   reason ....   refer him ....   rely ....
   separate something ....   stem ....

⟫➔

179

B Some verbs can be used with a prepositional phrase (but they needn't be):

> *I think he **applied** last week.*
> *Yes, but what did he **apply** for? Who did he **apply** to? When did he **apply**?*
> *He **applied** to his father's company for a job.*

Add the missing prepositions. The verbs in **bold italics** can be used with two prepositional phrases (like *apply* in the examples).

agree .... *apologise* .... *approve* .... **bargain** ....
care .... *decide* .... *despair* .... *experiment* .... *hope* ....
insist .... *interfere* .... *intrude* .... *look* ....
negotiate .... *object* .... **quarrel** .... *resign* ....
retire .... *smell* .... *struggle* .... *succeed* .... *suffer* ....
talk .... *vote* .... *watch* .... *worry* ....

C Some verbs normally followed by an object can be used with prepositional phrases.

> *She accused someone. Yes, but what did she **accuse** them of?*
> *He borrowed something. Yes, but who did he **borrow** it from?*

Add the missing prepositions:

accuse them .... *admire him* .... *blame her* .... *borrow it* ....
cheat them .... *congratulate him* .... *consult her* ....
convince them .... *cure him* .... *deliver it* .... *mention it* ....
punish him .... *rescue them* .... *respect her* .... *take it* ....
thank her .... *threaten them* .... *use it* .... *warn him* ....

D ▨ Highlight TEN verbs + prepositions you want to remember from A, B and C. Write sentences using them.

E Fill each gap in this news article with a suitable preposition.

Computers are being given elocution lessons so that they can announce the comings and goings .... French trains .... regional accents. Computer-controlled synthesised voices are said to be more reassuring .... passengers than man-made announcements .... railway staff.

According .... a survey, travellers bristle when they hear announcements .... the refined tones adopted .... airports. What they like best is a deep voice .... a touch .... regional homeliness, even when they know it comes .... an electronic throat. Apparently, not even the voice .... the stationmaster can produce the effect as well as computers.

Experiments to find the perfect electronic announcer were started two years ago when the station .... the Champagne town of Rheims was used .... tests. Those were considered a success but .... trying out the voice .... other stations it was found that the reassuring effect was increased if regional accents were added.

The generalised use .... synthetic announcers will be put .... effect .... the next few months but the reason is not entirely psychological. The synthesiser is considered more reliable and flexible. It will not depend .... recorded messages: the announcements will be put together .... computer keyboards just before they are needed.

.... the meantime, the voices are

being put .... service elsewhere, including information offices. Already, travellers .... Paris-Austerlitz can consult an experimental audio-visual information robot that chats away .... four languages. Ticket offices are also to be equipped .... automatic dispensers that respond .... travellers' oral commands because half .... the system's passengers are said to prefer talking .... an inanimate object that does not answer back or go .... strike.

But there are no statistics available .... the train drivers' reaction .... electronic voices. Some drivers .... mainline services are now getting their instructions .... robot voices, linked .... centralised computers who nag them when they go too fast.

Paul Webster

12.4 Ocean City

A   You'll hear a broadcast about a plan to build a city in the Pacific Ocean. Fill the gaps in this summary with facts and figures from the recording.

1 The population of Japan is .... million. Only ....% of its land area of .... sq km is inhabitable.

2 Kiyohide Terai and his team want to build a huge new city .... km offshore to accommodate .... million people.

3 *Fill in the missing details in this diagram:*

Distance between decks:	Top deck: ....
	2nd deck: ....
	3rd deck: ....
	Lowest deck: ....

4 It would be supported by .... hollow steel cylinders, each .... metres apart – not resting on the sea bed, but ....

5 Each cylinder would contain .... , the level of which would be constantly .... by computers to keep the city level.

6 It wouldn't be affected by .... or .... because of its size and ....

7 For residents the advantages of living in Ocean City would be:

1 No .... to pay

2 Mainland-style leisure facilities – not like an ocean ....

3 Lots of .... activities

4 Warm and pleasant weather – few .... and low ....

5 No risk of .... (unlike mainland Japan)

B   Work in groups and discuss these questions:

1 What would be the advantages and disadvantages of living in Ocean City?

2 Do you think this scheme will ever be realised? Give your reasons.

3 What would it be like to live in such a place?

⟫➔

C Work in groups. Design your own ideal city of the future. What facilities would it have? How would it be constructed? How large would it be?

➡ Give a short presentation of your ideas to another group or to the whole class.

12.5 Suffixes

Suffixes can be used to form nouns from verbs, or from abstract nouns:

-er	adviser computer employer examiner gangster office cleaner reviewer timer tranquilliser vacuum cleaner
-ee	absentee addressee employee trainee
-or	impersonator inventor juror operator perpetrator supervisor
-ist	environmentalist scientist technologist terrorist

A Work in pairs. Look at these pairs of words ending in *-er*, *-ee* and *-or*:
- How are they different? What do they have in common – if anything?
- What abstract noun or verb is associated with each noun – or does a phrase have to be used instead?

astrologer – astronomer
Both an astronomer and an astrologer study the stars. Astronomers look through telescopes but astrologers work out horoscopes.
– Astrology and astronomy.

administrator – dictator   attacker – hijacker   bartender – moneylender
commuter – computer   councillor – counsellor   demonstrator – spectator
designer – diner   employer – employee   fortune-teller – storyteller
housebreaker – heartbreaker   landowner – loner   messenger – passenger
miner – minor   moonlighter – ghostwriter   pawnbroker – stockbroker
payer – payee   persecutor – prosecutor   photographer – choreographer
picnicker – drug-trafficker   plumber – latecomer   predecessor – successor
researcher – searcher   rioter – proprietor   shareholder – householder
synthesiser – sympathiser   troubleshooter – troublemaker

Now do the same with these nouns ending in *-ist*:

archaeologist – meteorologist   cartoonist – humorist   chauvinist – feminist
conservationist – philanthropist   guitarist – telephonist
opportunist – humanist   pharmacist – perfectionist
psychologist – psychiatrist   scientist – technologist

B These suffixes can be used to form verbs from adjectives and nouns:

-en dampen ripen harden
-ise/-ize* modernise advertise popularise

Form verbs from these adjectives and nouns, using *-ise / -ize* or *-en*:

context deaf emphasis familiar general glamour hard loose
moist national ripe sharp straight strong subsidy summary
sweet sympathy synthetic thick tight victim visual wide

* These verbs can be written *-ize* or *-ise* (as you prefer) in British English – but in American English *-ize* is usual.

C 🖊️ Highlight the words you'd like to remember – and any spellings you find troublesome. Use a dictionary, paying particular attention to the examples.

D Work in pairs. Write a short exercise with gaps and give the sentences to another pair to do.

e.g. **A person who is sent for to deal with problems is a** .... (troubleshooter)

A Read the article below and answer the questions on the next page in writing.

Coming soon – a robot slave for everyone

THE HUMAN brain contains I am told, 10 thousand million cells and each of these may have a thousand connections. Such enormous numbers used to daunt us and cause us to dismiss the possibility of making a machine with human-like ability, but now that we have grown used to moving forward at such a pace we can be less sure.

Quite soon, in only 10 or 20 years perhaps, we will be able to assemble a machine as complex as the human brain, and if we can we will. It may then take us a long time to render it intelligent by loading in the right software or by altering the architecture but that too will happen.

I think it certain that in decades not centuries, machines of silicon will arise first to rival and then surpass their human progenitors. Once they surpass us they will be capable of their own design. In a real sense they will be reproductive. Silicon will have ended carbon's long monopoly. And ours too, I suppose, for we will no longer be able to deem ourselves the finest intelligence in the known universe.

In principle it could be stopped. There will be those that try but it will happen none the less. The lid of Pandora's box is starting to open.

But let us look a little closer to the present: by the end of this decade manufacturing decline will be nearly complete – with employment in manufacturing industries less than 10 per cent in Britain. The goods are still needed but, as with agriculture already, imports and technical change will virtually remove all employment.

The Japanese are aiming to make computers dealing with concepts rather than numbers with thousands of times more power than current large machines. This has triggered a swift and powerful response in the American nation. There is a large joint programme of development among leading US computer companies, and IBM, though it says nothing, may well have the biggest programme of all.

These projects are aimed at what are loosely termed fifth-generation computers. These are really a new breed of machine entirely and will be as different from today's computers as today's computer is from an adding machine.

The simple microprocessor provides sufficient intelligence for current assembly line robots. As robots learn to see and feel, their brains will grow. Eventually, and not too far in the future, they will make decisions on the production line currently delegated to a supervisor.

Outside the factory we employ men's minds in two principal ways; as founts of knowledge and as makers of decisions. The former of these attributes is now falling prey to the machine with the development of "expert systems" whereby the acquired knowledge of a man, an expert in mining for example, is made to repose in the memory of a computer. The transfer of data from human to machine mind is neither easy nor swift but once attained it may be copied at will and broadcast. A formerly scarce resource can thus become plentiful.

The ability to reach wise conclusions, as we expect of a doctor or lawyer, from much or scant data will long remain man's monopoly – but not always.

Fifth-generation computers will share this prerogative. Tomorrow we may take our ailments to a machine as readily as to a man. In time that machine will be in the house, removing the need to journey to the doctor and providing a far more regular

85 monitoring of the state of health than it is now economic to provide.

The computer as surrogate teacher may bring even more benefits. Today, and as long as we depend on humans, we must
90 have one teacher to many pupils. The advantage of a tutor for each child is clear and if that tutor is also endlessly patient and superhumanly well-informed we may expect a wonderful improvement in the standard of
95 education. What, though, is the purpose if, in this imagined future, there are no jobs?

Curiously we can find analogies in the past. Freemen of Periclean Athens led not such different lives as we might live, for
100 where we will have the machines, they had slaves who served both to teach and as menials. Thanks perhaps to their fine education, the freemen of Athens seem not to have found difficulty in filling their time.
105 Just as they did, we will need to educate our children to an appreciation of the finer things of life, to inculcate a love of art, music and science. So we may experience an age as golden as that of Greece.

As the intelligence of robots increases to 110 emulate that of humans and as their cost declines through economies of scale we may use them to expand our frontiers, first on earth through their ability to withstand environments inimical to ourselves. Thus, 115 deserts may bloom and the ocean beds be mined.

Further ahead, by a combination of the great wealth this new age will bring and the technology it will provide, we can really 120 begin to use space to our advantage. The construction of a vast, man-created world in space, home to thousands or millions of people, will be within our power and, should we so choose, we may begin in earnest the 125 search for worlds beyond our solar system and the colonisation of the galaxy.

Sir Clive Sinclair

1 Explain the meaning of these words and phrases used in the passage:
   daunt (line 4)   *progenitors* (line 19)   *deem* (line 24)   *triggered* (line 43)
   founts of knowledge (line 63)   *falling prey* (line 65)   *surrogate* (line 87)
2 How will it be possible for machines to become more intelligent than humans?
3 How will Britain's need for manufactured products be satisfied?
4 What is meant by an 'expert system' (line 67)?
5 How will teachers be threatened by computers?

B Using information from the article, and from this letter prompted by it, write a paragraph of about 80 words explaining how our home lives are likely to change in the future.

Chip thrills

Sir, Struggling through Sir Clive Sinclair's ruptured syntax (April 24) it appears that what he and IBM have in store for us is a life of sitting around in long flowing robes drinking wine and eating kebabs, discussing Art, Science and Philosophy and all that stuff while just out of eye and earshot there are these silicon machines gliding effortlessly around waiting to fulfil our slightest needs in our huge tastefully furnished machine-designed drawing rooms. . . . A treacherous thought intrudes however: if these machines are going to be so damned smart, why won't they be the ones sitting around discussing all the really interesting stuff while the little carbon-based squirts like Sir Clive and me scuttle around doing the housework?
– Yours, Peter Smee

"And when you're finished cleaning upstairs, you can give me a hand in the kitchen."

A Fill the gaps in these examples from earlier in this unit, using the verbs below.

1 TIME TO CRACK THAT TIMER
The TV series .... by cartoonist and engineer Tim Hunkin.
Most modern machines have their roots in a time before electronics ....
Some people .... to feel inadequate by their colleagues.

2 ELECTRONIC ANNOUNCERS
Experiments to find the perfect electronic announcer .... two years ago
    when the station at the Champagne town of Rheims .... for tests.
After trying out the voice at other stations it .... that the reassuring
    effect .... if regional accents ....
The synthesiser .... to be more reliable and flexible.
The use of synthetic announcers will .... into effect in the next few months.
In the meantime, the voices are .... into service elsewhere.
Ticket offices are also .... with automatic dispensers.

3 OCEAN CITY
Only 18% of Japan's land area can .... for living space.
Ocean City wouldn't .... by typhoons or storms.
If Ocean City is a success, more similar cities could ....
The only thing that would need to .... in would be food.
It would .... by an off-shore fund: tax benefits would .... to investors.

add   affect   build   equip   finance   find   find   increase
invent   make   offer   present   put   put   ship   start   use   use

➡ Try rephrasing each sentence in the active. What is the effect of using the
passive in each example?

B Look at these examples and then make up ten sentences about real people or
events using the same patterns with any of the verbs in italics:

Marie Curie was ..**thought**.. to be ..**the greatest scientist of her generation.**
She is ..**known**.. to have ..**succeeded where all others had failed.**
It used to be ..**said**.. that she ..**owed her success to her husband, Pierre.**

acknowledged   alleged   believed   claimed   considered   feared   felt
imagined   known   reported   said   supposed   thought   understood

It was ..**taken for granted**.. that ..**they would be getting married in the spring.**
It could never be ..**explained**.. why/how ..**the accident happened.**

admitted   agreed   announced   assumed   confirmed   denied   disclosed
explained   mentioned   pointed out   realised   regretted   revealed

C Rewrite each sentence using the passive, starting with the words on the right.

1 You'll have to get rid of all those old magazines.   Those old magazines . . .
2 Everyone looks down on her and she's fed up with it.   She's fed up with . . .
3 The children's grandparents looked after them.   The children . . .
4 My assistant is dealing with this matter.   This matter . . .
5 They have accounted for all the survivors of the accident.   All the . . .
6 Customers must pay for any breakages.   All breakages . . .
7 You can't rely on Tony to finish the work on time.   Tony can't . . .   ➤➤➡

8 I'll get someone to see to the repairs right away.   The repairs . . .
9 Someone had broken into her apartment during the night.   Her apartment . . .
10 People often look on scientists as experts.   Scientists . . .
11 Someone pointed out to me that I was wearing odd socks.   It . . .
12 People might refer to him as 'technophobic'.   He . . .
13 Without permission for a new runway they can't expand the airport.
    Until permission . . .
14 Electronics might intimidate some people, but not me.   Some . . .

12.8   Thinking about the reader

A   Read the passage through before looking at the questions below.

Over the years I have fumbled my way through life, walking into doors, failing to figure out water faucets, incompetent at working the simple things of everyday life. "Just me," I would mumble. "Just mechanical ineptitude." But as I studied psychology and watched the behavior of other people, I began to realize that I was not alone. My difficulties were mirrored by the problems of others. And we all seemed to blame ourselves. Could the whole world be mechanically incompetent?

The truth emerged slowly. My research activities led me to the study of human error and industrial accidents. Humans, I discovered, do not always behave clumsily. Humans do not always err. But they do when the things they use are badly conceived and designed. Nonetheless, we still see human error blamed for all that befalls society. Does a commercial airliner crash? "Pilot error," say the reports. Does a Soviet nuclear power plant have a serious problem? "Human error," says the newspaper. Do two ships at sea collide? "Human error" is the official cause. But careful analysis of these kinds of incidents usually gives the lie to such a story. At the famous American nuclear power plant disaster at Three Mile Island, the blame was placed on plant operators who misdiagnosed the problems. But was it human error? Consider the phrase "operators who misdiagnosed the problems". The phrase reveals that first there were problems – in fact, a series of mechanical failures. Then why wasn't equipment failure the real cause? What about the misdiagnoses? Why didn't the operators correctly determine the cause? Well, how about the fact that the proper instruments were not available, that the plant operators acted in

5

10

15

20

25

30

ways that in the past had always been reasonable and proper? How about the pressure relief valve that failed to close, even though the operator pushed the proper button and even though a light came on stating it was closed? Why was the operator blamed for not checking two more instruments (one on the rear of the control panel) and determining that the light was faulty? (Actually, the operator did check one of them.) Human error? To me it sounds like equipment failure coupled with serious design error.

And, yes, what about my inability to use the simple things of everyday life? I can use complicated things. I am quite expert at computers, and electronics, and complex laboratory equipment. Why do I have trouble with doors, light switches, and water faucets? How come I can work a multimillion-dollar computer installation, but not my home refrigerator? While we all blame ourselves, the real culprit – faulty design – goes undetected. And millions of people feel themselves to be mechanically inept. It is time for a change.

(from the Preface to *The Psychology of Everyday Things* by Donald A. Norman)

B   Work in pairs. Go through the passage and answer these questions.

1   Highlight three sentences that seem to sum up the writer's message.
2   Look at the cases where he uses *I*, *me* or *my* and underline them – what is the effect of this?
3   How many times does the writer use *we* or *ourselves*?
4   How many times does he use *you* or *your*, addressing the reader directly?
5   How many times does he use imperatives, addressing the reader directly?
6   How many questions does the writer ask? What is the effect of this? Put a ring round all the question marks: ⓐ
7   How many answers does he give? How many questions are unanswered?
8   How well does the writer succeed in involving the reader?
9   What kind of reader does the writer seem to have in mind? To what extent are you that kind of reader?
10 How does the kind of reader he has in mind affect:
    a) the content of the passage?
    b) the style of the passage?

C   Work in pairs. Think of another subject you feel strongly about and which you have some personal knowledge of (traffic problems in your city, bureaucracy, energy conservation, etc.) and make notes on your experiences and your views.
    Then write a paragraph in a similar style to the passage, using the first person and answered or unanswered questions.

A 🔲 The first part of the broadcast is about airport design. Note down your answers to the questions:

AIRPORT DESIGN

1 Describe (or draw) the layout of a 'conventional' airport.
2 What are the two problems that all airport architects have?
3 Why do some airports have two terminals?
4 Why do passengers get confused at Heathrow Airport?
5 Label each of these diagrams. The airports shown are:

ATLANTA SOUTH   ATLANTA NORTH   LONDON GATWICK   MUNICH
PARIS CHARLES DE GAULLE 1   PARIS CHARLES DE GAULLE 2   RIYADH   WASHINGTON

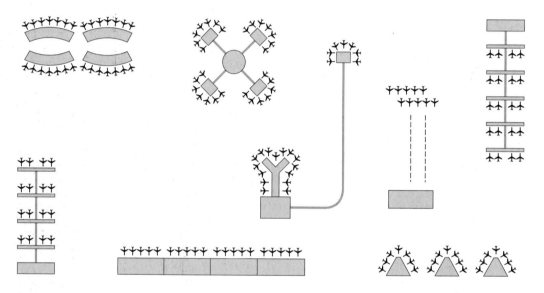

B 🔲 The second part is about airport convenience. Answer the questions.

AIRPORT CONVENIENCE

1 Match the information given in each column.

Airport	Distance to city	Surface connection to city centre
Atlanta	35 km	taxi *or* limousine to major hotels
Gatwick	15 km	fast bus
Munich	70 km	rapid transit train *or* bus
Paris	45 km	direct train
Riyadh	40 km	direct train
Tokyo (Narita)	30 km	direct train (30 mins)
Washington	25 km	direct coach *or* shuttle bus and train

2 Why is it less convenient to get from Central London to Heathrow than Gatwick?
3 What's the quickest way of getting from London to Paris?

C Work in groups and discuss these questions:
- Which of the information in the broadcast interested or surprised you most?
- Describe the design and convenience of your local airport – perhaps comparing it with another airport you've visited or flown from.
- If you've flown a lot, which is the nicest airport you know – and the worst?
- What do you like and dislike about visiting an airport? And about flying?

12.10 Modern design

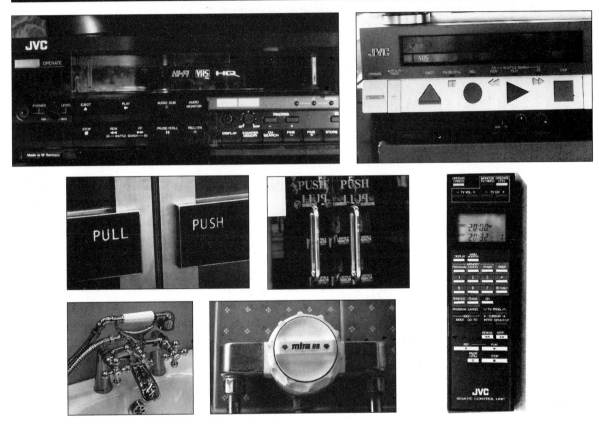

A Work in groups of three and discuss these questions:
- Which of the things shown above look easier to use? Why is this?
- Can you programme a video recorder to record a TV programme? Have you ever set one wrong? Was it your fault or the designer's?

Now one of you should look at Activity 11, one at 27 and one at 40. You'll have some more questions to ask each other about the design of everyday equipment (based on the ideas of Donald A. Norman – see 12.8).

B Spend some time researching and thinking about the ideas you discussed earlier, and looking at the way you interact with doors, watches, switches, numbers, etc.
Work in groups and find out about each other's ideas and experiences.
Discuss how you will organise and sequence your ideas in an essay on this topic:

Modern design does not pay enough attention to the average user.

C Write your essay in about 300 words, giving examples you discussed in B and discovered in your research. Make notes before you start.

Show your completed essay to another student and ask for comments.

12.11 Give + take

A Which of the following would you GIVE and which would you TAKE?

a photograph   advice to someone   an answer   an explanation
an interest in something   encouragement   evidence   issue with someone
a liking to someone or something   part in something   permission
pity on someone   pride in something   someone a kiss   someone a lift
someone a ring   someone a shock   someone some help
your time over something

B Find synonyms for the phrases in italics, or explain their meaning.

1 Don't *take it for granted* that everything's going to be easy: you should be prepared to *take the rough with the smooth* when you *take up* a new job.
2 When we criticised him I half expected him to *take offence*, but he *took it in good part*, and in the ensuing discussion he *gave as good as he got*.
3 She was quite *taken aback* when I *took* her *up* on her offer.
4 They *were* quite *taken with* each other on their first meeting.
5 She nearly *took* us *in*, but she *gave* herself *away* when she started giggling.
6 There was so much information that I couldn't *take it* all *in*.
7 I know you're annoyed but don't *take it out on* me – *take* it *up* with the people who were responsible.
8 Cheer up! Why don't you *take* him *out* for a meal, it may *take you out of yourself*.
9 She can *take off* her father's voice and mannerisms brilliantly – especially the way he *takes off* his glasses when his patience is about to *give out*.
10 He *took exception* to the fact that she was starting to *take* him *for granted*.

C Fill the gaps in these sentences with suitable phrases from the list below. You may need to change the form of the verbs.

1 The sight was so beautiful it .... her breath ....
2 I remember .... the message but I've forgotten where I put it.
3 About 75% of the land area of Britain is .... agriculture.
4 You really should .... insurance before you travel.
5 You've .... more work than you can manage and it seems to be .... it
.... of you. Why don't you .... a few days .... ?
6 I apologise. I .... all those things I said about your new hairstyle.
7 I'm feeling a bit tired of driving, would you mind .... for a while?
8 I used to go jogging but now I .... it .... Perhaps I'll .... swimming instead.

*give over to   give up   take away   take back   take down   take off
take on   take out   take out   take over   take up*

D Write the first paragraph of a story, using as many of the expressions from above as you can. Begin like this:

I knew I had to give up but . . .

13 Relationships

A   Work in pairs. Look at the photos and discuss these questions:
- What seems to be the relationship between the people?
- What do you think has just happened? What are they saying now? What is likely to happen next?

B   ⊡ You'll hear five people talking about 'best friends'. Answer these true/false questions:

1 At school, **Anne** frequently dropped one friend and took up with another.
2 The schoolfriend she still knows well wasn't one of her best friends at school.
3 **Mike**'s friend Buzz was aggressive and tough.
4 Mike and Buzz always shared the same political views.
5 **Rupert** and his family do sometimes have rows.
6 **Elaine** and her friend laughed at the same things.
7 Elaine's friend now lives in Austria.
8 **David** thinks that people who are too alike don't get on well together.
9 It sounds as if David's enemy at school was a bully.
10 David sometimes can't be bothered to make an effort to like certain people.

⟫→

C Work in groups and discuss these questions:

- Which of the experiences you heard about in B struck a chord with you?
- Describe the person who was your own best friend as a child – how has your relationship changed since you first got to know each other?
- What do you appreciate about the friends you have now? Explain why you get on well with them.
- Is it better to have just one or two close friends, or quite a few friends you don't know so well?

D Work in pairs and discuss the relative importance of the following in a friendship or a relationship. What important qualities are missing from the list?

cheerfulness commitment communication compassion compatibility considerateness enthusiasm generosity good looks honesty intelligence kindness loyalty optimism passion patience politeness punctuality realism reliability responsibility sincerity thoughtfulness trust

And how important are the following in a friendship or a relationship?

age family background mutual interests sense of humour social class shared attitudes to religion, politics, etc. similar personalities

➡ Which FIVE features from the two lists are the most important and why? Which are the five least important features?

E 🔲 You'll hear the same words spoken in different ways:

> Well, good evening. Thank you both for getting here on time and for waiting so patiently. Everyone else seems to be rather late, or maybe they haven't been able to make it. Anyway, we'll make a start I think, and if any of the others do come we can always fill them in on what's happened so far...

Decide which word from the list below best describes each speaker's mood or tone:

1 .... 4 ....
2 .... 5 ....
3 .... 6 ....

annoyed anxious businesslike despondent eager impatient jaded patient sarcastic timid

➡ Discuss how each speaker's tone of voice conveyed their mood. Consider their speed of delivery, the amount of hesitation, the pitch of their voice, the way they emphasised words, the way they sighed or laughed or made other noises, etc.

A   Read the three extracts and discuss the questions that follow.

THIS is the story of a five-year sojourn that I and my family made on the Greek island of Corfu. It was originally intended to be a mildly nostalgic account of the natural history of the island, but I made a grave mistake by introducing my family into the book in the first few pages. Having got themselves on paper, they then [5] proceeded to establish themselves and invite various friends to share the chapters. It was only with the greatest difficulty, and by exercising considerable cunning, that I managed to retain a few pages here and there which I could devote exclusively to animals.

I have attempted to draw an accurate and unexaggerated picture [10] of my family in the following pages; they appear as I saw them. To explain some of their more curious ways, however, I feel that I should state that at the time we were in Corfu the family were all quite young: Larry, the eldest, was twenty-three; Leslie was nineteen; Margo eighteen; while I was the youngest, being of the [15] tender and impressionable age of ten. We have never been very certain of my mother's age, for the simple reason that she can never remember her date of birth; all I can say is that she was old enough to have four children. My mother also insists that I explain that she is a widow for, as she so penetratingly observed, you never know [20] what people might think . . .

I did not kill my father, but I sometimes felt I had helped him on his way. And but for the fact that it coincided with a landmark in my own physical growth, his death seemed insignificant compared with what followed. My sisters and I talked about him the week after he died, and Sue certainly cried when the ambulance men tucked him [5] up in a bright red blanket and carried him away. He was a frail, irascible, obsessive man with yellowish hands and face. I am only including the little story of his death to explain how my sisters and I came to have such a large quantity of cement at our disposal.

In the early summer of my fourteenth year a lorry pulled up [10] outside our house. I was sitting on the front step rereading a comic. The driver and another man came towards me. They were covered in a fine, pale dust which gave their faces a ghostly look. They were both whistling shrilly completely different tunes. I stood up and held the comic out of sight. I wished I had been reading the racing page [15] of my father's paper, or the football results.

'Cement?' one of them said. I hooked my thumbs into my pockets, moved my weight to one foot and narrowed my eyes a little. I wanted to say something terse and appropriate, but I was not sure I had heard them right. I left it too long, for the one who had spoken [20] rolled his eyes towards the sky and with his hands on his hips stared past me at the front door. It opened and my father stepped out biting his pipe and holding a clipboard against his hip . . .

I was born poor in rich America, yet my secret instincts were better than money and were for me a source of power. I had advantages that no one could take away from me – a clear memory and brilliant dreams and a knack for knowing when I was happy.

I was at my happiest leading two lives, and it was a satisfaction to me that the second one – of the dreamer or the sneak – I kept hidden. That was how I spent my first fifteen years. Fifteen was young then and I knew this: The poor don't belong. But one summer out of loneliness or impatience my second self did more than wake and watch, and more than remember. He began to see like a historian, and he acted. I have to save my life, I used to think.

Early that summer I was walking down a lovely crumbling little street lined with elms, called Brookview Road. The city of Boston, with its two tall buildings, was visible from one end of the road looking east. . .

Work in pairs. Discuss these questions and note down your answers.

1 Which extract comes from which of these books?

2 Which of the extracts makes you want to read on? Give your reasons.
3 What do the extracts have in common?
4 What are the main differences between the three extracts?
5 What kind of young person does each narrator seem to be?
6 In the first extract, how did the narrator's family 'invite various friends to share the chapters'? And what does he mean by 'their more curious ways'?
7 In the second extract, why do you think the narrator was 'rereading a comic'? Why did he 'wish he had been reading the racing page of his father's paper'?
8 In the third extract, what is meant by 'The poor don't belong'?
9 What do we learn of the relationship between the narrator and his family in each extract?

B Join another pair and compare your answers to the questions. Then discuss which of the qualities you discussed in 13.1 D are most important in relationships between parents and children, and between sisters and brothers.

D It's often hard to differentiate between associations and collocations – as this pseudo-Freudian word association game may show:

Work in pairs. Take it in turns to say the first word or phrase that comes into your mind, like this:

'Word' 'association' 'football' 'referee' 'whistle' 'flute' 'violin' 'bow' 'arrow' 'question' 'answer' and so on . . .

If you perceive no connection, ask your partner to explain why she or he said that word:

'Why 'question'?'
'There's a question after the ➡ in section A opposite.'
'Ah.'

13.6 The narrator

A Read the passage and then discuss the questions below with a partner.

My career has always been marked by a strange mixture of confidence and cowardice: almost, one might say, made by it. Take, for instance, the first time I tried spending a night with a man in a hotel. I was nineteen at the time, an age appropriate for such adventures, and needless to say I was not married. I am still not married, a fact of some significance, but more of that later. The name of the boy, if I remember rightly, was Hamish. I do remember rightly. I really must try not to be deprecating. Confidence, not cowardice, is the part of myself which I admire, after all. 10

Hamish and I had just come down from Cambridge at the end of the Christmas term: we had conceived our plan well in advance, and had each informed our parents that term ended a day later than it actually did, knowing quite well that they would not be interested enough to check, nor sufficiently *au fait* to 15 ascertain the value of their information if they did. So we arrived in London together in the late afternoon, and took a taxi from the station to our destined hotel. We had worked everything out, and had even booked our room, which would probably not have been necessary, as the hotel we had selected was one of those large 20 central cheap-smart ones, specially designed for adventures such as ours. I was wearing a gold curtain ring on the relevant finger. We had decided to stick to Hamish's own name, which, being Andrews, was unmemorable enough, and less confusing than having to think up a pseudonym. We were well educated, the two 25 of us, in the pitfalls of such occasions, having both of us read at one time in our lives a good deal of cheap fiction, and indeed we both carried ourselves with considerable aplomb. We arrived, unloaded our suitably-labelled suitcases, and called at the desk for our key. It was here that I made my mistake. For some reason I was requested to sign the register. I now know that it is by no means customary for wives to sign hotel registers . . .

30

(from *The Millstone* by Margaret Drabble)

1 What kind of person does Rosamund, the narrator, seem to be?
2 Find an example of the narrator poking fun at herself.
3 How would you describe the tone or style of the passage?
4 What do you think is going to happen in the rest of the novel? What clues are given in the passage? Why is it called *The Millstone* do you think?

B The author wrote the story in the first person. Why do you think she did this? What would be the effects of changing the pronouns to the third person?

Look again at 13.4. If the extracts from *Wilt* and *The Wimbledon Poisoner* were in the first person, what effect would this have on them?

If the extracts in 13.2 were in the third person, what effect would this have?

C Work in pairs. Think of an embarrassing, amusing or memorable experience you have had (or imagine yourselves having). Write TWO versions of the opening paragraph of a story about the experience, one in the first person (using *I/me/my*), the other in the third person, as if you're writing about a 'character'.

➡ Compare your paragraphs with a partner. Discuss which version was easier to write and which was most convincing.

★★ If you choose to write a narrative in the exam, using the first person can make it easier for you to identify with your protagonist – even if the personality of the protagonist is not like you at all really.

A fictional or semi-fictional narrative can be easier to handle than one which sticks strictly to the truth.

A Work in pairs. Discuss any differences in style or meaning between these sentences:

1 If it weren't for the children they would have split up by now.
 If it wasn't for the children they would have split up by now.
 Were it not for the children they would have split up by now.
 If they didn't have children they would have split up by now.

2 If you should see Terry could you give him my regards?
 When you see Terry could you give him my regards?
 If you happen to see Terry could you give him my regards?
 If you see Terry could you give him my regards?
 Should you see Terry could you give him my regards?

3 If you wouldn't mind waiting I'll let them know you're here.
 If you don't mind waiting I'll let them know you're here.
 If you wait I'll let them know you're here.

4 Had it not been for your help, I couldn't have done it.
 Without your help I couldn't have done it.
 If it hadn't been for your help I couldn't have done it.
 If you hadn't been so helpful I couldn't have done it.
 I'm glad you helped me, otherwise I couldn't have done it.

➡ There are no commas in most of the above sentences – which of them would be easier to understand if they were to have commas?

B Finish the incomplete sentences in such a way that each one means the same as the complete sentence before it.

1 Please do take a seat and I'll bring you some coffee.   If you …
2 Their relationship was doomed because of their incompatibility. Had …
3 I might miss my connection, if so I'll try to call you to let you know. Should …
4 They didn't get married because their parents were against it.   But …
5 You probably won't have time – but I'd like you to come and see us. If …
6 There was such a lot of traffic: that's why we're late.   Had …
7 She could tell him she's leaving, but it would upset him.   If …
8 They have a wonderful relationship, and have decided to get married. Were …
9 She's very patient and loyal, that's why she hasn't left him.   If it …
10 If you don't work hard at a relationship it's not likely to last. Without …

C Work in pairs. Write five sentences about your own friends and relations, and your relationships with them using the following structures:

 Had …   If it weren't for …   Were …   Should …   Without …

Join another pair and compare your sentences.

Edward Hopper: 'Nighthawks', 1942 (detail)

A Work in pairs and discuss these questions about the picture:
- Where are the people? Who are they? How do they feel?
- What has happened earlier, what's happening now and what's going to happen?
- What have they said to each other earlier? What are they saying now? What are they going to say? What is their relationship?
- How does the picture make *you* feel? Would you like to be one of the people? Give your reasons.

B Work in pairs. One of you should look at Activity 12, the other at 29. You'll each have another picture to look at and describe. Ask each other questions to find out how the picture illustrates the relationships between the people.

C Choose any ONE of the three pictures you have discussed. Imagine that it shows the first scene in a novel or short story.
Write TWO openings to the story (about 150 words each):
- one from the point of view of one of the characters (using *I*, *we*, etc.)
- the other as a conventional narrator (using *he, she, they*, etc.)

★★ One of the composition topics in the exam may require you to put yourself into the position of two different people. For example, you might have to write two people's statements to the police about an accident or a robbery, or two speeches about an

14 Earning a living

A   Work in groups and discuss these questions about the photos:
- What are the pros and cons of each person's job?
- Which of the jobs would you prefer to have? Give your reasons.
- What would be the ideal job for you, and why?

B   Fill the gaps with suitable words from the list below, using plurals as necessary.

1   A large company is owned by its ...**shareholders**..., who may be individual .... or major financial ...., but it is controlled by a board of ....
2   Universal Studios and Columbia Studios are .... of Matsushita and Sony respectively, both of which are .... companies with their .... in Japan.
3   National airlines used to have a .... of European air routes, but now there is .... between different airlines.
4   Cars are .... by putting together the various .... on an ....
5   In marketing ...., people often refer to 'the 4 Ps':
Marketing consists of providing the customer with the right p................. at the right p................., and ensuring that the goods are available to the customer in the right p................. through appropriate channels of distribution, as well as p.................
(including packaging and advertising).
6   The selection of new staff is the responsibility of the .... department. They are also responsible for the .... and .... of ....
7   Sales representatives are paid a monthly .... but they also receive travelling .... and may earn a .... on the sales they make.
8   When the company went .... all the workers in the .... were made ....

*assembly line   bankrupt   commission   competition   component   director   employee
expenses   headquarters   institution   investor   jargon   manufacture   monopoly
multi-national   personnel   place   plant   price   product   promotion   redundant
salary   shareholder   subsidiary   training   welfare*

A Read the article through, preferably before the lesson, before answering the
questions on the next page.

 Begin by highlighting the first mention of each of the women interviewed.

Million dollar dealers

The young man shouts "Eighty-
eighty-eight dollar yen!" as he
hurls the telephone receiver at his
desk. A few feet away, a fat man with
5   a moustache rears up from his seat.
He glares across the table. "What *is*
going on?" he demands. His
colleague cowers.
    "What have you got?"
10   "94:98."
    "94:96?"
    "One at 96."
    "Forget it. Why don't you *listen*?"
    The fat man is angry because he
15 has just lost a multi-million pound
deal. His colleague's mind wandered
for a moment and he got hit by
another dealer somewhere on the
other side of the world. The dollar-
20 mark table at Foreign Exchange
Brokers R P Martin is extremely
volatile. Prices shift hundreds of
points a day. Get it wrong and you
can let five million pounds slip
25 through your fingers.

All around there are likely lads
called Gary and Ron and Glen who
are screaming into colour-coded
telephones and stabbing at computer
keyboards. The game they are   30
playing is fast, furious and hellishly
complicated. "Forex," as it is called is
the riskiest and sexiest in the City.
The object is to put buyers and
sellers in touch with each other   35
before someone else can beat you to
it. Like market places everywhere,
the dealers shout their prices. Most
of them react with outbursts of
theatrical aggression. They're   40
shouting so loudly, in fact, it's easy to
overlook the trio of females lurking
among them.

Teresa Caira wears a dark suit as
sombre as her male colleagues. But,   45
while they bellow, she murmurs
calmly into her telephones. Her
hushed tones are deceptive. At 28,
her boss describes her as the best

spot (instant deal) lira broker in London. Nevertheless, she is one of only three female Forex dealers he employs. Women may be gaining ground elsewhere in the City, but only about a dozen have entered the jungle of Foreign Exchange.

"You have to be thick-skinned in this job," Teresa explains, juggling a handful of telephone receivers. "A woman has to be firm without appearing masculine. It's tricky to get the balance right. You must be extrovert and get yourself noticed but not as a *woman*." These additional stresses certainly don't attract many women recruits. Half of all trainees fail to make the grade. Vacancies are not advertised. Most women have never even heard of the job.

How do the men react to women brokers? "Well, they test you out at first to see how far they can push you. They want to know if you're going to burst into tears. It's no advantage to play on your femininity. But you can't be one of the boys either – drinking and swearing as much as they do. I think of myself as 'quietly confident'," says Teresa. Across the table, a young man catches her eye.

"I need spaghetti* for Düsseldorf, 85:90."

"Give you one," says Teresa.

"Mine at one."

In just five seconds, she's earned herself more commission to top up her salary and team bonus. "The salary's pretty good if you don't spend it all living it up," she admits. "I try to put a bit by. I hope to invest in property or start my own business after I leave here. Forex brokers don't do it for life. The official retirement age is 55 but most of them are burnt out by 40. Nobody is taken on over the age of 25. It's a young person's game."

Teresa left school at 16 to work in a bank. She has the same kind of East End accent as most of the lads. The pace and excitement suits anyone from ex-cab drivers and bookies to university graduates. "I like to be busy," says Teresa, "when things are quiet it gets boring. If you relax you make mistakes. They don't carry passengers here. You have to keep up." It's a long day. Trading starts before eight and can go on until past seven at night if the market is still "frothy".

"The responsibility does worry me sometimes," says Teresa. "You must admit it when you've made a mistake. If you try to cover it up it gets even more expensive. People have very low tolerance here because they are under so much pressure. You get screamed at all the time. But you can't be a tearful little woman. You have to fight back without seeming to. I suppose I'm a sort of honorary man." As if to prove her point one of the blokes yells out in triumph:

"I hammered 'im, Teresa!"

Teresa smiles back at him like a perfect gent.

Behind a hardboard partition on their Forward Dollars desk, Jackie Taylor, 20, is still working on acquiring that kind of self-possession. She joined the firm a year ago straight from school. A trainee like her earns about £10,000 a year. When she qualifies this should shoot up to £40,000 and above. It all depends on how well she serves her collection of banks.

"You have to get your clients to trust you," she explains, "you ought to be working together." On the other hand, all the banks she represents are vying with each other. In a way, she is competing with herself. A lot of lunchtime wining and dining of elderly bankers is required to resolve that contradiction. "That's one area," she smiles, "where hopefully I have an advantage over the men."

But she has no illusions about the popularity of women brokers. "When I first started here I was called every name under the sun." She was also warned she'd become unfeminine. She's certainly got a lot louder. The trouble is there just aren't enough women in the job yet. One or two can't hope to challenge the gung-ho

* *spaghetti*: lire

205

macho atmosphere and support one
another. If more women realised how
exciting and profitable it was, she
says, things would improve.

"Men still think women aren't
interested in making money. But we
are."

A football crowd roar greets
another victory over at dollar-yen.
Jackie frowns. "I see the worst side
of the men who work here," she says.
"I couldn't possibly be married to one
of them now I know what they're like.
It's a purely male atmosphere and
they like their own company. They
still believe a woman's place is
behind a sink or changing nappies.
I'm staying single while I'm here. You
can't be a married woman in the
market. And children would be
impossible." She knows Teresa
manages with a child-minder for her
nine-year-old son. But, well, Teresa is
special.

On the other side of the partition
the third member of the female trio is
a sun-tanned woman in her twenties.

Susie McElney is a tough nut to crack
and she doesn't mind who knows it.
"The men's crude comments never
upset me," she insists. "I give as
good as I get." She was brought up by
her father and brothers and attended
a boys' public school. "I'm used to
being surrounded by men," she says
with a grin.

"I need dollar yen here," she
shouts suddenly in a harsh voice.

"I'm ready for you!" booms back a
masculine voice.

"Five at 85!" screams Susie, waving
her phone receivers.

"Are we going to give it to these
people, lads?" challenges a second
male.

"80:75 I give," bellows Number
One.

"Thank you, guys," says Susie,
another deal richer. Five million
dollars have just changed hands. "If
you *thought* in millions, you'd never
do this job," she adds, fingering the
modest clutch of diamonds at her
throat.

Helen Chappell

B Highlight each of these phrases in the passage. Then decide which of the
two meanings in italics below is correct.

slip through your fingers   (line 24)
   a) *get lost*   b) *be difficult to deal with*
thick-skinned   (line 57)
   a) *insensitive*   b) *not easily hurt*
fail to make the grade   (line 67)
   a) *don't perform well enough in their work*   b) *don't pass their exams*
They don't carry passengers   (line 106)
   a) *You have to pull your weight*   b) *They are ruthless employers*
vying with each other   (line 143)
   a) *competing with each other*   b) *cooperating with each other*
wining and dining   (line 145)
   a) *taking them out for an expensive meal*   b) *preparing a meal for them*
the gung-ho macho atmosphere   (line 158)
   a) *warlike male-dominated atmosphere*   b) *brave manly atmosphere*
a tough nut to crack   (line 186)
   a) *difficult to deal with*   b) *not easily dominated*
changed hands   (line 208)
   a) *been bought and sold*   b) *been lost*
the modest clutch of diamonds   (line 211)
   a) *discreet diamond necklace*   b) *small diamond brooch*

C Choose the best alternative to fill each blank:

1 The purpose of foreign exchange dealing is to ....
  bring buyers and sellers together   buy and sell currency
2 There are about .... female foreign exchange dealers in London.
  3   6   12   28
3 Most Forex dealers don't go on working after the age of ....
  25   40   55
4 To become a Forex dealer you .... well-educated and highly qualified.
  should be   don't need to be   mustn't be   can't be   must be
5 In foreign exchange dealing large sums of money are made ....
  in a few seconds   after a lot of careful planning
6 Forex dealers .... go on working till after 7 p.m.
  always   usually   sometimes   never   rarely
7 Forex dealers ....
  easily get angry with each other   are tolerant of each other's mistakes
8 A single Forex dealer acts on behalf of ....
  one bank   several competing banks   several collaborating banks
9 Female dealers are better than their male counterparts when entertaining
  business clients for lunch because they ....
  don't drink heavily   are less forceful   can be more charming
10 Women brokers are .... by their male colleagues.
  well liked   not well liked   ignored   pursued
11 Susie McElney doesn't get upset by her male colleagues because ....
  she has a good sense of humour   she has lived among males all her life
12 The most experienced woman broker at R P Martin is ....
  Jackie   Teresa   Susie

D Work in groups and discuss the pros and cons of:

- working as a foreign exchange dealer
- husbands and wives working together
- being a single parent, having to earn a living and raise a young child
- working as a woman in a man's world – or as a man in a woman's world
- making money as an investor on the stock market or the money market

E Work in pairs. One of you should look at Activity 7, the other at 46.
You'll each see an advertisement for a scheme to make you rich – rich beyond
your wildest dreams!

➡ Explain to your partner how the advertised scheme works. Decide why the
claims are preposterous: What are the flaws in the reasoning behind each ad?

A Study the examples and fill the gaps in the sentences. Highlight any phrasal verbs that you're unfamiliar with and look them up.

1 Some phrasal verbs are intransitive (they don't take an object):

*When we challenged him to justify his point of view he **backed down**.*
*He wasn't being serious, but I didn't **catch on** until he started smiling.*

But not: I didn't catch immediately on. ✗

check up   climb down   cool off   close in   die out   fall apart   fall behind
pass away   pay up   ring off   settle down   settle up   shop around
speak up   stand out   stay on   stop over   wear off

a) If you want to save money you should .... before making a purchase.
b) The effects of the wine .... by the next morning.
c) After a few moments' silence, one of them .... and asked a question.

2 With most transitive phrasal verbs (i.e. verbs that take an object) the object can come in various positions, but not if the object is a pronoun:

*They've **brought** the meeting **forward**.*   *They've **called** the meeting **off**.*
*They've **brought forward** the meeting.*   *They've **called off** the meeting.*
*They've **brought** it **forward**.*   *They've **called** it **off**.*
*The meeting's been **brought forward**.*   *The meeting's been **called off**.*

But not: They've brought forward it. ✗   They've called off it. ✗

carry out   cut back   dream up   drive out   explain away   follow up
hand in   leave behind   pay back   rip off   send up   sort out   think up
tone down   trade in   try out   use up   win over   write out

a) Thanks for lending me the money, I promise I'll .... on Friday.
b) Everyone was .... by the force of her arguments.
c) The little boy was very upset because his mother ....

3 With some transitive phrasal verbs the **object** must come immediately **after** the verb:

*The twins look so alike that I couldn't **tell them apart**.*
*I couldn't **tell the twins apart**.*
*They tried to **catch me out** by asking me a trick question.*
*They tried to **catch the interviewees out** by asking them trick questions.*

But not: I couldn't tell apart them. ✗   They tried to catch out me. ✗

call back   count in   cut off   give up   invite out   order about   see out
show around   start off   tear up

a) When they left I went downstairs with them and ....
b) Pam is a new student, could one of you ...., please?
c) I wanted to .... on Friday night, but she said she was washing her hair.

4 Some phrasal verbs can be followed by a preposition:

*I was trying to **catch up** on the work I'd missed.*
*I've missed a lot of work and I'm trying to **catch up**.*

*He was annoyed at having to **clean up** after his guests.*
*He was annoyed at having to **clean up**.*

*He was annoyed at having to **clean** everything **up**.*

> tidy up after   check up on   crack down on   creep up on   miss out on
> play along with   wait up for

a) I wasn't invited to the party and I was afraid I might be .... the fun.

b) I'm just interested in how you're getting on – I'm not ....

5 Some three-word phrasal verbs **must** be used with a preposition:

*You shouldn't **talk down to** children.*
*She finds it hard to **live up to** her mother's expectations.*

> come up against   talk someone out of   face up to   grow out of   lead up to
> stick up for

a) When they set up their new business they .... a lot of problems.

b) She was being unusually polite to me and I wondered what it was all ....

6 The object of a **verb + preposition** (see 12.3) must come after the preposition:

*We were **counting on** her to help us.   We were **counting on** Liz to help us.*
*Liz didn't realise she was being **counted on**.*

But not: We were counting her on. **✗**   We were counting Liz on. **✗**

> account for   bank on   call for   deal with   dispose of   long for   look after
> look into   part with   provide for   stand for   stem from

a) If you tell me what the problem is, I promise to ....

b) He's very mean and always hates to ....

c) The abbreviation *plc* .... public limited company.

B Fill each of the blanks with a suitable phrasal verb from 1 to 5 above.

1 If you've got a parking ticket you can't just .... – you'll have to ....

2 It was clearly my fault but I was able to .... an excuse to ....

3 He was threatening to .... his notice, but I managed to .... and persuade him to ....

4 I'm relying on you to .... if there's any trouble.

5 She used to be a very sulky little girl, but she .... eventually.

6 If you already have a car, you can .... when you buy a new one.

7 I'm going to be back very late tonight – don't ....

8 He eventually .... after we'd presented all the arguments.

9 Customs officers have been .... people who are over the duty free limit.

10 Let's hope you aren't .... by this last question!

*"The job may interest you **now**, Mr Harvey, but do you honestly feel the interest would be sustained?"*

A   Read this article and then answer the questions that follow in writing.

JANE McLOUGHLIN

No job to go to

EVERY weekday, Dick Derwent (which is not his real name) is driven out of bed by the alarm clock he leaves outside the bedroom door. Stopping its
5 din means he must get up first, not simply turn it off and settle back to sleep. He brings his wife Jean a cup of tea, dresses in his office suit while she makes toast and a sandwich which he
10 packs in his brown briefcase. He leaves the house at precisely 7.55 am to walk the half mile to the station to catch the 8.15 suburban stopping train to town.
15   The routine hasn't changed in the 25 years since he and Jean first moved to their neat little house in a Lego-built street in a suburb of a London suburb. Dick sees the same people on the
20 platform every morning – by now he even nods to one or two. The only difference is that until two years ago he used to buy a paper from the kiosk outside the station and now he picks
25 one up if a fellow passenger discards it on the journey.
    Two years ago, Dick was fired. He no longer has a job to go to with the others in the pin-stripe tide rushing
30 out of Waterloo to go to the office. He starts an eight hour day doing nothing.

His wife doesn't know. He couldn't tell her he'd lost his job, so he simply carried on as though he goes to work.
35 He believes she believes the elaborate myth he has created round his working day. His boss objects to private telephone calls, so please don't ring him at work: the other blokes at
40 work come and go these days, he doesn't really know them well enough to talk about them at home; if he's lucky and picks up a Standard in the afternoons, he can pretend that he
45 had the kind of day that Bristow* had at work, and she's so bored she doesn't want to hear.
    Two of his ex-colleagues did drop by his home one weekend, and he rushed
50 them down to the pub. He told Jean they'd both been fired so it was nice to see them after so long, to explain the way they greeted him. They mentioned afterwards to his friends
55 that Dick and Jean seemed to have very little furniture around, and they said they'd given up the television because there was so much rubbish on these days. The furniture? Oh, they
60 were going to redecorate, so they'd sold the old stuff and Jean would go to the sales when they'd got the new decor.
    She *must* know. There's no way of
65 finding out without asking her, and that's the one question no one can ever ask.
    Dick pays for his season ticket out of the fast-dwindling redundancy money
70 he put in the bank. He takes £1 a day spending money and collects his dole weekly from the DHSS office near his old workplace. He gives Jean the same money he always did, but the
75 bills for rates and gas and electricity he grabs up on his way out in the morning and stuffs in a wastebin near the station. When they go to cut him off, Jean gives them a cheque,
80 thinking he has forgotten, so he doesn't really know the state of his bank account. He told her he took a

---

* *Bristow*: an office worker in a cartoon strip (see page 212) pay cut last year because the firm was in trouble. "She doesn't actually think I've forgotten; she thinks I've been on a drinking spree again," he says.

His days are a precarious triumph over mind by matter, or lack of it. A typical day starts at Waterloo, when you've no idea how hard it is to hold back to his slow pace as the commuters stampede from the platform to an imperative march. "No, no tea. It's too expensive, and it's a waste of your resources because there's no chance of a return on investment. At lunchtime, if you get in the bar early and buy someone a drink, that's the first round, and when his friends come in they include you in their rounds. You've got to pick your moment to get out, of course."

He grins sideways at you and puts a lot of energy into the height of his steps rather than their length. We walk slowly along the river by the National Theatre and the Festival Hall. The wind is in the wrong direction and it's very cold. From behind, Dick's valiant old suit shows its age in the daylight and you notice how scuffed his shoes are. You can see people hurrying by, trying to avoid catching his eye. "They think I'll ask for a handout. They can smell something off me."

He sits in the park after a while, and two women on the seat break off their conversation, fidget, and loudly ask each other the time. They've got to go; never knew it was so late.

"I don't like dogs, you know, but after what I've seen I'd never speak against them. They make friends for you, for people on their own. Everyone will talk to someone with a dog in a park."

There's something which happens gradually as the hours drag by; wherever he loiters, it seems to be with intent. He can't window shop or watch the people go by without feeling that people are wondering what he's doing. During the day, we go into a public library to read the papers. He used to take the Times at home, now he reads the Sun first. It makes no demand, and provides some form of comfort in its simplistic attitudes. "It's really irritating reading those papers where people seem to take themselves so seriously. Same goes for the magazines."

It's the contrasts that make Dick's misery worse. It had been his slowness in the morning; and all through the morning it was having nothing to do when everyone else seemed to be busy and intent. Except the down and outs, who wouldn't speak to him. "Perhaps they think I'm a copper," he joked.

At lunchtime, his drinks trick didn't work. He sat through opening hours with a half pint, a black hole among the noise and camaraderie. "I remember what it was like. You don't want some guy in trouble to bring you down when you're having a good time."

But after lunch his spirits pick up. The worst is over. He finds a park bench, or tramps back to Waterloo on a rainy day and takes out his sandwiches. He has pet pigeons. "It's nice in the summer. You can sit out in the Embankment Gardens near Charing Cross and watch everyone. All sorts of stories going on day after day. It's like Coronation Street, down there."

We walk past his old workplace. He does it every day. "The odd time, someone I knew comes out and thinks I'm just passing, so we have a chat. I always say I'm doing fine – it doesn't do to let people know the truth; it frightens them away from you, as though your wife had died or something."

He says you get used to spending 9 to 5 deliberately doing nothing. "What you miss is feeling you belong somewhere. That's why I go to the same places. If I didn't go one day, someone might notice."

One day, he'd spent 50p on a horse, sitting in the betting shop getting quite excited about the race. He'd won £5. The next day, he'd spent a wet afternoon watching a dirty movie near Trafalgar Square.

"At 6 pm sharp everyone there got up and hurried up to Charing Cross. Home to their wives, that was it. Didn't want them to know they hadn't got jobs any more. I'm not alone, you know."

B Highlight the following words and phrases used in the article and explain their meanings in a short phrase:

> *din* (line 5)   *suburb of a London suburb* (line 18)   *discards* (line 25)
> *elaborate myth* (line 36)   *season ticket* (line 69)   *fast-dwindling* (line 70)
> *dole* (line 72)   *a precarious triumph* (line 88)   *simplistic attitudes* (line 140)
> *camaraderie* (line 157)

C Look at the article and explain who or what is referred to by the words in italics in these quotations from the passage:

> He told Jean *they'd* both been fired   (line 52)
> *They* mentioned afterwards to his friends   (line 54)
> *they* said *they'd* given up the television   (line 57)
> When *they* go to cut him off, Jean gives *them* a cheque   (line 79)
> *they* include you in their rounds   (line 101)
> *They* think I'll ask for a handout   (line 115)
> *They*'ve got to go   (line 121)
> *They* make friends for you   (line 125)
> Perhaps *they* think   (line 152)
> it frightens *them* away   (line 179)
> Didn't want *them* to know   (line 197)
> *they* hadn't got jobs any more   (line 197)

D Describe a typical day in the life of Dick Derwent (about 120 words). Before you start, make notes and compare them with a partner.

E Work in groups and discuss these questions:

- What was your reaction to the passage?
- Could you ever behave like Dick Derwent? Why did he behave the way he did?
- What are the best ways of coping with being unemployed?

⚠️ This section deals with only a small portion of a vast topic. The only way to learn collocations of this kind is by reading and listening carefully – and by referring to a dictionary to check up when necessary.

A   Work in pairs. Which of the following things **break**? And which can **change**?

waves   traffic lights   a boy's voice   a storm   the weather   your mood   day

B   Which of the following things can you **break**? And which can you **change**? (Some can be used with either verb, with different meanings.)

a promise   a world record   an appointment   a tablecloth   crockery
direction   gear   money   someone's heart   the bed or the sheets   a habit
the ice   the law   the news to someone   the silence   the subject   trains
your clothes or your shoes   your leg or your arm   your mind

And in what circumstances might you break or change each of them?

C   Which of the following things can you **follow**? And which can you **lose**? (Some can be used with either verb, with different meanings.)

an argument   a line of argument   a route or directions   a story
a trade or profession   advice or instructions   control over something
someone's example or their lead   an idea   face   heart   a football team
a football match   interest in something   the fashion or a trend
the thread of a story   track of something   weight   your job   your nerve
your temper   your voice if you have a cold   your way or bearings

And in what circumstances might you follow or lose each of them?

D   Fill the gaps in these sentences with suitable words from the list below, changing the form of the verb as necessary.

1 Can I .... you a favour? I'd like you to .... me a hand with .... this heavy package.
2 If you want to .... a bank account, they may ask you to .... references.
3 I'd like to .... the order which I .... last week – I've .... my mind.
4 Always .... careful attention to what the interviewer says. You should answer clearly but there's no need to .... your voice above the normal level. Don't reply too quickly: give yourself time to .... your thoughts.
5 When he .... me the chocolates, I couldn't .... the temptation to .... them even though I was trying to .... weight.
6 Although she .... a very busy life, ... her own business, she tries to .... a balance between the demands of her work and her private life.
7 She tried to .... light on the situation by .... our attention to the fact that we would have to .... the costs of the scheme.
8 No one .... any objection when we .... the decision to .... the next meeting on Sunday.

accept   ask   bear   cancel   change   collect   draw   hold   lead   lend   lift   lose
offer   open   pay   place   raise   raise   reach   resist   run   strike   supply   throw

A   Work in pairs. Which of these students' endings to a job application letter are most effective? Which encourage the reader to look favourably on the application?

1

Dear Sirs,

   Referring to your advertisement in the Cambridge Evening News on Monday 9th September I wish to apply for the job as a commercial banker.

 . . .

  In order to improve my English skills I would like to work for about two years in England and I think the position as a junior commercial banker would fit with my imagination. I am ready for further discussions. Give me a ring or write to me.

   Yours faithfully,

2

Dear Sirs,

   I would like to apply for the post of International Corporate Finance Manager, advertised in last Tuesday's Daily Telegraph.

  . . .

I have a good knowledge of English and German, and I am learning Spanish.

  I enclose my curriculum vitae and will be available for interview any day after September 1. My present position is subject to one month's notice.

  I look forward to your reply.

   Yours faithfully,

3

Dear Sir or Madam,

   I should like to apply for the post of assistant manager in your Sales Development Department, Far East, advertised recently in the Financial Times.

. . .

Besides my mother tongue, German, I can also speak English and Japanese fairly well.

  If you feel that my qualifications meet with your requirements, I shall be pleased to come for an interview.

  Please find enclosed a curriculum vitae, educational reports and certificates of training.

   Yours faithfully,

4

Dear Mr Barnwell,

   I am a 24 year-old girl and I am interested in your advertisement for the job of secretary/receptionist advertised in yesterday's newspaper.

  . . .

   I can type and take shorthand, I enjoy contact

```
with people and I am a willing and responsible person.
          I am very interested in the job you are
offering and reckon myself to be the right person for
it.
          I look forward to hearing from you,
               Yours sincerely,
```

B Work in pairs. Look at the final paragraphs of the passages in 9.4, 9.7, 9.9, 12.2, 12.6, 14.2 and 14.4, taking account of the very last sentence in particular.

Discuss these questions:

- Which one has the least effective ending?
- Which one has the most effective ending? Why?
- Do short sentences seem more effective than long, complex ones? Why (not)?
- Why is a good ending important?

C Now look at the final paragraphs of your own recent compositions:

- Which of them are you most pleased with? Why?
- Which of them could be improved? Rewrite the last sentences of these with your partner's help.

These exercises revise grammar and vocabulary points covered in earlier units.

A Finish the incomplete sentences in such a way that each one means the same as the complete sentence before it.

1 If you're lucky you might get the job you have applied for. There …
2 He said, "Arrive on time for the interview tomorrow." He reminded …
3 I didn't know I had to write my name in block capitals. I wish …
4 FACTORY TO CLOSE SAYS MANAGER. According to …
5 No one ever explained why she was asked to leave. It was …
6 I read about the closure of the factory only yesterday. It …
7 The factory could not have been built without a government subsidy. Had …
8 I believe the company may well make a profit this year. I wouldn't be …

★★ When doing a transformation exercise like the one above, make absolutely sure that you've included all the information given in the original sentence, and that you haven't inadvertently changed the meaning or emphasis of the sentence.

B Fill each of the blanks with a suitable word or phrase.

1 Apart …………… highly qualified, she has plenty of …………… in doing this kind of work.
2 …………… no doubt that she …………… got the job …………… she hadn't …………… her nerve in the interview.
3 They promised me that …………… the job unless my qualifications ……………
4 Foreign exchange dealers …………… to be under a great deal of pressure: if their minds …………… they …………… losing millions of pounds.
5 The world of business is sometimes …………… as dull, but this is a ……………
6 …………… his cowardice, Dick Derwent …………… told his wife that he …………… his job.
7 …………… some time before I …………… that I couldn't …………… his line of argument, so in the end I …………… interest and gave up.
8 I'd rather you …………… make so much noise, it's time the children …………… sleep.

★★ Usually several points are being tested in sentences like these. Both grammar and vocabulary may be involved, so check your work carefully. If you can think of more than one way of filling a gap, decide which seems the best in the context.

A You'll hear part of a seminar for job-seekers. Listen to the recording and tick (✓) only the advice and information that the speakers actually give.

APPLICATION FORM
1 Photocopy it and practise filling in the copy first. □
2 Write your final version neatly and clearly. □
3 Use a separate sheet for any extra information you want to give. □

4 Personnel officers read application forms very carefully. ☐
5 Use words that show you want to be successful. ☐
6 Mention any unusual hobbies or jobs. ☐

THE INTERVIEW
7 Be confident. ☐
8 Avoid answering questions about your leisure interests. ☐
9 Do some research into the company's competitors. ☐
10 Ask the interviewer to explain what his or her company does. ☐
11 Expect to be surprised. ☐
12 You may have to have lunch with the interviewer. ☐
13 The interviewer may insult you. ☐
14 Remain calm whatever happens. ☐
15 Arrange to participate in some mock interviews beforehand. ☐
16 Tell the interviewer that you are sensitive and clever. ☐

'CREATIVE JOB SEARCHING'
17 This technique is better than applying for jobs in the conventional way. ☐
18 Get in touch with employees working in companies in your chosen field. ☐
19 You will get a job if you are persistent enough. ☐
20 If you're personally known to a company you stand a better chance. ☐

B Work in groups and discuss these questions:
- Which of the advice given do you disagree with?
- From your own experience, what other advice would you give to job-seekers?
- If you were looking for an employee, what qualities would you be looking for?
- How many job interviews have you been involved in? Describe one of them.

➡ What do you find most difficult about *exam* interviews? What aspects of your performance would you most like to improve?

C Write a composition on one of these topics:
1 *Find an advertisement for a job you find attractive, or which is suitable for someone with your talents, experience and qualifications. Write a letter of application, describing yourself and explaining why you are the ideal person for the job.* (about 300 words, not including the address, etc.)

OR

2 *Write an account of a job application you were involved in, starting from the time you found out about the vacancy and ending with the time you heard whether you got the job.* (about 350 words)

D Work in pairs. If you wrote C 1, role-play the interview following your job application, taking it in turns to be the interviewer and interviewee. If you wrote C 2, imagine that you have applied for a job and role-play the interview.

★★ In questions like C 1 and C 2 in the exam, there is no need to be completely honest. It may be easier and more interesting to embroider the truth a little by using your imagination.
In a real job application, it *is* advisable to tell the truth, however!

A Find synonyms for the phrases in italics, or explain their meanings. Refer to a dictionary if necessary.

1 'What do you enjoy most about your work?' *'That's a good question!'*
2 I know it's a very old car but I think it's still *good for* a few more years.
3 I asked him to apologise and he did so, but *with bad grace*.
4 I made 10 photocopies and then one more *for good measure*.
5 Don't do someone *a good turn* in the hope of getting something in return.
6 Have you finished in the shower, or are you planning to stay in there *for good*?
7 I'm not myself today – I had rather *a bad night*.
8 Is it *bad manners* to read while you're eating a meal?
9 After that things *went from bad to worse*.
10 I didn't get the job, but it's *all to the good* because it wasn't really right for me.
11 He can't be trusted: he's *good for nothing* and a thoroughly *bad lot*.
12 'Work hard and play hard' is an old saying that still *holds good* today.

B Fill the gaps in these sentences with suitable phrases from the list below.

1 You can .... as a foreign exchange dealer.
2 She used to take .... time off work, but then the boss gave her .... and since then her attendance has been exemplary.
3 Make sure you arrive .... for the interview – that usually ....
4 She promised to phone me first thing today and she was ....
5 There has been .... between Tony and Liz since Liz was promoted.
6 I've had the machine overhauled and serviced – now it's ....
7 I can't run because I've got ....
8 The company is ....: more staff are being made redundant.
9 The service here is terrible – I .... complain to the manager.
10 I know the managing director personally, so I'll .... you.
11 I took the machine to pieces but found it impossible to fix – in the end I ....
12 Things may go wrong if we continue, I think we should stop now ....
13 We made the offer .... and didn't expect these problems would arise.
14 You can't expect him to hurry – he'll do the work ....
15 Lunchtime already! It's .... I brought some sandwiches.

> *a bad leg / ankle / knee*   *a good job*   *as good as new*
> *a good deal of*   *as good as her word*   *bad blood*
> *earn good money*   *a good talking to*
> *give up as a bad job*   *have a good mind to*
> *in a bad way*   *in good faith*   *in good time*
> *in his own good time*   *make a good impression*
> *put in a good word for*   *while the going's good*

E In the last part of the recording, Steve talks about the rewards of his work and looks into the future. Note down:

- what Steve enjoys – and what he doesn't enjoy
- what he wants to do in the future
- the reasons why he might decide to stop working in the film industry

➡ Compare your notes with a partner. Then discuss your reactions to the whole interview.

15.3 Show business   Interview practice

In this section you'll be asking each other questions – playing the part of examiner and candidate. A one-to-one examination interview lasts 15–20 minutes, but this practice is likely to take longer. Don't work with the same partner for every part of this section.

A *Photographs* Work in pairs. One of you should look at Activity 16, the other at 33. You'll each have a picture to describe and discuss. Take it in turns to be the 'examiner' and the 'candidate'.

B *Passages* Work in pairs. One of you should look at Activity 14, the other at 31. You'll each have two short passages to look at. Comment on their source and intention, as well as your reactions to them. You may quote from them, but *don't* read them aloud.

C *Tasks* Work in pairs. One of you should look at Activity 15, the other at 21. You'll each have some questions to ask your partner about his or her tastes in entertainment and the arts. Take it in turns to be the 'examiner' and the 'candidate'.

★★ In the examination interview, candidates are assessed on their:

fluency	**pronunciation of individual sounds**
grammatical accuracy	**interactive communication**
pronunciation of sentences	**vocabulary resource**

★★ In the exam, don't be the passive partner – take the initiative just as you would in a normal conversation. If you're reticent, it may be quite difficult for the examiner to find out how well you speak English. Remember that it's how you communicate that's being assessed, not whether your answers are correct, intelligent or sensible – or even true!

A cheerful, confident manner is also very helpful in the interview. If you're feeling nervous the examiner will try to put you at your ease by asking you a few things about yourself before you have to speak about the photograph(s).

A Fill the gaps in these sentences with suitable prepositions from the list. Some are used more than once.

> above   at   before   below   beside   besides   by   during   for   from
> in   into   in front of   next to   on   on top of   opposite   over   to
> under   with

1 There's a free seat .... me here – sit .... me and keep me company.
2 The temperature .... the South Pole .... winter is usually .... 50 degrees .... zero.
3 The Mona Lisa, which is .... the Louvre .... Paris, was painted well .... 400 years ago.
4 Would you prefer to go .... car, ... the bus or .... foot?
5 The Odeon is directly .... the bus station, a few metres .... the square. If you're approaching it .... the west, turn .... the left when you see the university .... your right.
6 'Try to arrive .... time .... future,' he said to me .... a whisper.
7 I couldn't see very well because someone .... a big hat was sitting .... me .... the cinema. And I couldn't hear the soundtrack because some people were talking .... loud voices .... the film.
8 .... painting lovely pictures she's very good .... sculpture.
9 G comes .... F .... the alphabet, and .... H.
10 He was working .... the painting .... five weeks .... the spring.
11 Instead of keeping his money .... the bank he hides it .... the carpet. He keeps his small change .... a biscuit tin .... the wardrobe.
12 When they walked .... the room hand .... hand, they saw her sitting .... an armchair .... the window .... a big smile .... her face.

B Work in pairs. Look at the pictures opposite and discuss with your partner how the optical illusions are created, using suitable prepositional phrases:

> *at the top of   on the other side of*   etc.

and adjectives:

> *horizontal   vertical   diagonal   parallel   curved*   etc.

For example:

> The box in the top left-hand corner looks three-dimensional, but it isn't really. If you look at it closely, you'll see that it's composed of one-dimensional lines, not two-dimensional sides. It looks as if it has an open lid, but it's not clear whether the lid is slightly open and pointing towards us, or open a long way and pointing away from us...

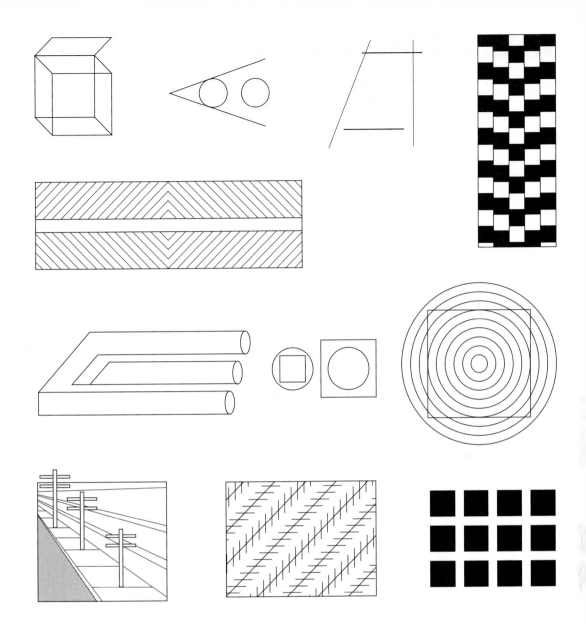

C Work in pairs. First draw a simple sketch without letting your partner see. Then turn the sketch upside down. Explain to your partner how to draw the same sketch as if it is an abstract drawing, by referring to the positions and shapes of all the parts, not what they represent (i.e. *a large oval* not *a face*, *a semi-circle* not *a smile*, etc.).

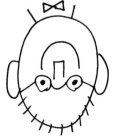

A   Before you listen to the interview, discuss these questions:
- What kinds of music do you like to listen to?
- What pleasure do you get from listening to music?
- What kind of person becomes a composer or songwriter?
- What kind of person becomes a pop musician? Or a classical musician?

B   Listen to the interview and answer these multiple-choice questions.

Vince Cross

1 How did it come about that Vince Cross became a composer?
    a) Because he is not a particularly good keyboard player
    b) Because keyboards are important in most modern music
    c) Because of his education and training

2 Vince composes pieces of music . . .
    a) and then tries to sell it to clients
    b) for clients who want music for children
    c) when a client commissions him

3 Vince says that he . . .
    a) is an innovative composer
    b) is good at copying any style of music
    c) sometimes uses other composers' tunes

4 Why does Vince consider himself to be fortunate?
    a) Because everything is going well at the moment
    b) Because he makes a good living
    c) Because his work is his hobby

5 Unlike an employee, Vince . . .
    a) doesn't have to work very hard
    b) has to rely on getting commissions himself to earn his living
    c) has to work long, unsocial hours

6 As a songwriter, Vince . . .
    a) depends on well-known singers to inspire him
    b) has no time for writing songs for his own satisfaction
    c) gets ideas for songs irregularly

7 Vince would like to write a musical one day when he . . .
    a) can afford to take a break from commissioned work
    b) has become very rich
    c) has plenty of free time

8 The feeling Vince gets from composing music is almost like the feeling . . .
    a) a poet might feel
    b) a sculptor or carpenter might feel
    c) a good teacher might feel

9 Like many musicians, Vince is obsessive because he . . .
    a) enjoys his work so much
    b) has to practise many hours a day
    c) is a perfectionist

C Work in groups and discuss these questions:

- What do you think is the 'downside' that Vince mentions of combining his hobby with his job?
- What aspects of Vince's way of life do you envy? Why would you like / not like to lead the same kind of life?
- How important is it to enjoy your job? How much of a perfectionist are you?
- How much attention do you pay to the kind of background music (in films or TV commercials) that Vince composes? What is the purpose of this kind of music?

15.6 Exam practice

A Section A of the Reading Comprehension paper consists of 25 multiple-choice questions. These may focus on vocabulary or grammar, or both.
Look at these annotated exam-style questions and then do the remaining ones unaided.

1 The review didn't actually say that it was a terrible film but that was what was .... by the sarcastic style.
A implicated   B implied ✓   C inferred   D hinted **+ at**
in a crime   **the reader**
                                  infers

2 She's a very .... writer – she publishes three books a year.
A fertile   B fruitful   C copious   D prolific ✓
...imagination   ...collaboration   ...notes   COLLOCATION

3 .... you wish to see the play, tickets can be obtained at the box office.
A Should ✓   B Did   C Were   D Had **+ past**
              in a question   ...you intending   GRAMMAR

4 Professional musicians are not .... to enter for the music competition.
A enabled   B capable   C permissible   D eligible ✓
= given the   of —ing   'permitted'
opportunity   would be OK

5 The building of the new theatre is .... gaining the support of local people.
A thanks to   B responsible for   C dependent on   D reliant on
'was built   doesn't really   not very good, but   '...the support'
thanks to the   make sense   the 'least bad' answer   would be OK
support' would be OK

6 I'll enter the competition if you ....
A would   B should   C will   D shall

7 He was so convincing that we were completely taken .... by his lies.
A along   B in   C about   D down

8 Before the performance the actors spent many hours ....
A repeating   B rehearsing   C practising   D training

9 The art gallery couldn't survive without a .... from the government.
A subsidiary   B subsidy   C subsidence   D subscription

10 The performance will begin at 7.30 unless .... indicated on your ticket.
A further   B differently   C below   D otherwise

⟫➔

B Question 4 in the Use of English paper also tests both vocabulary and grammar. Look at the annotated answers to the first questions and then do the rest unaided.

For each sentence, write a new sentence as similar as possible in meaning to the original sentence, using the word given. The word must not be altered in any way.

1 As it was raining the only thing we could do was go to the art gallery.
   alternative
   As it was raining our only alternative was to go to the art gallery.
      – meaning changed
   As it was raining there was no alternative but to go to the art gallery.
      – 'we' omitted
   We had no alternative but to go to the art gallery. – 'rain' omitted
   There were no alternatives to going to the art gallery as it was raining.
      – word changed
   As it was raining we had no alternative but to go to the art gallery. ✓
   In the rain we had no alternative but to go to the art gallery. ✓

2 I remember very few things about the film.
   scarcely
   I (can) scarcely remember a thing about the film. – brackets not advisable
   I can scarcely remember the film. – meaning changed
   I can scarcely remember anything about the film. ✓
   I scarcely remember anything about the film. ✓
   I can scarcely remember a thing about the film. ✓

3 A silent movie can't be compared to a modern film.
   comparison
   I can't make a comparison between a silent movie and a modern one. – 'I' added
   It's difficult to make a comparison between a modern film and a silent movie.
      – meaning changed
   Comparisons between a silent movie and a modern one are difficult to make.
      – word altered
   There's no comparison between a silent movie and a modern film. ✓

4 Not many people are expected to attend the show.
   poorly

5 You can't possibly expect me to pay for the tickets.
   question

6 Before he made *American Friends*, Steve Abbott produced *A Fish Called Wanda*.
   previous

7 It was stupid of her to turn down the offer of free tickets for the opera.
   fool

8 I never thought of taking up painting as a hobby.
   occurred

★★ In questions like the ones opposite there are often several possible ways of rewriting the sentences. Make sure you have included all the information and not changed any of it. Questions of this kind often rely on collocations and common phrases – you should look out for these in your reading.

15.7 Guernica Questions & summary

A This passage describes Pablo Picasso's *Guernica*, which was painted after the bombing of a Basque town during the Spanish Civil War. The painting itself is nearly eight metres across, but the reproduction below gives an idea of what it looks like and will help you to follow the description in the first two paragraphs.

➡ Before you read it, discuss your reactions to the picture with a partner.

Guernica is the most powerful invective against violence in modern art, but it was not wholly inspired by the war: its motifs – the weeping woman, the horse, the bull – had been running through Picasso's work for years before *Guernica* brought them together. In the painting they become receptacles for extreme sensation – as John Berger has   5
remarked, Picasso could imagine more suffering in a horse's head than Rubens normally put into a whole Crucifixion. The spike tongues, the rolling eyes, the frantic splayed toes and fingers, the necks arched in spasm: these would be unendurable if their tension were not braced against the broken, but visible, order of the painting . . .   10

. . . it is a general meditation on suffering, and its symbols are archaic, not historical: the gored and speared horse (the Spanish Republic), the bull (Franco) louring over the bereaved, shrieking woman, the paraphernalia of pre-modernist images like the broken sword, the surviving flower, and the dove. Apart from the late Cubist style, the only specifically modern elements in *Guernica* are the eye of the electric light, and the suggestion that the horse's body is made of parallel lines of newsprint like the newspaper in Picasso's collages a quarter of a century before. Otherwise its heroic abstraction and monumentalized pain hardly seem to belong to the time of photography and bombers. Yet they do: and Picasso's most effective way of locating them in that time was to paint *Guernica* entirely in black, white, and grey, so that despite its huge size it retains something of the grainy, ephemeral look one associates with the front page of a newspaper.

B Highlight these words in the description above and explain their meanings:

> *invective* (line 1)   *motifs* (line 2)   *receptacles* (line 5)   *archaic* (line 11)
> *bereaved* (line 13)   *paraphernalia* (line 14)   *ephemeral* (line 23)

C Now read the continuation of the passage and write your answers to the questions that follow, using your own words as far as possible.

Guernica was the last great history-painting. It was also the last modern painting of major importance that took its subject from politics with the intention of changing the way large numbers of people thought and felt about power. Since 1937, there have been a few admirable works of art that contained political references – some of Joseph Beuys's work or Robert Motherwell's *Elegies to the Spanish Republic*. But the idea that an artist, by making painting or sculpture, could insert images into the stream of public speech and thus change political discourse has gone, probably for good, along with the nineteenth-century ideal of the artist as public man. Mass media took away the political speech of art. When Picasso painted *Guernica*, regular TV broadcasting had been in existence for only a year in England and nobody in France, except a few electronics experts, had seen a television set. There were perhaps fifteen thousand such sets in New York City. Television was too crude, too novel, to be altogether credible. The day when most people in the capitalist world would base their understanding of politics on what the TV screen gave them was still almost a generation away. But by the end of World War II, the role of the 'war artist' had been rendered negligible by war photography. What did you believe, a drawing of an emaciated corpse in a pit that looked like bad, late German Expressionism, or the incontrovertible photographs from Belsen, Maidenek, and Auschwitz? It seems obvious, looking back, that the artists of Weimar Germany and Leninist Russia lived in a much more attenuated landscape of media than ours, and their reward was that they could still believe, in good faith and without bombast, that art could morally influence the world. Today, the idea has largely been dismissed, as it must be in a mass media society where art's principal social role is to be investment capital, or, in the simplest way, bullion. We still have political art, but we have no *effective* political art. An artist must be famous to be heard, but as he acquires fame, so his work accumulates 'value' and becomes, ipso facto, harmless. As far as today's politics is concerned, most art aspires to the condition of Muzak. It provides the background hum for power. If the Third Reich had lasted until now, the young bloods of the Inner Party would not be interested in old fogeys like Albert Speer or Arno Breker, Hitler's monumental sculptor; they would be queuing up to have their portraits silkscreened by Andy Warhol. It is hard to think of any work of art of which one can say, *This* saved the life of one Jew, one Vietnamese, one Cambodian. Specific books perhaps; but as far as one can tell, no paintings or sculptures. The difference between us and the artists of the 1920s is that they thought such a work of art could be made. Perhaps it was a certain naïveté that made them think so. But it is certainly our loss that we cannot.

(from *The Shock of the New* by Robert Hughes)

1 Before 1937, when *Guernica* was painted, how did artists believe that they could make political statements?
2 How do people in the West nowadays form their political opinions, according to the writer?
3 Why did it become meaningless to paint scenes of war during World War II?
4 What is the function of art in the modern capitalist world?
5 What is the role of art in politics nowadays?

D In one paragraph, using your own words as far as possible, summarise the changing role of art in Western society between the 1920s and the present day (about 60 words).

First make notes and compare them with a partner.

E Work in groups and discuss these questions:
- To what extent do you agree with the writer's views?
- What do you think is the purpose of a work of art?
- What influence could a painting, or any other work of art, have on your own feelings and attitudes?
- Does a critic like Robert Hughes perform a useful function in explaining works of art as well as evaluating and interpreting them?
- Does the same hold good for a film critic, a music critic, a TV critic or a sports writer?

➡ Discuss these exam tips with a partner. Which of them might work for you? Are there any other tips you can add?

★★ 1 Section B (Question 5) of the Use of English paper is worth 40 to 45% of the marks for the whole paper. Aim to spend about 40 minutes on it and don't spend too long on it at the expense of the other questions.

2 Do the easier questions in Section B first and come back to the harder ones later.

3 Use a highlighter or a pencil to help you to see all the vocabulary in context in the passage.

4 Make notes before you put pen to paper – space is limited and there may not be enough room for extensive corrections later.

5 You might prefer to do Section B before the other questions, when you feel fresher, rather than later when you're more tired – or make your notes for the answers earlier and then write them out later, when you've had time to mull them over.

6 If time is running out, give some answers in note form and don't leave any blank spaces.

7 Your answers have to be 'coherent and relevant' so check for any irrelevancies in your answers, especially in the summary.

8 In the summary, try to rephrase some of the information in your own words, but don't waste too much time trying to think of a synonym for every word – just avoid direct quotation as far as possible!

15.8 Conjunctions and connectors – 2   Advanced grammar

A Replace the conjunctions in these sentences with the words given.

1 I don't know much about art but I know what I like.
Despite ....

2 Not only does she paint in oils, but she also paints watercolours.
Besides ....

3 You won't get seats for the show if you don't go to the box office today.
Unless ....

4 The performance was cancelled because the tenor and soprano were both ill.
Due to ....

5 I like all kinds of music but I don't like jazz.
Except for ....

6 He was missing his wife and he was missing his children too.
As well as ....

7 You didn't enjoy the film, and neither did I.
Like ....

8 The soloist gave a wonderful performance, otherwise I wouldn't have enjoyed the concert.
But for ....

B Fill each of the gaps in this passage with a suitable word or phrase from the list below (some are used more than once).

Critics should never imagine that they are powerful, ...1...... it would be culpable of them not to realise that they are bound to be influential. There is no reason, ...2......, to be crushed flat by the responsibility of the job. It is, ...3......, a wonderfully enjoyable one, ...4...... at its most onerous. The onerousness, ...5......, springs more from the fatigue of trying to respond intelligently than from the necessary curtailment of one's night-life. Television critics soon get used to being asked about how they can bear the loss of all those dinner parties. Don't they pine for intelligent conversation? The real answers to such questions are usually too rude to give, ...6...... the interrogator is a friend. Formal dinner parties are an overrated pastime, barely serving their function of introducing people to one another, ...7...... nearly always devoid of the intelligent conversation they are supposed to promote. Most people severely overestimate their powers as conversationalists, ...8...... even the few genuinely gifted chatterers tend not to flourish when surrounded by bad listeners. The talk on the little screen is nearly always better than the talk around a dinner table. For my own part, I hear all the good conversation I need ......9...... lunching with drunken literary acquaintances in scruffy restaurants. In London, the early afternoon is the time for wit. At night, it chokes in its collar.

What I miss in the evenings is not dinner parties but the opera house. ......10...... I finally give up reporting the tube, it will probably be ......11...... the lure of the opera house has become too strong to resist. ......12...... sitting down to be bored while eating is an activity I would willingly go on forgoing. The box is much more entertaining – a fact which even the most dedicated diners-out occasionally admit, ...13...... from time to time it becomes accepted in polite society that dinner may be interrupted in order to watch certain programmes. It was recognised, ...14......, that *The Glittering Prizes** might justify a collective rush from the dinner table to the television set, ...15...... I confess that ......16...... my own inclination was to rush from the television set to the dinner table.

Clive James

*after all although and because But but even for example
however in this one case incidentally since unless When when
while*

* *The Glittering Prizes*: a TV serial about university life

C Look at these phrases that are used when making generalisations:

*as a rule   broadly speaking   everyone would agree that   generally speaking
in many cases   in most cases   in some cases   it is often said that
it is recognised that   it is sometimes said that   many people believe
on the whole   some people believe   to a certain extent   to some extent*

and giving exceptions:

*apart from   but   but all the same   but every so often   but now and then
but in other cases   but in this one case   but there are exceptions to every rule
except for   however   on the other hand*

Fill the gaps and write a continuation for each of these sentences using the phrases above.

1 ...**Some people say that**... modern art is overrated and .... I do agree, but . . .
2 .... artists lead a good life: their hobby is their profession, but . . .
3 .... Hollywood movies are ephemeral, ... you see one you can't forget.
4 .... watching television is rather a waste of time, . . .
5 .... politicians are honourable, dedicated people, . . .
6 .... reading is a wonderful source of pleasure, . . .
7 .... people work because they have to, not because they want to, . . .
8 .... I enjoy all kinds of music, . . .

*"For heaven's sake, Harry! Can't you just relax and enjoy
art, music, religion, literature, drama and history,
without trying to tie it all together?"*

2 What does the writer mean by 'corpulence' (line 4)?
   a disease affecting executives   – it's not a disease (this looks like a guess)
   the condition of being overweight   – fine, not too long or short
   being plump or chubby   – OK, but these words seem rather too informal
   fat   – not bad, but 'fatness' might be better

3 What does the writer mean by 'fad' (line 13)?
   fashion   – OK, not bad
   craze   – fine, this is exactly right
   desire to take part in this form of relaxation or therapy
       – looks like a guess, but better to bluff like this than not answer the question at all!
   crazy idea   – this is wrong and looks like a guess too

4 What does the writer mean by 'euphoric' (line 19)?
   feeling extremely happy   – fine: good, straightforward answer
   exhilarated   – good answer, but it depends on knowing this word
   glad   – too weak, doesn't convey the meaning adequately
   full of euphoria   – this may be true, but it doesn't show any understanding

    Now highlight these words in the passage and explain what they mean, in the context of the passage:

    seedy (line 25)   *seasoned* (line 31)   *surge* (line 31)   *snatches* (line 54)
    vivid (line 55)   *chemicals* (line 67)   *tedium* (line 67)   *bustle* (line 70)

C   Look at these annotated answers and then write your answers to the remaining questions unaided:

1 How, according to the writer, did stressed executives 'unwind' before 'floating'?
   They used to unwind with a few cigarettes and a pint of lager.
       – a direct quotation from the passage
   They smoked and slurped.   – another direct quote
   They found that smoking and drinking helped them to relax.   – good answer
   They relaxed drinking and smoking.   – fine: good idea to reverse the sequence

2 What is the principle underlying floating?
   Deprive the body of physical sensations and you free the mind for medication.
       – don't quote verbatim from the passage, and if you do, don't misquote!
   If the body can't feel anything, the mind can do nothing but meditate.   – OK
   When your body is deprived of feelings, your mind can be freed to meditate.
       – changing the structures is good, but the vocabulary hasn't been changed
   If you take away the body's sensations, the mind can meditate without restraint.
       – fine: there aren't really any suitable synonyms for 'sensations' and 'meditate'

3 What does a tank look like?
4 How do the owners of tanks help to put their clients in the right mood?
5 What happens to people once they have been floating for some time?
6 How do floaters know it's time to stop meditating and 'wake up'?
7 What are said to be the disadvantages of taking drugs and meditation?
8 Why might floaters feel worse after a session in the tank?

D   Summarise the history of floating.   (about 80 words)

A When telling a story or describing your experiences, the use of illustration and allusion can help to make your writing more vivid, especially if you can give personal examples or make interesting comparisons.

Work in pairs. Look at these examples and decide which of the alternative endings sounds more vivid:

1 The weather was so hot that . . .
   . . . a river of sweat was pouring off him.
   . . . he was sweating like a pig.
   . . . he felt very uncomfortable.

2 They were so unfriendly that . . .
   . . . I wished I had stayed at home.
   . . . I regretted having left home.
   . . . I felt unwanted and unwelcome, as if I was an outsider.

3 The lecture was so dull that . . .
   . . . we found it hard to concentrate.
   . . . we could hardly keep our eyes open.
   . . . we all started to nod off.

4 I was so looking forward to the holidays that . . .
   . . . I couldn't keep my mind on my work.
   . . . I was very excited.
   . . . I couldn't sit still.

5 There was such a lot of rain that . . .
   . . . we were soon soaked to the skin.
   . . . we soon looked like drowned rats.
   . . . we got extremely wet.

6 She was so beautiful that . . .
   . . . he kept on looking at her.
   . . . he couldn't keep his eyes off her.
   . . . his heart skipped a beat every time he looked at her.

B Work in pairs. Decide how to fill the gaps in this story about 'A visit to the doctor'. When you've finished, compare your ideas with another pair.

I woke up feeling as if ....: my head was throbbing and my joints were aching so much that .... And I felt so dizzy that ....

I called the doctor to make an appointment. Over the phone the receptionist spoke to me as if .... but when I walked in she smiled at me as if ....

I found a seat in the corner of the waiting room, which looked like .... Sitting there waiting for my turn among the other patients reminded me of .... Looking round, my eyes came to rest on a young man smoking a cigarette, who looked as if .... He had such a bad cough that it sounded as if .... With him was a little girl who looked so unhealthy that ....

By the time my name was called I was feeling rather better — it seemed as if .... I stepped into the doctor's room.

"What seems to be the trouble?" asked the doctor in a such a
.... voice that I .... I described my symptoms to her,
feeling a bit like ....

"You've just got the flu," she said. "Go home, go to bed and
don't waste my time." I felt so foolish that ....

C Look at two or three of your own recent compositions. How many times have
you used phrases like the ones illustrated in A? Can you find any places where
you could have used such phrases – or are they better without such phrases?

D In these idiomatic expressions, match the words in the two columns:

drink too much alcohol – He drinks like . . .   wildfire
drive fast   – She drove like . . .   cat and dog
have a row   – They fought like . . .   a sieve
forgetful   – I have a memory like . . .   a fish
run fast   – She ran like . . .   a fish
sleep well   – I slept like . . .   a house on fire
extravagant   – He spends money like . . .   the wind
swim well   – She swims like . . .   the wind
be good friends   – We got on like . . .   a log
very quickly   – The news spread like . . .   water

⚠ Illustration and allusion are less common in formal writing, such as essays,
reports and formal letters. Overuse may seem strange – as in the story in B.

16.7 Synonyms   Vocabulary development

A 🔲 You'll hear the same words spoken in different ways – pay attention to the
underlying meaning conveyed by each speaker's tone of voice:

> Ah, there you are. I was wondering where you'd got to. Luckily
> I had some work to get on with so I wasn't bored. Anyway, even
> if the film has started by the time we get there, I don't think
> it'll matter, do you?

Decide which word from the list below best describes each speaker's tone:

1		5	
2		6	
3		7	
4		8	

amused   bored   cross   friendly   furious   kind   sad   unemotional

➡ Listen to the recording again and note down at least one other adjective (or
phrase) to describe the tone of each speaker. Compare ideas with your partners.

⟫➤

B Look at these words and match them with their synonyms below.

amazed   annoyed   clever   confused   cured   depressed   determined different   disappointed   dull   encouraged   exciting   frightened   glad respected   revolting   shocked   upset   worried   worrying

admired   anxious   astonished   better   bewildered   delighted   despondent disgusting   disillusioned   distressed   disturbing   diverse   dreary heartened   horrified   indignant   persistent   scared   talented   thrilling

C Replace each adjective in italics with a suitable synonym which might impress the examiners more than simple words – or which can help you to avoid repetition. You may have to rewrite the whole sentence in some cases.

1 Surfing can be *dangerous*, but hang-gliding is much more *dangerous*.
2 There are many *good* ways of keeping fit – jogging is very *good*.
3 I was *happy* to meet my old friends again. It was *good* to talk about old times.
4 I'm sorry that you were *unwell* yesterday. You look *all right* today.
5 It was *kind* of you to offer to help, but the work wasn't *difficult*.
6 We went for a *nice* walk at the weekend, ending up at a *nice* restaurant.
7 The original novel was *interesting*, but the film they made of it was *boring*.
8 The meal we had last night was *good*, but the wine wasn't *good*.
9 Keeping in shape is *important* and keeping your weight down is also *important*.
10 I *like going to* the cinema but I *like going to* the theatre more.

D Replace the verbs in italics with suitable phrasal verbs. (This exercise revises some of the phrasal verbs you have come across in previous units.)

1 I *withdraw* that remark I made about you.
2 If you have a pain in your back you'll just have to *endure* it.
3 Would it *inconvenience* you if I stayed for dinner?
4 I hope you aren't *delayed* in the rush-hour traffic.
5 She *invented* the whole story and she *deceived* us all!
6 His suitcase *disintegrated* on the luggage carousel.
7 He *had* the brilliant idea of immersing his assistants in salt water.
8 Having heard all the arguments I've decided to *support* your idea.
9 I find that stress at work often *causes* a headache.
10 I couldn't *make them understand* that I wanted to go to bed early and this really *depressed* me.

1 The writer's parents . . .
   a) became very anxious at holiday times.
   b) couldn't understand his dreams.
   c) spoke calmly about their dreams.
   d) weren't interested in hearing about his dreams.

2 Most people the writer knows . . .
   a) are irritated by their dreams.
   b) do not enjoy their dreams.
   c) are bored by hearing about his dreams.
   d) wish they didn't dream.

3 Brown, Smith and Robinson are . . .
   a) dead friends of the writer.
   b) living friends of the writer.
   c) people you or I might know.
   d) people who were well-known when the piece was written.

4 In our dreams we experience . . .
   a) deeper anxiety and unhappiness than in our waking lives.
   b) greater fear, despair and joy than in our waking lives.
   c) more interesting events than in our waking lives.
   d) premonitions of future events.

5 The writer reproaches people who belittle dreams because . . .
   a) they are daft and don't understand how important dreams are.
   b) they think dreams are less important than their waking lives.
   c) they don't agree that dreams are just as important as being awake.
   d) each dream is a tangible part of our experience.

B Work in groups and discuss these questions:

- To what extent do you agree with what the writer says about dreams?
- Do you have vivid dreams? Do you remember a nightmare you have had?

➡ Think of a dream you've had recently and describe it vividly to your partners – or make one up. The others should guess whether you really had that dream.

★★ In the exam read each passage twice: once quickly to get the gist and again more carefully to find the answers. Each correct answer gains two marks. Some of the alternatives are designed to be tricky and distract you from the right answer – so don't jump to conclusions.

Use a highlighter or pencil to mark any questions that you're still unsure about. It may be best to come back to them later on, rather than reading the passage again straight away.

A   Work in pairs. Discuss the notes below and add your own views to them.
Decide which of the points you'll include and which you'll leave out in a
composition on this topic:

> *We are constantly bombarded with advice from experts on ways of
> staying healthy and surviving to a ripe old age. Which aspects of their
> advice do you think it is practicable to follow?*   (about 350 words)

DIET

High fibre intake   →   better digestion + less disease
                                          connected with digestion
Reduced salt intake →   lower blood pressure
Reduced fat intake   →   less heart disease
Reduced sugar
   intake   →   less tooth decay + control of
                                          weight
Sufficient vitamins →   higher resistance to infection
A well-balanced
   diet   →   control of weight

EXERCISE   →   higher resistance to infection
                              →   lower susceptibility to heart
                                          disease, muscular pains,
                                          arthritis, etc
                              →   control of appetite
                              →   feeling of well-being and
                                          physical fitness

HABITS

Cigarette smoking →   cancer, bronchial disease
Alcohol   →   liver disease, addiction
Stress at work &   →   heart disease + stress-related
   home   illness (migraine, mental
                                        illness, depression, etc

HEREDITY

Parents' medical history passed on to children

B   Make your own notes before writing the composition.

➡ Show your completed composition to your partner and ask for comments.

A   Find synonymous words or phrases to replace the phrases in italics, using a dictionary if necessary.

1   She *gave me her word* that she would pay me back the next day.
2   Being insured costs a lot of money but it gives you *peace of mind*.
3   I was so annoyed that I couldn't resist *giving him a piece of my mind*.
4   Don't expect him to spare your feelings: he always *speaks his mind*.
5   She's so indecisive: she can never *make up her mind* what to do.
6   We *were in two minds* whether to phone you or not.
7   He's so garrulous that you can't *get a word in edgeways*.
8   It'll all end in tears, *mark my words*!
9   I can still see the whole scene *in my mind's eye*.
10 I'm sorry I didn't post the letter, it *slipped my mind*, I'm afraid.
11 Their new car is *the last word in* luxury.
12 'No, you can't stay out all night.' 'Is that *your last word*?' 'Yes.'

B   Fill the gaps in these sentences with suitable phrases from the list below. You may need to change the form of the verbs.

1   I couldn't think what to do, then suddenly I had a .... ?
2   You're an expert on this subject, would you mind if I ....?
3   She's usually so trustworthy, she's the last person I'd expect to ....
4   Actors have to be .... before they go on the stage.
5   Sit down, listen to some music and try to .... your problems.
6   I'm so angry about the way I was treated that I .... write a letter of complaint.
7   Idioms like these can't be translated .... into another language.
8   Who are you going to believe? We both denied responsibility so ....
9   You look preoccupied, as if you ....
10 Many English jokes depend on a ....
11 If you .... about coming with us, just give me a call.
12 I was .... but I couldn't solve the problem.

brainwave   change your mind   go back on his/her word
have a good mind to   have something on your mind   take your mind off
word for word   word perfect   it's his/her word against mine   pick your brains
play on words   rack my brains

➡ Can you think of any more phrases using *mind*, *brain* or *word*? Write them down and compare them with a partner.

17 The past

A   Work in pairs. Before you listen to the recording, look at this list of events which happened in 1974, 1976 and 1978. Pencil in any information you already know.

IN THE WORLD:
     Emperor Haile Selassie was .... in Ethiopia ....
     Gerald Ford became US President ....
     Greece became a .... and the monarchy was abolished ....
     Isabel Peron ousted in .... coup in Argentina ....
     Jimmy Carter elected President of the USA ....
     Presidents Sadat and Begin shared Nobel Peace Prize ....
     US President Nixon .... after Watergate tapes scandal ....
     Pope John Paul II became first non-Italian pope since 1542 ....
DEATHS:
     Agatha Christie, age 85 ....   Aldo Moro murdered, age 62 ....
     Duke Ellington, age 75 ....   Juan Peron, age 78
     Mao Tse-tung, age 82 ....   Georges Pompidou, age 62 ....
SPORT:
     Austrian driver Niki Lauda crashed in German Grand Prix ....
     Olympic Games in Montreal ....
     Winter Olympics in Innsbruck ....
     West Germany beat .... 2–1 in Soccer World Cup ....
     Argentina beat Holland 3–1 in Soccer World Cup ....
OSCARS FOR BEST FILM OF THE YEAR:
     The Deer Hunter ....   *Rocky* ....
     The Godfather Part 2 ....
TECHNOLOGY & MEDICINE:
     First commercial flight of Concorde ....
     First .... operation ....
     Many killed when poisonous gas escaped at Seveso, Northern Italy ....
IN BRITAIN:
     First .... opened in London ....
     The musical *Evita* opened in London ....
     Very hot summer: Minister for .... appointed ....

B  You'll hear two people giving a talk about historical events that happened in the years they were born: 1974 and 1976. Fill in the missing years and missing information opposite, but be careful: some of the events happened in 1978.

C Do some research on the events that happened in the year (or the month) *you* were born. Then give a short talk to the members of your group.

D Work in pairs. Discuss which word or phrase makes best sense in these quotations:

1 'History repeats itself; historians repeat ....' (Philip Guedalla)
 history   lies   themselves   dates
2 'History is little more than the register of the crimes, follies and .... of mankind.' (Edward Gibbon)
 achievements   mistakes   events   misfortunes
3 'Our chief interest in the past is as .... to the future.' (W. R. Inge)
 a warning   an omen   a guide   a signpost
4 'What experience and history teach us is this – that people and governments never have .... history, or acted on principles deduced from it.' (Hegel)
 benefited from   forgotten   paid attention to   learnt anything from
5 'The past is a foreign country: they do things .... there.' (first line of *The Go-between* by L.P. Hartley)
 similarly   differently   again   earlier
6 'No great man lives in vain. The history of the world is but the .... of great men.' (Thomas Carlyle)
 history   biography   achievement   success

E Work in groups and discuss these questions:
- Which of the quotations above do you agree with? Give your reasons.
- Why do we hear about so few women in history? Who are the most famous women in your country's history?
- Name three significant events in your country's history. Why are they memorable?
- What was the most significant world event of the last ten years?
- What do you think is the point of studying history?

"This could be great! They could do all the menial jobs no one else will do."

A Read these poems before you look at the questions on the next page.

THE SOLDIER

If I should die, think only this of me;
  That there is some corner of a foreign field
That is for ever England. There shall be
  In that rich earth a richer dust concealed;
A dust whom England bore, shaped, made aware,
  Gave, once, her flowers to love, her ways to roam,
A body of England's breathing English air,
  Washed by the rivers, blest by suns of home.

And think, this heart, all evil shed away,
  A pulse in the eternal mind, no less
    Gives somewhere back the thoughts by England given;
      Her sights and sounds; dreams happy as her day;
  And laughter, learnt of friends; and gentleness,
    In hearts at peace, under an English heaven.   Rupert Brooke

FUTILITY

Move him into the sun –
Gently its touch awoke him once,
At home, whispering of fields unsown.
Always it woke him, even in France,
Until this morning and this snow.
If anything might rouse him now
The kind old sun will know.

Think how it wakes the seeds, –
Woke, once, the clays of a cold star.
Are limbs, so dear-achieved, are sides,
Full-nerved – still warm – too hard to stir?
Was it for this the clay grew tall?
– O what made fatuous sunbeams toil
To break earth's sleep at all?   Wilfred Owen

THE GENERAL

'Good-morning; good-morning!' the General said
When we met him last week on our way to the Line.
Now the soldiers he smiled at are most of 'em dead,
And we're cursing his staff for incompetent swine.
'He's a cheery old card,' grunted Harry to Jack
As they slogged up to Arras with rifle and pack.

But he did for them both with his plan of attack.   Siegfried Sassoon

B Work in pairs. Discuss which of the alternatives you consider best reflects the meaning and mood of each poem.

1 In Rupert Brooke's *The Soldier*, the poet is praising . . .
   England's brave soldiers.
   England's scenery and people.
   England's free and democratic society.

2 The England described in the poem is England . . .
   during peacetime.
   in spring or summer.
   during the poet's youth.

3 If he dies the poet is sure that . . .
   he will be remembered.
   England will remain unchanged.
   his Englishness is immortal.

4 If the idea of 'England' were replaced in the poem by 'Germany' or another country . . .
   the poem would no longer make sense.
   the poem would still mean the same.
   the poem would have a different significance.

5 The tone of *The Soldier* is . . .
   sentimental   optimistic   pessimistic

6 In Wilfred Owen's *Futility*, the soldier described . . .
   has only just died.
   has been dead for a long time.
   is sure to die soon.

7 According to the poem it is pointless that . . .
   any man should die in war.
   a dead man should be moved into the sun.
   a man should grow up to die in this way.

8 The tone of *Futility* is . . .
   resigned   sardonic   lyrical

9 In Siegfried Sassoon's *The General*, the smiling general is . . .
   insincere   incompetent   happy

10 'Harry and Jack' are . . .
   two typical private soldiers.
   two now-dead friends of the poet.
   two young officers.

11 The soldiers who marched past the general last week . . .
   disliked him
   respected him
   liked him

12 The tone of *The General* is . . .
   serious   humorous   sarcastic

C Work in groups of three. Student A should look at Activity 10, student B at 37 and C at 43. You'll each have some information about each poet's life and death to share with your partners. Then discuss:

- To what extent does knowing more biographical information about each poet influence your response to the poems?
- Which of the poems made the greatest impact on you? Give your reasons.
- Which poems or works of literature came out of wars that your country has been involved in?
- Why is it that people find reading (and seeing films) about war fascinating?

★★ When tackling a reading passage in the exam, you may prefer to read quickly through it to get the gist before looking at the questions – or to look at the questions first and then read the passage through.

Some of the alternatives given in the questions may be tricky or deceptively plausible, which may distract you from the best alternative – so don't jump to conclusions. Be ready to eliminate the wrong answers and find the right one by a process of elimination.

Read carefully through the passage to find the answers, highlighting any relevant parts so that you can find them again quickly later. In the exam each correct answer gains two marks.

17.3   The end of the war   Reading

Read this extract, which describes the last months of the First World War, as seen from one young man's point of view. Then answer the questions that follow.

Nancy's brother, Tony, had also gone to France now, and her mother made herself ill by worrying about him. Early in July he should be due for leave. I was on leave myself at the end of one of the four-months' cadet courses, staying with the rest of Nancy's family at Maesyneuardd, a big Tudor house near Harlech. This was the most haunted house that I have ever been in, though the ghosts, with one exception, were not visible, except occasionally in the mirrors. They would open and shut doors, rap on the oak panels, knock the shades off lamps, and drink the wine from the glasses at our elbows when we were not looking. The house belonged to an officer in the Second Battalion, whose ancestors had most of them died of drink. The visible ghost was a little yellow dog that would appear on the lawn in the early morning to announce deaths. Nancy saw it through the window that time.

The first Spanish influenza epidemic began, and Nancy's mother caught it, but did not want to miss Tony's leave and going to the London theatres with him. So when the doctor came, she took quantities of aspirin, reduced

5

10

15

262

her temperature, and pretended to be all right. But she knew that the ghosts in the mirrors knew the truth. She died in London on July 13th, a few days later. Her chief solace, as she lay dying, was that Tony had got his leave prolonged on her account. I was alarmed at the effect that the shock of her death might have on Nancy's baby. Then I heard that Siegfried had been shot through the head that same day while making a daylight patrol through long grass in No Man's Land; but not killed. And he wrote me a verse-letter from a London hospital (which I cannot quote, though I should like to do so) beginning:

I'd timed my death in action to the minute . . .

It is the most terrible of his war-poems.

Tony was killed in September. I went on mechanically at my cadet-battalion work. The new candidates for commissions were mostly Manchester cotton clerks and Liverpool shipping clerks – men with a good fighting record, quiet and well-behaved. To forget about the war, I was writing *Country Sentiment*, a book of romantic poems and ballads.

In November came the Armistice. I heard at the same time of the deaths of Frank Jones-Bateman, who had gone back again just before the end, and Wilfred Owen, who often used to send me poems from France. Armistice-night hysteria did not touch our camp much, though some of the Canadians stationed there went down to Rhyl to celebrate in true overseas style. The news sent me out walking alone along the dyke above the marshes of Rhuddlan (an ancient battlefield), cursing and sobbing and thinking of the dead.

Siegfried's famous poem celebrating the Armistice began:

Everybody suddenly burst out singing,
And I was filled with such delight
As prisoned birds must find in freedom . . .

But 'everybody' did not include me.

(from *Goodbye to All That* by Robert Graves)

1 According to the writer, the invisible ghosts . . .
    a) really did not exist.
    b) really did exist.
    c) were visible only to Nancy.
    d) were the ghosts of soldiers who had died at the Front.

2 The doctor who came to see Nancy's mother . . .
    a) knew she was dying.
    b) did not realise she was very ill.
    c) gave her tablets to bring down her temperature.
    d) did not examine her thoroughly.

3 The writer mentions the deaths of . . .
    a) five people he knew well.
    b) four people he knew well.
    c) three people he knew well.
    d) two people he knew well.

4 The writer, at the time, was . . .
   a) fighting at the Front.
   b) training new recruits.
   c) training soldiers who wanted to be officers.
   d) training would-be officers, fresh from school.
5 When the Armistice was announced the writer . . .
   a) was overjoyed.   c) became hysterical.
   b) had mixed feelings.   d) was overwhelmed with grief.
6 The tone of the writing in the extract seems . . .
   a) emotional. b) cynical. c) detached. d) careless.

➡ Discuss your reactions to the passage with a partner.

17.4 Adjectives + prepositions   Grammar review

A Work in pairs. Discuss the differences in meaning between the adjectives in
these sentences. What (or who) might *it* or *them* refer to in each sentence?

1 Drink up: it's good for you.   She is very good at it.
   He was very good about it.   She was very good to them.

2 She was angry with them.   He was angry about it.

3 I knew I was right about them.   The choice was right for them.

4 We were pleased with them.   We were pleased for them.
   He sounded pleased about it.

5 She was sorry for them.   He was sorry about it.

6 She was very popular with them.   He became popular for it.

B Work in pairs. Decide whether *of* or *to* is used after each of these adjectives:

accustomed ahead allergic ashamed aware capable comparable
conscious courteous critical cruel devoid devoted envious
equivalent guilty hurtful identical impolite indifferent inferior
intolerant irrelevant kind loyal preferable proud scared
sensitive short similar superior susceptible unfaithful unworthy
wary weary

C Which of these prepositions are used after these adjectives?

vague   annoyed   consistent
sceptical   absent   bewildered   compatible
responsible   apprehensive   comparable   conversant
patient *about for from on with* curious
dependent
level keen intent fussy famous free familiar dubious
indignant   guilty   far

➡ Look up any words you're unsure of, and study the examples in the dictionary.

D Fill each gap with one word only, chosen from the exercises opposite:

1 We felt .... about the reception we might get, even though we knew that we'd be forgiven when we explained how .... we were for being late.

2 He is .... to his children and feels .... of them, but he does get .... with them if they are ever .... to people. Usually he feels .... about this afterwards, even though he knows it is .... for them.

3 I know I'm being .... of your staff but I'm not .... to being treated in this way. Who is the person who is .... for this?

4 She pretended to be .... to our sarcastic remarks, but in fact she's quite .... to being made fun of. Personally I'm .... about the effectiveness of sarcasm and I'm .... of the fact that it can be very .... to people.

5 Although he's usually .... on getting his own way, he didn't seem to be .... of convincing anyone at the meeting – on this occasion I felt quite .... for him, but I was .... of telling him so.

A You'll hear part of a seminar about emigration. Listen to the recording and fill the gaps in questions 1 to 4, and choose the best alternatives in 5 to 10:

1 In the 19th century the emigrants were escaping from:
   .... in Ireland;   .... in Russia;
   .... in industrial areas;   .... in agricultural areas.

2 All the emigrants had one thing in common: they had .... to ....

3 But the streets were not 'paved with ....' – the reality was more work in the sweat shops of .... or hunger on a barren farm in ....

4 MOVEMENTS OF POPULATIONS – add the nationalities and countries to the map:

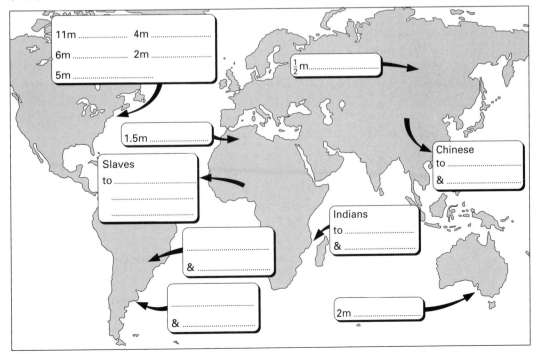

$\gg\!\!\rightarrow$

5 The present-day mixture of people in the New World was established in the . . .
  18th century   19th century   early part of the 20th century

6 The total number of US immigrants between 1821 and 1920 was . . .
  30 million   33 million   130 million   133 million

7 German and Italian are still spoken by South American citizens who . . .
  have recently arrived.   are the descendants of immigrants.
  cannot speak Portuguese or Spanish.

8 One can deduce the origins of American citizens of European origin by . . .
  noticing their foreign accents.   looking at the colour of their skin.
  looking through a telephone directory.

9 According to the speaker, more recent immigrants . . .
  form large, permanent communities in some countries
  send money home to their families   are unlike immigrants in the past

10 The speaker implies that immigration has contributed to . . .
  prejudice against immigrants.   a rich mixture of different cultures.
  the loss of immigrants' cultural heritage.

17.6 Collocations

★★ In the exam, you should read the whole passage through before filling in the blanks.
If you can't think what to put in some of the gaps, leave them blank and allow
yourself enough time to come back to them later. If you are unsure of an answer,
write it in pencil and come back to it later.
    Make sure the words you choose not only make sense in the context but are
grammatically correct and that you spell them correctly.

Fill each gap with **one** suitable word.

Between 1815 and 1914 Europe thrust out into the world, impelled by the force of its own
industrialisation. Millions of Europeans poured overseas and into Asiatic Russia, seeking and
finding ......1...... opportunities in the wider world. Between 1880 and 1900 Africa, a
continent four times the ......2...... of Europe, was parcelled out among the European powers.
And when in 1898 the United States of America, following the European ......3...... annexed
Puerto Rico, the Philippines and other islands of the Pacific, and asserted a controlling voice
in Latin American affairs, it seemed as though European expansion was turning into the
......4...... of the white ......5...... over the coloured majority. But expansion carried with it the
seeds of its own ......6...... . Even before European rivalries plunged the continent into the
......7...... of 1914–18, the beginnings of anti-European reaction were ......8...... in Asia and
Africa, and no sooner had the United States occupied the Philippines than they were met by a
nationalist ......9...... under the great Philippine leader, Aguinaldo.
    Today, in ......10......, we can see that the age of expansive imperialism was a transient
......11...... of history; while it lasted, it left a European ......12...... on the world. The world in
1914 was utterly different from the world in 1815, the ......13...... of change during the
preceding century greater than previously during whole millennia. Though industry in 1914

was only beginning to ......14...... beyond Europe and North America, and life in Asia and Africa was still regulated by age-old ......15......, the nineteenth century inaugurated the ......16...... of transformation which dethroned agricultural society as it had existed through the ......17......, and replaced it with the urban, industrialised, technocratic ......18...... which is spreading – for good or for ......19...... – like ......20...... through the world today.

(from *The Times Atlas of World History*)

17.7   The life and achievements of . . .   Composition

A Work in pairs. Decide which of this information you would certainly include, and which would have to be omitted in a 350-word essay on this topic:

Describe the life and achievements of a famous historical figure.

Napoleon

Personal Life

1769 born in Corsica

1796 married Josephine Beauharnais

1810 divorced Josephine as she had borne him no son

1810 married Archduchess Marie Louise of Austria

1811 birth of son

1821 death on remote island of St Helena in Atlantic

Political Life

1799 appointed First Consul of France

1800 reorganised political and educational system in France

1804 Napoleonic legal code introduced (basis of French and many other countries' legal systems, even Japan's)

1804 crowned Emperor of the French

1814 abdicated and sent to Island of Elba

1815 escaped from Elba – ruled again as Emperor for 100 days

1815 exiled to St Helena

Military Victories

1797 against Austrians at Rivoli (Northern Italy)

1805 against Russians and Austrians at Austerlitz

1806 against Prussians at Jena

1807 against Russians at Friedland

1809 against Austrians at Wagram

1812 against Russians at Borodino – Moscow taken, but in flames

*French forces not personally commanded by Napoleon

Military Defeats

1805* by British at Trafalgar (confirming British naval supremacy)

1812 retreat from Moscow (only 100,000 of the original 600,000 strong army survived)

1813 by Russians, Prussians and Austrians at Leipzig

1814* by British at Vitoria – French driven out of Spain

1814 Paris taken

1815 by British and Prussians at Waterloo

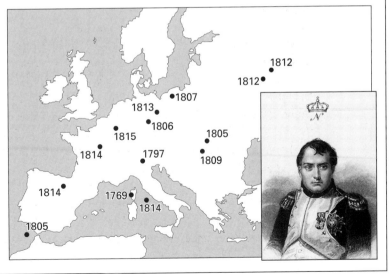

B Make your own notes and then write a composition on the same topic, not about Napoleon but about a historical figure from *your* country.

267

A Which of these sentences look right – and which are wrong?

They were extremely pleased with my work.
It was very delightful to have met you.
It is extremely important to read the question carefully.
It is very essential to make notes before you start writing.
It is extremely vital to check your answers for slips of the pen.

Work in pairs. Tick the adjectives and participles that are 'gradable' (i.e. they can be intensified by words like *very* or *extremely*) and put a cross by the ones that are 'non-gradable' or 'absolute' (and are not usually intensified by *very*).

livid ✗ · indignant ✓ absurd · preposterous · improbable
genuine · believable intelligent · sensible · brilliant happy · euphoric
identical · similar priceless · valuable amazed · surprised · astounded
interesting · fascinating worthless · futile · inexpensive
delightful · pleasant · magnificent · enjoyable vital · essential · important
fatal · hazardous · deadly · harmful · hurtful terrifying · frightening

B Fill each gap with a suitable modifier from the list, but without repeating the same one in the same sentence.

absolutely badly considerably deeply exceptionally extraordinarily
fully highly perfectly quite really reasonably remarkably
seriously thoroughly totally unexpectedly utterly widely

1 He was .... determined to succeed, and he was .... disappointed when he didn't. We were .... amused, but pretended to be .... sympathetic.
2 Many people were .... injured in the accident, which was .... reported in the press.
3 The amount of work that is required is .... greater than we expected, and we'll have to make a(n) .... great effort to finish it on time.
4 We were .... delighted to hear he was getting married, especially to such a(n) .... nice woman.
5 He was feeling .... depressed after his illness, but he made a(n) .... quick recovery, and was .... cheerful after that.
6 We felt we had been .... let down when they told us the application had been rejected. We were .... embarrassed because we'd told all our friends.
7 I'm sure her business will be .... successful, as she is a(n) .... capable person, even though it's .... true that most new businesses don't succeed.
8 It was a(n) .... wonderful film and I thought the performances were .... moving. It was .... different from any other film I've ever seen.
9 They made a .... good job of the report and we were .... pleased with it.
10 The role of women in history is not .... recognised by many historians, who tend to be .... traditional in their attitudes.

C For each sentence, write a new sentence as similar in meaning as possible to the original sentence, using the word given but without altering it in any way.

1 Some people simply can't remember historical dates.	impossible
2 We should be very happy indeed to accept your invitation.	delighted
3 It happened so long ago that no one remembers it at all now.	forgotten
4 There's no point at all in asking him to be tactful.	futile
5 She was very angry indeed when she found out.	livid
6 There is no likelihood of his succeeding.	improbable
7 You *must* remember to check your work through for mistakes.	essential
8 We were extremely interested in the lecture.	fascinating

17.9 Under exam conditions   Composition

★★ **Checking your work**

Look carefully for any mistakes or slips of the pen you may have made, like the ones illustrated here:

> *Its important to emphasise that . . .*
> *Perhaps it should pointed out that . . .*
> *Historie can be a facsinating subject.*
> *Rarely it is possible to . . .*
> *I decided to do a long journey . . .*
> *We enjoied the peformance.*

By now you're probably familiar with the kind of 'silly mistakes' that you make yourself when you're under pressure. As long as these are spotted and corrected before your work is handed in, there's nothing to worry about – but make sure you do allow yourself enough time for this!

Look back at two or three of your most recent compositions and highlight any 'silly mistakes' you made. Make sure you check your work for mistakes like these in the exam.

Prepare and write *one* of these composition exercises, allowing yourself 60 minutes only. This hour includes: time to think, to make notes and, afterwards, to check your work through for mistakes. Do this without using any reference books.

1 *How useful is it to teach history in schools?*   (about 350 words)

2 *Write a report of a historical event in the style of a modern newspaper article.* (about 350 words)

3 *Write a first-person narrative about a historical event, as if you were one of the people present at the time, ending with the words: ". . . only then did I realise that I had been involved in a historic moment in history."*   (about 350 words)

A   Photographs   In this part of the interview you are asked to comment on one
or more photographs, but you aren't expected to describe it/them in detail.
This is intended as a stimulus for discussion.

Work in pairs. Discuss these questions about the first photograph:

- What's happening in this picture? What kind of people are they?
- What would it have been like to be a member of this family, do you think?
- What might they be talking about?
- Describe a typical Sunday lunch in YOUR family or with YOUR friends. How is it different from the family meal shown in the photo?
- How have eating habits changed in your country during your lifetime?

Then discuss these questions about the second photograph:

- What's going on in this picture?
- What would it have been like to be a member of the class?
- What kind of lives could these girls look forward to?
- How has life for young women changed since that time?

B Passages   In this part of the interview you are asked to comment on the content, style and source of one or more passages. You aren't expected to read the passage(s) aloud, though you may quote a line or two if you wish.

Work in pairs. One of you should look at Activity 13, the other at 28.

C Communicative activity   In this part of the interview you take part in an activity, to show how well you can communicate in different situations.

Work in pairs. Both of you should look at Activity 20. Take it in turns to play the role of the examiner – or do this as a discussion in pairs.

★★ If you're doing the interview as an individual (one-to-one with the examiner) the whole interview lasts 12–15 minutes. If you do the interview in pairs (with another student) it lasts about 20 minutes, or about 25 minutes if you do it in groups of three.
  In the exam the photographs and passages may be connected, and you may have to comment on the differences between them.
  Before the exam, spend some time doing practice interviews from *Cambridge Proficiency Examination Practice Books* – with a partner playing the role of 'examiner'. This will help you to feel more confident about the procedure for the

"Come along, dear, we're off now."

18 Modern life

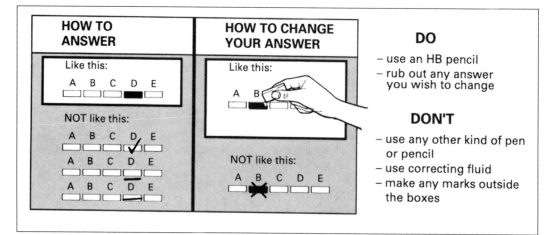

18.1 Vocabulary and usage
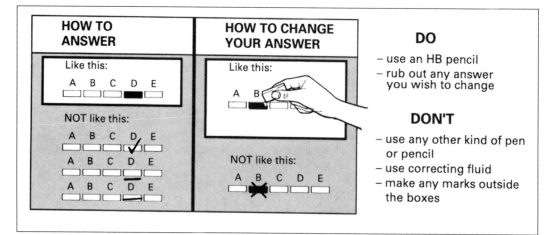

Paper 1 Section A

A Choose the word or phrase which best completes this sentence. In the exam (Paper 1 Section A) questions like these are answered on the 'MULTIPLE-CHOICE ANSWER SHEET'.

1 Every member of the community has their own personal .... to make.
   A announcement   B contribution   C donation   D endowment
2 In this very poor neighbourhood many youths belong to ....
   A bands   B gangs   C groups   D packs
3 At the end of the match the .... went wild with excitement.
   A audience   B congregation   C witnesses   D spectators
4 We're looking for new blood to join our dynamic ....
   A circle   B clique   C set   D team
5 Let's .... together after work and thrash this out between us.
   A come   B gather   C get   D meet
6 Someone who prefers not to join in with everyone else is a(n) ....
   A deviant   B individual   C loner   D pervert
7 I didn't take up his recommendation, as he sounded so .... about it.
   A half-baked   B half-hearted   C half-timbered   D half-witted
8 .... had the thieves entered the bank than the police arrived.
   A Scarcely   B Hardly   C No sooner   D Rarely
9 To enter a skilled trade a new recruit may have to serve a(n) ....
   A apprenticeship   B education   C initiation   D training
10 He turned to a life of crime .... he had had a normal, happy childhood.
   A as long as   B despite   C even though   D provided that
11 Society .... on laws to regulate the behaviour of its anti-social members.
   A exists   B depends   C trusts   D is organised
12 If you .... a crime being committed, you ought to report it to the police.
   A are seeing   B had seen   C should see   D were to have seen

13 One person .... ten will commit a crime at one time in their lives.
       A from   B in   C of   D over
14 Technically speaking, anyone who .... the law is a criminal.
       A could have broken   B has been breaking   C has broken
       D may have broken
15 Even if you kill someone in self-defence you may be charged with ....
       A bumping him off   B homicide   C lynching   D manslaughter
16 Supposing I .... to tell you how much I admired you, what would you say?
       A am   B could   C were   D would
17 The louts who mugged two old ladies have been convicted of ....
       A arson   B assault   C looting   D vandalism
18 A prisoner serving a life sentence may eventually be released on ....
       A bail   B leave   C parole   D probation
19 The defendant was found guilty by the jury and given a suspended ....
       A conviction   B fine   C sentence   D verdict
20 Some people say that all mentally ill people should be ....
       A locked in   B locked out   C put away   D put up
21 The judge .... the witness for his frivolous attitude.
       A abused   B commended   C prosecuted   D reprimanded
22 Most members of society are perfectly .... citizens like you and me.
       A law-abiding   B legal   C legitimate   D obedient
23 Don't give in to the .... of cheating in an exam – you may get caught!
       A allure   B inducement   C provocation   D temptation
24 In a multiple-choice exercise it's sometimes easier to .... the wrong answers
    before choosing the correct one.
       A dismiss   B eliminate   C obliterate   D omit
25 And it's always better to make an educated .... than to leave a blank.
       A attempt   B endeavour   C chance   D guess

B   Work in groups. Discuss these questions:
   ● What do you each find most difficult about answering multiple-choice questions?
   ● Is there any advice you can offer each other?
   ● What tips from previous units do you try to follow when doing this kind of test?
   ● Do you prefer to read all the questions quickly through first, before going through
     marking your answers on the Answer Sheet?

★★   Each of the multiple-choice questions in Paper 1 Section A is worth one mark,
     making a total of 25, but the fifteen questions in Section B are each worth two marks
     – making a total of 55 for the whole of Paper 1. You should aim to get at least 33
     marks (about 60%).
         Section B is likely to take a few minutes longer than A. Don't spend longer than
     about 25 minutes on either Section, allowing time to come back later to any
     questions you were unsure of.

★★   Practice in doing tests like these from one of the *Cambridge Proficiency Examination
     Practice Books* will help you to develop your speed, and give you practice in making
     educated guesses.

Read each passage and choose the answers that fit best, according to the passage. There are three passages, with 15 questions in all. There are discussion questions on all three passages in D.

A   FIRST PASSAGE

There is nothing that man fears more than the touch of the unknown. He wants to *see* what is reaching towards him, and to be able to recognize or at least classify it. Man always tends to avoid physical contact with anything strange. In the dark, the fear of an unexpected touch can mount to panic. Even clothes give insufficient security: it is easy to tear them and pierce through to the naked, smooth, defenceless flesh of the victim.

All the distances which men create round themselves are dictated by this fear. They shut themselves in houses which no one may enter, and only there feel some measure of security. The fear of burglars is not only the fear of being robbed, but also the fear of a sudden and unexpected clutch out of the darkness.

The repugnance to being touched remains with us when we go about among people; the way we move in a busy street, in restaurants, trains or buses, is governed by it. Even when we are standing next to them and are able to watch and examine them closely, we avoid actual contact if we can. If we do not avoid it, it is because we feel attracted to someone; and then it is we who make the approach.

The promptness with which apology is offered for an unintentional contact, the tension with which it is awaited, our violent and sometimes even physical reaction when it is not forthcoming, the antipathy and hatred we feel for the offender, even when we cannot be certain who it is – the whole knot of shifting and intensely sensitive reactions to an alien touch – proves that we are dealing here with a human propensity as deep-seated as it is alert and insidious; something which never leaves a man when he has once established the boundaries of his personality. Even in sleep, when he is far more unguarded, he can all too easily be disturbed by a touch.

It is only in a crowd that man can become free of this fear of being touched. That is the only situation in which the fear changes into its opposite. The crowd he needs is the dense crowd, in which body is pressed to body; a crowd, too, whose physical constitution is also dense, or compact, so that he no longer notices who it is that presses against him. As soon as a man has surrendered himself to the crowd, he ceases to fear its touch. Ideally, all are equal there; no distinctions count, not even that of sex. The man pressed against him is the same as himself. He feels him as he feels himself. Suddenly it is as though everything were happening in one and the same body. This is perhaps one of the reasons why a crowd seeks to close in on itself: it wants to rid each individual as completely as possible of the fear of being touched. The more fiercely people press together, the more certain they feel that they do not fear each other. This reversal of the fear of being touched belongs to the nature of crowds. The feeling of relief is most striking where the density of the crowd is greatest.

(from *Crowds and Power* by Elias Canetti)

Public Enemy No 1

PICTURE the scene. Dozens of theatregoers leave for their cars after an enjoyable evening watching *Evita*. There's a gentle buzz of conversation as couples praise or criticise the show. A smartly-dressed group heads towards the multi-storey car park where a couple of hours earlier they left their vehicles with a paid-for ticket stuck on the windscreen. And then it grips them – that Clamping Feeling.

For this particular party the experience was too much to bear. They had been clamped for allegedly parking in spaces reserved for others. Finding the clampers still at work, the motorists vented their frustration, reportedly setting about the clamper and his 22-year-old female assistant with a fury that took even the hardened victims by surprise.

What the incident confirmed is that car clampers have taken over the role of Public Enemy No 1 once held by traffic wardens.

While most small businesses talk of recession, there is a boom in the number of clamping firms being hired by owners of private land and car parks.

There are, of course, many respectable firms operating for councils and police forces, de-mobilising cars in city centres and charging a set fee for freedom. And although it can be argued that the very act of immobilisation leads to greater traffic jams and more public annoyance, there is no doubt that clamping has an immediate impact on the car owner which a parking ticket does not. But it is the explosion in private clamping which is causing most friction.

The distress felt by readers of *Auto Express* who had fallen victim to the clampers prompted us to investigate the tactics and legality of the private firms. We found that clamping was generally carried out by small outfits which could obtain a franchise for as little as £115.

The firm involved in the *Evita* incident has a large network of franchise holders. It charges them a joining fee of £46 plus £11.50 for a sign to erect at the site. They must buy six signs when they join up. The company sets its de-clamping fee at £46 and operators must pay back £8 for each "hit". This means they are in profit after 15 clampings – and from then on have the potential to make a small fortune.

We approached the firm for a job managing one of its franchises. Our reporter said he was an out-of-work security guard who had been in prison for three years after being convicted of theft and that he was a big, aggressive, bullying type. It did not put them off.

"We'd only turn you down if you've been inside for rape or murder," was the reply.

The most worrying aspect, as far as the motorist is concerned, is that the growing breed of operators are working in a twilight legal world. Our investigation revealed that there is no law regulating the operators or the often exorbitant fees they charge.

Andrew Bordiss

1 Why were the people who had been to *Evita* clamped?
    A For blocking an entrance or exit.
    B For displaying their tickets in the wrong place.
    C For not paying enough for their car park tickets.
    D For parking in unauthorised spaces.
2 Before clampers, the most disliked people in the country were . . .
    A car park attendants.
    B estate agents.
    C politicians.
    D traffic wardens.
3 If their cars are clamped, motorists have to pay . . .
    A a fixed amount of money.
    B a sum equivalent to the cost of a parking ticket.
    C at least £46.
    D £11.50.
4 Clamping is effective because it . . .
    A causes embarrassment.
    B costs more to have a car freed than a parking ticket.
    C is more inconvenient for motorists than a parking ticket.
    D leads to more annoyance for other drivers.
5 Operating a clamping franchise is a very . . .
    A enjoyable occupation.
    B hazardous occupation.
    C profitable occupation.
    D unpredictable occupation.

D Work in groups and discuss your reactions to the first two passages.
  - Have you ever been robbed or had your pocket picked? How did you feel and what did you do about it?
  - How long does it take you to get from home to the place where you work or study? What are the pros and cons of living in the suburbs and commuting?

E Before discussing the third passage, read the article below and compare your reactions to it.
  - Have you ever been given a parking ticket or had your car clamped?
  - How effective is clamping as a way of controlling unauthorised parking?
  - In what circumstances is it justifiable to take the law into your own hands?

Wheelclamper carried away by vengeful forklift driver

THE motoring public tends to come off worst in encounters with wheel-clampers: yesterday the boot was on the other wheel. A West Country wheelclamper was swept 10 feet into the air, complete with his Fiesta van, on the end of a forklift truck.

At this point Alan Pearman struck lucky. The forklift driver had intended to dump him into Torquay harbour, but the lift jammed.

The trouble began when Mr Pearman spotted a Saab car on the harbourside, belonging to Steve Carter, a crane driver. It had a parking permit, but it also had a tide table on the dashboard, obscuring the expiry date.

Mr Pearman rang his boss at A1 Securities, and followed the advice to go ahead and clamp.

Retribution immedi-ately followed, in the form of Mr Carter's boss, John Thompson, driving a fiery forklift truck.

"He lifted me up twice," Mr Pearman said. "The first time it was about 4½ feet in the air. Then he dropped the van suddenly on to the concrete on the harbourside. Then he went back a couple of feet, rammed me, and lifted me up again, this time a lot higher. I don't mind telling you it was pretty frightening."

The firm said the van was considerably damaged.

Mr Thompson, who insists the Saab was legally parked in a company space, was interviewed by the police, but told he would not be charged.

Maev Kennedy

18.3 Two compositions Paper 2

Write two of the following composition exercises in 2 hours. Allow enough time to make notes before you start writing and to check your work through before you hand it in.

1 Describe the aspects of living in *your* city, suburb, town or village that give you most personal pleasure.   (about 350 words)

2 "The punishment should fit the crime." To what extent do you agree with this well-known saying?   (about 350 words)

3 Write a short story beginning or ending with the words: "Free at last!"   (about 350 words)

4 You have been sent the following cutting from a newspaper in your country. Prepare a suitable document that can be handed to visitors and tourists arriving at airports and frontiers.   (about 300 words)

Reports in the foreign press

THERE have been a growing number of reports in newspapers abroad that there is a "crime wave" in this country. The Minister of Tourism fears that this may cause concern among foreign visitors, who may assume they are likely to be robbed once they set foot in the country.

What is needed is a short, persuasive handout warning tourists of the dangers of pickpockets and thieves but which does not alarm them unduly. It should offer advice on how to minimise the risks by taking the right precautions.

A prize will be given to the originator of the material used.

5 Basing your answer on your reading of the prescribed text you have studied, answer ONE OF THE FOLLOWING.   (about 350 words)

a) Describe and give examples of the way in which the writer builds up a sense of excitement and tension as the plot unfolds.

b) What makes the text stand out as a 'work of literature' above the common run of popular fiction (or drama)?

c) "Any good work of fiction has just the same ingredients as a detective story." To what extent is this view applicable to the text you have read?

★★ **Marking** 40 marks are given for Paper 2 – 20 for each composition. The examiners' first priority is to assess your efforts at communication and give you credit for that, including the clarity and organisation of your composition. Questions 1 to 3 allow for a variety of approaches, including personal reminiscence and anecdote, dialogue and humour. If you fail to answer the question, there are penalties for reproducing 'blatantly irrelevant material learned by heart' and for 'grossly or wantonly misinterpreting the question'.

Length For Questions 1, 2, 3 and 5 this is usually 350 words, but 'exceptional candidates may provide excellent answers using fewer words or they may substantially exceed this number without becoming dull or repetitive'. But you don't get credit for extra length, which anyway will probably increase the total number of inaccuracies in your work.

Question 4 In this directed writing task, structured information is provided and a shorter length is specified – highlight the number of words required, so that you keep it constantly in mind. You have to respond to a clearly-defined task and the appropriateness of your response and style and register are particularly important. If there are two tasks, a single combined mark is given out of 20. If you only do one of the two specified tasks, it is normally marked out of 10.

Question 5 In Question 5 you have to show that you have read and enjoyed a set text and can demonstrate this in an appropriately illustrated description and discussion. Credit is given for breadth, development and relevance of argument, and for the abundance and appropriateness of illustration and quotation.

18.4 Use of English

1 Cloze test

Fill each gap with one word only.

There are few .... (1) which can guarantee a conversation in a bar or railway carriage, but sex, the weather, beer and the dreadful .... (2) of the city's traffic are among them. City traffic has .... (3) a standing joke (or a running sore) in most cities, as roads .... (4) for past eras try to cope with today's cars, bicycles, taxis, buses and lorries. Traffic is a most difficult .... (5).

Traffic jams are .... (6). Being passed by old ladies pushing squeaky prams is an indignity .... (7) drivers welcome. Traffic jams are a waste of everyone's time. Yet every morning M4 commuters into London know that just past London Airport, and all the .... (8) into town, will be an .... (9) jam. The remedies are not .... (10); indeed they may be counterproductive. Building new roads generates more traffic; one-way .... (11) try to squeeze a quart into a pint pot; providing off-street parking .... (12) even more traffic; disincentives (narrowing roads, clamps) do not deter, they .... (13) infuriate, and pedestrian .... (14) damage trade.

Florence has just .... (15) the car from its centre because of the pollution. Whether it works or not will be .... (16) watched, but to

.... (17) no one has died from withdrawal symptoms. But in cities like London or New York this would not .... (18), because the traffic jams in the periphery and the .... (19) are as bad as they are in the centre.

Tinkering will not .... (20). Florence's solution will work for smaller cities, but ideas for larger ones are needed..

2 Transformations

Rewrite each sentence so that its meaning remains unchanged.

1 We'll always remember these days together at our meetings in the future.
Whenever ....

2 I admire her achievements a great deal but as a person I loathe her.
Much ....

3 It's because he was reprimanded that he is feeling so upset.
If ....

4 You should admit that you're to blame, not try to conceal it.
I'd rather ....

5 The realisation that I had been swindled came later.
Only ....

6 The police are advising vigilance as there have been more robberies lately.
Due to ....

7 It is fairly unlikely that he will be convicted of the offence.
There ....

8 I'm sorry that my story sounded so unconvincing.
I wish ....

3 Fill the gaps

Fill each gap with a suitable phrase or word.

1 Difficult .... I was able to answer most of the questions.

2 'She said she'd kill me!' 'My word, she .... awfully upset then.'

3 We look forward to receiving your donation, ... it may be.

4 Never in my life .... such a monstrous crime!

5 The robbers were locked up in a top security prison. .... they succeeded .... from it.

6 'So you both found it hard to get used .... in a foreign country?'
'No, not at all. I didn't find it at all difficult and .... my friend.'

4 Use the word given

Write a new sentence as similar as possible in meaning to the original sentence, using the word given. This word must not be altered in any way.

1 Without the cooperation of the public, the work of the police would be impossible.
depends ....

2 She was afraid to scream because she didn't want to wake up the neighbours.
fear ....

3 No one is to blame for the accident.
fault ....

4 Their flat has been broken into twice this year.
had ....

5 She has a one-hour journey to work every day.
takes ....

6 They may not arrive on time because of the heavy traffic.
   doubtful ....

7 He may not be as dependable as you think.
   rely ....

8 I hate the stresses and pressures of modern life.
   what ....

★★ Do the easier questions first. Double-check each answer for grammatical accuracy
and spelling. Make sure you haven't unwittingly changed the meaning. Return to any
difficult ones later (mark them in pencil so that you don't overlook them) – you may
have got inspiration by then!

---

5 Questions and summary

Read the following passage, then answer the questions that follow it.

A first in Cambridge

THE university city of Cambridge could be the first in Britain to introduce road pricing. A meeting of the county council on November 20th is expected to give the go-ahead in principle to "congestion-metering". The idea is to charge all motorists who enter the city for the congestion their cars cause. The money raised would help pay for a super-tram line from the north to the south of the city.

Cambridge should be a good test-bed for road pricing. It is a compact place, with little urban sprawl – so the boundaries of the city centre are easily defined – and many people commute by car. The city's traffic has become as congested as London's, after rising by 47% in the past decade. It is expected to go up by another 40% in the 1990s, partly because the city hopes for another 25,000 jobs during them. The council fears that, unless it reduces congestion, the traffic bottleneck could strangle the commercial expansion which is supposed to bring those jobs. But any new roads would risk ruining the city's character and undermining its booming tourist business.

The road-pricing scheme is the brainchild of the county surveyor, Mr Brian Oldridge, who has been working with technical help from Newcastle University. The organisers would provide a meter, free of charge, to all vehicles in the area. The meters would be switched on automatically by a set of beacons around the perimeter of Cambridge as a vehicle entered the city. The driver would then be charged in direct proportion to the congestion he encountered. (The meter would identify congestion by the stop-start-stop pattern of driving.)

This sounds unfair. Why should a driver be penalised for encountering a jam? The theory is that jams are caused by all the vehicles in them, so their drivers should all pay. The system would thus provide an incentive for drivers to avoid jams, for example by travelling in off-peak periods.

Drivers would pay by a "smart card", which would carry a fixed number of pre-paid units like a phonecard. One feature may not appeal to Cambridge folk. Once the card's units have been used up, the

65 meter would cut off the petrol supply on the next occasion when the engine was switched off; so it would be impossible to restart a car until a new card had been inserted. 70 That could mean lots of pay-as-you-jam motorists fuming behind the stalled cars of the forgetful.

If the council agrees, further research will be carried out; then there would be a pilot scheme; then 75 Parliament would have to approve a private bill, and the system could be in operation by 1995. Enthusiasts think it could be a model for the rest of Britain's cities. 80

(from *The Economist*)

1 What is meant by 'give the go-ahead in principle' in line 5?
2 Why is Cambridge considered such a 'good test-bed for road pricing'?
3 Why is such a scheme needed so urgently in Cambridge?
4 Why can't new roads be built in the city?
5 What is meant by 'brainchild' in line 35?
6 What is the justification for making motorists suffer for getting in a jam ?
7 How much will local motorists pay to have their cars fitted with meters?
8 What, according to the article, is the most inconvenient aspect of the scheme?
9 What steps would be necessary before the scheme could be fully operational?
10 How will motorists from out of town be made to pay?
11 In 80 to 100 words, explain how the Cambridge scheme would work.

★★ This Questions and summary exercise is shorter than the one you will encounter in the exam. You should do further practice using tests from one of the *Cambridge Proficiency Examination Practice Books*. Do these against the clock, spending no more than 50 minutes on the section.
Look again at the exam tips on page 232.

"The jury finds the defendant guilty – and advises him to get a better lawyer next time."

283

Your teacher will play each part twice, allowing you time to read the questions through before each playing.
(There are discussion questions on all three passages in D opposite.)

A RULES AND VALUES

Listen to the interview with a sociologist and answer the questions.

1 'Rules' are different from 'laws' in that . . .
   A there is no threat of punishment involved.
   B rules are more powerful.
   C rules are not understood by people.
   D rules are not recorded.

2 Society has rules in order to . . .
   A control how people spend their time.
   B regulate people's behaviour.
   C give guidance on how to behave.
   D maintain political stability.

3 A parent or teacher is in a similar position to that of a . . .
   A chess player.
   B criminal.
   C judge.
   D policeman.

4 Most of us would never break the law because we . . .
   A want to be the same as everyone else.
   B are afraid of being caught.
   C are afraid of being punished.
   D would feel embarrassed.

5 If the members of a society did not share the same set of rules . . .
   A a new set of rules would soon evolve.
   B there would be no more crime.
   C there would be social harmony.
   D no one would know how to behave.

6 Our circle of friends consists of people who . . .
   A like what we like.
   B obey the same rules.
   C share the same values.
   D think the same way as we do.

7 In the United States many people drop out of society because they . . .
   A are black or Hispanic.
   B cannot achieve success.
   C don't share the same values as anyone else.
   D take drugs.

8 When a society's values are challenged 'positively' by rebels . . .
   A society's rules and values may change.
   B a social revolution may follow.
   C criminal values may be substituted.
   D the rebels are persecuted.

B A NEW YORK COP

Listen to the interview and fill each gap with the **exact word** the speaker used.
Write your answers in the boxes on the right.

1 Many of the people a cop deals with are mentally ....
2 People don't call a cop unless there's a ....
3 A cop sees the .... side of society.
4 On the whole, a cop's job is very stressful, but some
   of the situations you are in, as a cop, are very ....
5 He remembers the two occasions when he .... a baby,
   which was an experience that .... him.
6 He has never had to .... a life.
7 Cops represent .... – without law
   you would have ....
8 In law everything is black and white, but when dealing
   with people there are .... areas.

C A BRITISH POLICE OFFICER

You will hear an interview with a senior police officer. For each question, tick one
box to show whether the statement is true or false.

	TRUE	FALSE
1 Britain has a single country-wide police force, divided into six regions.	☐	☐
2 Police work in a rural area is entirely different from that in an urban area.	☐	☐
3 Women who join the police now start in the policewomen's department.	☐	☐
4 Kate joined the police because there was no work for a customs officer in the area.	☐	☐
5 Most of a police officer's time is spent dealing with people and their problems.	☐	☐
6 A good police officer should try not to be sympathetic or compassionate.	☐	☐
7 A police officer is expected to deal with distressing events without feeling upset.	☐	☐
8 Police officers do have bad dreams about very unpleasant experiences.	☐	☐
9 Some police officers don't want to talk to their family about a horrific experience.	☐	☐
10 In general, members of the public are mistrustful of the police.	☐	☐
11 Most people feel uneasy if a police officer comes to their door.	☐	☐
12 Members of the police force have a strong feeling of fellowship.	☐	☐

D Work in groups and discuss your reactions to the interviews.

• Why do people commit crimes, in your opinion? How can they be deterred from this?
  How should they be punished, or what treatment should they be given?
• What is the attitude of the general public in your country to the police?
• Do you like to watch or read crime stories? Give your reasons.

★★ The complete listening comprehension test in the exam lasts about 30 minutes –
make sure you remain alert during the second listening, even if the recordings are
not particularly interesting to listen to.
    Practise doing exam-style tests by using the cassettes that accompany one of the
Cambridge Proficiency Examination Practice Books.

For each part of this section, work in pairs, taking turns to play the roles of 'examiner' and 'candidate'.

A   Introductory phase

EXAMINER: Welcome the candidate, and ask a few general questions:

- Where are you from?
- How long have you been studying English?
- What do you do?
- Tell me something about yourself.

B   Photograph

EXAMINER: The candidate should be invited to discuss these questions:

- How would you describe the people, the setting and what is going on?
- What has happened and why?
- How would you feel in this situation?
- What are your views on traffic in cities?
- How is illegal parking dealt with in your country?
- What is the role of the police in modern society?

C Passages

EXAMINER: The candidate should be invited to:

- comment on the source of one of the texts
- comment on its register (style)
- comment on the content and discuss any issues arising from it

1

! WARNING !
PRIVATE   PROPERTY

VEHICLES PARKED WITHOUT AUTHORITY
WILL BE WHEEL CLAMPED.
RELEASE FEE £45 INC. V.A.T.
FAILURE TO COMPLY WILL RENDER YOU LIABLE TO PROSECUTION,
HAVE YOUR VEHICLE TOWED AWAY & IMPOUNDED, RELEASE FEE £90
CLAMPDOWN SECURITY BOURNEMOUTH   +£2.50 Per Day
HEAD OFFICE (0202) 429162

2 Private clampers have no special permission or licence to ply their trade. Instead they work under obscure laws designed to stop sheep straying, which date back to the Middle Ages.

On public highways the position is clear cut. Police are authorised to clamp vehicles and local authorities can pass bye-laws enabling them to do so or private contractors to do so on their behalf.

3 I was absolutely furious. This was the first time it had happened to me. I'd only left it for ten minutes and when I got back ... well, you can imagine how I felt. Anyway, I phoned the number on the sticker and about an hour later along came this white van, driven by a very tough-looking man in some sort of uniform. £35 plus VAT — and, yes, they do take plastic, believe it or not.

★★   In the examination the examiner will be awarding you marks for:

FLUENCY   GRAMMATICAL ACCURACY
PRONUNCIATION OF PROSODIC FEATURES (stress, rhythm and intonation)
PRONUNCIATION OF INDIVIDUAL SOUNDS
INTERACTIVE COMMUNICATION   VOCABULARY RESOURCE

Try to give a good impression of your spoken English. Don't just wait to be asked questions – behave and speak as you would in a real conversation. Each part of the interview is based on the same general topic, but you won't lose marks if you go off at a tangent.

⟫➔

D   Communication activity

1   EXAMINER: Ask the candidate to discuss which of the measures listed below are DOs and which are DON'Ts for rich people who want to stay safe.
Which of the DOs are most important and which DON'Ts are the most risky? Give your reasons.

> One of the problems about being successful is that you may become rich and famous and thus become a target for kidnappers, who may take you hostage and demand an enormous ransom for your release...
>
> ### HOW NOT TO BE KIDNAPPED
> Travel in isolated areas
> Keep to a set routine at work or on holiday
> Keep a low profile
> Make reservations in your own name
> Carry identification documents and medical details
> Park in protected areas
> Carry luggage with your name and address on it
> Stop at the same bar/restaurant/park on your way home
> Tell family and friends where you are going
> Vary your route to and from the office
> Arrive early for appointments
> Arrive exactly on time at airports and stations
> Arrange covert signals to use with family on phone
> Be suspicious of everybody you don't know
> Think it could never happen to you
> Find out about the politics of any country you visit
> Ignore the possibility of danger to your family

2   EXAMINER: Ask the candidate to discuss these questions:

- Just supposing you or a member of your family were kidnapped and the criminals/bandits/terrorists demanded far more money than you could possibly pay, what would you do?
- What punishment would you recommend for a convicted kidnapper?
- How can would-be kidnappers be deterred from perpetrating such a crime?

One last word:
I do hope you've enjoyed using Progress to Proficiency and I'd like to wish you the best of luck in your examination.

Best Wishes,

Leo Jones

Communication Activities

1   This is the first part of the article:

At first light my tent collapsed around me; blown out of the ground by a Force 9 gale. I crawled out to find summer had disappeared for good, kicked in the teeth with a boot that had flattened everything from insects to trees. In minutes I was drenched and there was nothing I could do but start walking.

I kept going all day; so did the storm. That afternoon totally despondent, I trudged into Newport and took shelter in a launderette. I sat there in socks and shorts and tried to re-examine my motives.

Before I'd set out, I'd accepted that walking a long distance footpath wouldn't be a normal holiday. I mean, I wasn't doing it for the girls, the glamour and the night life. In fact I'd convinced myself a journey like this would awaken senses in me that years of travelling by motor car had blunted. I had a lightweight tent and sleeping bag, a little stove and some waterproofs, and I was set for a week or two of getting back to basics.

It was only after I'd completed the path ten days later that I came to realise how, on a walk of any distance, the bad times are as frequent as the good, and the sense of achievement at the journey's end is, more often than not, the result of some hard work. Certainly, the postcards I sent from that North Coast all read like suicide notes – "I can't take it any more, I've had enough . . . etc." – and all I gained from those first few days was a strange discoloration of the toes, which I could only diagnose as trenchfoot and the knowledge that there's no truth in the term "waterproof".

2

Using body language

If you want to seem friendly and cooperative, look at the other person's face, smile and nod when they are talking, have open hands and uncrossed arms and legs, lean forward slightly or move closer to them. If you want to appear confident, look into their eyes, don't blink, keep your hands away from your face, stay still and don't make sudden movements. If you want to appear thoughtful, tilt your head to one side, stroke your chin or pinch the bridge of your nose, lean forward to speak and back to listen and keep your legs still.

(from *So you think you can cope with customers?* – A Video Arts Guide)

3

Find out about your partner's photo by asking questions:

- What's going on in your photo?
- What's going to happen next?
- How would you like to be doing the same thing?

➡ Before you begin your conversation, note down THREE MORE questions to ask.

4   This is the next paragraph of the story in 6.2:

> The hotel people began to be more pleased with me too, so I thought Mr Yorum must be quite an important man. Several more times on other days I told them I didn't understand Turkish, and each time they rang Mr Yorum and he came, and sometimes I paid for the drinks and sometimes he did. He and the hotel staff must have thought I had taken a great fancy to him or else that I was working up to some deal I wanted to do with him. The fourth time he came I had a bright idea that I would give him one of the missionary manuals that aunt Dot had left behind in her rucksack, because I thought each manual which I got rid of would lighten the rucksack.

5

How red wine is made

Ingredients: grape juice, grape skins and stems

1 After the grapes have been picked they are taken to the winery where they are put into a machine which crushes them and removes the stems, but not the skins and pips*. This end product is called *must*. It takes 3kg of grapes to make one bottle of wine.

2 The must is emptied into tanks or vats. The grape skins have their own natural yeasts which ferment with the sugar in the grape juice to produce alcohol and carbon dioxide. During fermentation, the skins and pips form a thick layer on the surface.

3 Fermentation stops after a week or so. The new wine is drained off and the residue of skins and pips is pressed to extract another 20%.

4 Wine for everyday drinking is stored in glass-lined cement or stainless steel tanks: the secondary fermentation takes place, making the wine softer and rounder before it is ready to be bottled. Quality wine is often aged in oak casks, which imparts a special flavour to the wine.

5 During ageing the wine is *racked* – treated with egg white or another substance to carry the sediment to the bottom of the cask.

6 The wine is bottled, capped and labelled by machine. Quality wines can be further aged in their bottles, but everyday wine is ready for drinking right away.

* To make white wine, the juice is immediately separated from the skins and pips. It is separated after a day or less to make rosé wine.

6

Model summary for 8.6 B:

```
Although he claims to have 'the world's most wonderful
job', Michael Buerk seems to have had some awful
experiences. In El Salvador, for example, he was caught
in the middle of a gun battle and had to crouch in terror
in a ditch - compared to this a night in a Turkish jail
and being seasick in a lobster boat seem almost
luxurious! He says that his worst experience was a
sleepless night in northern Ethiopia searching
unsuccessfully for a scorpion in his room. In Ethiopia,
again, he witnessed terrible human suffering - an
experience which changed his way of looking at the world.
```

7 Describe the scheme advertised here to your partner. You should do this in your own words, but feel free to quote the odd line if you wish.

"I CAN MAKE YOU A MILLIONAIRE IN JUST 21 DAYS or your money back"

When I was 20 years old I asked my dad to loan me £10. **He turned me down.** Now 10 years later I'm incredibly rich and famous and I deny all knowledge of ever having a father.

Not that it's taken me 10 years to become a *millionaire. No!*

I MADE MY FIRST MILLION IN JUST 3 WEEKS.

Yes! 3 weeks. *Impossible, I hear you say,* but it's as true as I'm sitting here writing this.

Thanks to advice given to me by an ageing uncle I now have:
★ A thriving pan global business empire.
★ A bank balance bigger than the bill for national power.
★ 17 different houses all over the world and a cottage in Bigbury on Sea.

Sadly Uncle George is no longer with us but I have never forgotten those few words that changed the course of my life.

Now, I feel the time has come for me to share the secret of my good fortune with other men and women of business. *I seek no personal profit.*

I have more money than I could ever win at the 'Big Time Tombola'. Which is why I only ask £5.99. Just *£5.99* to become a millionaire in only 21 days. *GUARANTEED.*

I will hold your cheque for 21 days. *I promise,* and if you're not drinking champagne by the bucketful by then I'll refund your money. IN FULL.

Now that can't be bad can it?

ONLY £5.99

★ Please rush me my secret of earning lots of money in just 3 weeks as soon as possible please.
★ NAME ....
★ ADDRESS ....

8

Your behaviour creates an impression

People gain a general impression of you from a combination of your facial expression and head movements, your gestures with your hands and arms, and the rest of your body including your legs. They will tend to see you as defensive if you avoid looking at them, clench your hands or cross your arms, keep rubbing an eye, ear or your nose, lean away from them, cross your legs or swivel your feet towards the door. They will tend to see you as anxious if you blink frequently, lick your lips, keep clearing your throat, put your hand over your mouth while you are speaking, tug at your ear, fidget in your chair or move your feet up and down.

(from *So you think you can cope with customers?* – A Video Arts Guide)

9 Study these diagrams, then explain the process to your partner.

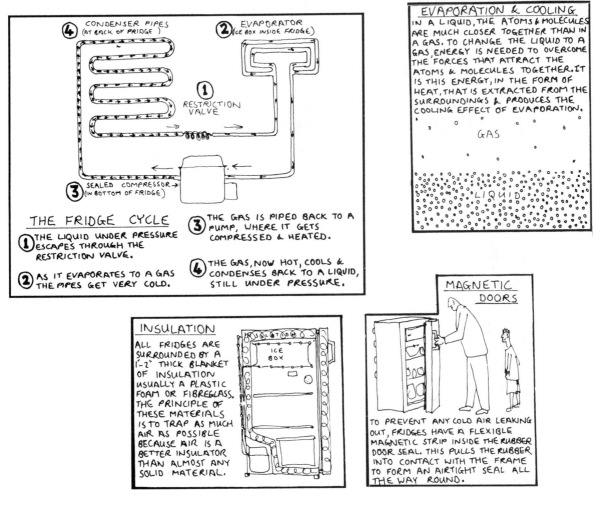

★ THE REFRIGERATOR ★

④ CONDENSER PIPES (AT BACK OF FRIDGE)

② EVAPORATOR (ICE BOX INSIDE FRIDGE)

① RESTRICTION VALVE

③ SEALED COMPRESSOR → (IN BOTTOM OF FRIDGE)

THE FRIDGE CYCLE

① THE LIQUID UNDER PRESSURE ESCAPES THROUGH THE RESTRICTION VALVE.

② AS IT EVAPORATES TO A GAS THE PIPES GET VERY COLD.

③ THE GAS IS PIPED BACK TO A PUMP, WHERE IT GETS COMPRESSED & HEATED.

④ THE GAS, NOW HOT, COOLS & CONDENSES BACK TO A LIQUID, STILL UNDER PRESSURE.

EVAPORATION & COOLING

IN A LIQUID, THE ATOMS & MOLECULES ARE MUCH CLOSER TOGETHER THAN IN A GAS. TO CHANGE THE LIQUID TO A GAS, ENERGY IS NEEDED TO OVERCOME THE FORCES THAT ATTRACT THE ATOMS & MOLECULES TOGETHER. IT IS THIS ENERGY, IN THE FORM OF HEAT, THAT IS EXTRACTED FROM THE SURROUNDINGS & PRODUCES THE COOLING EFFECT OF EVAPORATION.

GAS

LIQUID

INSULATION

ALL FRIDGES ARE SURROUNDED BY A 1-2" THICK BLANKET OF INSULATION USUALLY A PLASTIC FOAM OR FIBREGLASS. THE PRINCIPLE OF THESE MATERIALS IS TO TRAP AS MUCH AIR AS POSSIBLE BECAUSE AIR IS A BETTER INSULATOR THAN ALMOST ANY SOLID MATERIAL.

ICE BOX

MAGNETIC DOORS

TO PREVENT ANY COLD AIR LEAKING OUT, FRIDGES HAVE A FLEXIBLE MAGNETIC STRIP INSIDE THE RUBBER DOOR SEAL. THIS PULLS THE RUBBER INTO CONTACT WITH THE FRAME TO FORM AN AIRTIGHT SEAL ALL THE WAY ROUND.

10 Rupert Brooke (1887–1915) became an officer at the outbreak of the First World War in 1914. He died of blood poisoning from a mosquito bite on his way to the Turkish front by ship, and never saw active service. He was buried on the Greek island of Skyros. His best-known poems are patriotic and romantic, contrasting with the bitterness of Owen and Sassoon.

Rupert Brooke

11 Study these ideas and then ask your partners the questions:

Taps and showers

Think of the hot and cold water taps you have used:

- How do you know which is which? Which side is hot? Is it always that side?

Think of the showers you have used:

- How do you know how to turn it on? How do you know how to make it hotter? How do you know how to increase the flow?
- Do they all follow these conventions?
    increase/more ↑ ⌢ reduce/less ↓ ⌣
- Have you ever been scalded in a shower? Was it your fault or the designer's?

Sounds   Sounds can provide feedback.

- What noise does a zip make? If a zip was silent, what difference would it make?
- How can you tell if a car door isn't closed properly – does the driver have to look or can you hear the rattle?
- What other sounds can you think of that provide feedback when you're using a piece of equipment?

---

12 Describe this picture to your partner.

Find out about your partner's picture by asking the same questions as you discussed in 13.8 A.

Edward Hopper: 'Sunlight in a Cafeteria', 1958

13

Ask your partner these questions about his or her passage:

- Where do you think the passage comes from? Who was it written for?
- What is it about?
- What is your reaction to it?

➡ Then answer your partner's questions about this passage:

> IF YOU are comfortably settled in your beach-chairs, give a sigh of gratitude, and a guilty start, that you were born when you were. Seventy-five years ago this August summer's day your grandfathers were marching off to what they did not know would be the Great War, the smashing of the world the nineteenth century had created. Fifty years ago your fathers were pulling on their ammunition boots in preparation for an even greater war, because of the demons unleashed by the first one. On this double anniversary – of 1914 and 1939, look around your holiday beach for the ghosts of the myriad unborn, whose would-be fathers and grandfathers never had the chance to give them life.

14

Ask your partner to tell you about the two passages he or she has:
Which seems the better film and why?
What kind of publication does your partner think the passages came from?

➡ Then answer your partner's questions about these passages:

MIDNIGHT RUN
French/Portuguese
Starring Robert De Niro, Charles Grodin

Jack Walsh (De Niro), a private detective, is offered 100,000 dollars to find and return "Duke" Mardukas (Grodin), accountant to the mob, who has jumped bail in Los Angeles and fled to New York.

Catching the Duke seems simple until Walsh realises the accountant has a phobia of flying and must be transported back overland. What's more, there is a string of FBI agents and gangsters who want the Duke as desperately as he does, and will stop at nothing to get him.

De Niro displays a new comic side to his acting which is a perfect match to Grodin who gives the best performance of his career in this comedy adventure.

WORKING GIRL
110 mins
Starring Melanie Griffith, Harrison Ford, Sigourney Weaver

Tess McGill (Griffith) is a street smart working girl who's demonstrated the use of her brains and talent to pull herself out of the secretarial pool and into the upper echelons of New York brokerage industry.

When her high powered boss, Katherine Parker (Weaver), is hospitalised, Tess has the perfect opportunity to step up the corporate ladder and even finds herself dating her boss's ex-fiance – Jack Trainer (Ford). But Parker is never far away and proves to be a vicious enemy when she realises what is going on!

15   Find out about your partner's tastes in music, entertainment and the arts by asking these questions:

- Who are your favourite painters?
  Why do you enjoy / not enjoy looking at paintings?
- What are your favourite operas?
  Why do you enjoy / not enjoy opera?
- What are your favourite pieces of classical music?
  Why do you enjoy / not enjoy listening to classical music?
- Who are your favourite popular singers or groups?
  Why do you enjoy / not enjoy pop or rock music?
- Who are your favourite film stars?
  Why do you enjoy / not enjoy the cinema?
- What are your favourite TV programmes?
  Why do you enjoy / not enjoy watching television?

➡ Then answer your partner's questions about your own tastes.

---

16   Study this still in silence for a few moments, so that you can describe it in detail to your partner. What appears to be happening? What might have happened earlier and what might happen later? What kind of film is it from?

➡ First of all, ask your partner the same questions about his or her picture.

33 Study this still in silence for a few moments, so that you can describe it in detail to your partner.
What appears to be happening? What might have happened earlier and what might happen later? What kind of film is it from?

➡ Ask your partner the same questions about his or her picture.

34 This is the last part of the article:

For three days the walking was a joy, as I strode around St Brides Bay and the Dale Peninsula. The nights, too, were peaceful and I found some really wild places to camp. Then early one morning I rounded St Ann's Head and came into Milford Haven; as I did so the sun went in.

Nelson once called this harbour the finest he'd ever seen. Twenty-five years ago, the major oil companies came to the same conclusion and built the second largest oil refinery in Europe on its shores. Jetties and pipelines snake far out into the deep-water channel, collections of oil tanks sit on the hillsides like caravan sites, and the horizon is broken with the dark silhouettes of refineries and power stations. It's a sort of industrial Disneyland, and I walked through it for a while, awestruck. But after a mile or two it seemed a bit daft, and in the end I caught a bus.

Not until the path turned South again, past West Angle Bay did it recapture its craggy beauty, but soon after that the restricted military area around Castlemartin caused a lengthy diversion inland and it was St Govan's Head before I was able to rejoin the coast.

By then the rain had returned and I saw little of the last stretch as I walked head down, until I bumped into Tenby. There, children in school uniform queued at bus stops with holidaymakers – the surest sign that summer is over. I had a cup of tea in a beach café and pressed on to the walk's end at Amroth.

It had taken me 11 days to travel 300 kilometres; five hours later I was back in London.

35 Look at this reproduction of a Victorian 'narrative painting'. Tell your partners what you think is the story behind this picture. Their paintings show different parts of the same story. Then work out how the three scenes fit together and what events must have happened in between each scene. Decide on a suitable title for each of the paintings, and for the complete story.

36 Retell this news story in your own words, beginning: *There was . . .*

Rat runs amok on jumbo

A PET white rat running loose aboard a Boeing 747 en route from New York to Athens caused confusion and alarm among 400 passengers yesterday.

The rat, named Spiro, was asleep in its owner's travel bag for most of the flight but awoke while breakfast was being served and made its escape down the aisle.

Spiro's owner eventually managed to catch the rat, but sadly, on the orders of the captain, Spiro was confiscated for the rest of the flight and later destroyed. Conveying live animals on flights contravenes international regulations.

37 Wilfred Owen (1893–1918) served for three years in Flanders as an officer. He was killed by machine-gun fire on November 8th 1918, just a few days before the Armistice. Owen's poems on the futility and horror of modern warfare were not published until after the war.

Wilfred Owen

38 Retell this news story in your own words, beginning: *There was . . .*

Bird brained

A YEAR-long search by a British naturalist, Dick Watling, in Fiji for a bird thought to be extinct, ended when it crashed on his head. The bird, known as MacGillivray's petrel, was recorded for the first and last time 129 years ago. Mr Watling lured one in at night from the sea using flashlights and recordings. It crashed on his head and after examining the bird he let it go.

39

cliché /klɪːʃeɪ/, **clichés**; also spelled **cliche**. A cliché is an idea, expression, or way of behaving which has been used so much that it is no longer original or effective; used showing disapproval. EG *...sentimental clichés about 'peace' and 'the open air'... How true is the old cliché that trouble shows us who our friends really are?... I wanted to get right away from the usual clichés of historical films.*
N COUNT ⇑ platitude

collocation /kɒləˈkeɪʃəᵊn/ is the way that some words occur regularly whenever another word is used; a technical word in linguistics.
N UNCOUNT ⇑ occurrence

jargon /dʒɑːɡəᵊn/ is language containing words that are used in special or technical ways. Jargon is used to talk about particular subjects or by particular groups of people. EG *She could explain it without recourse to the jargon of psychoanalysis... I have endeavoured to avoid boring legal jargon in this book.*
N UNCOUNT : USU +SUPP ⇑ words = language, parlance

platitude /plætɪtjuːd/, **platitudes**. A platitude is a statement which is considered boring and unsatisfactory because it has been made many times before in similar situations; a rather formal word. EG *Given his liking for platitudes, he might well have added that, if a job was worth doing, it was worth doing well... ...empty platitudes about democracy.*
N COUNT = cliché, banality

sarcastic /sɑːˈkæstɪk/. Someone who is sarcastic uses words to mean the opposite of what they seem to say in order to mock or insult someone. EG *Although she had been crying earlier, she seemed her usual sarcastic self at dinner.* ▸ used of a person's speech or actions. EG *Her remarks can at times be bitterly sarcastic... He turned to me with a superior and sarcastic smile.* ◊ **sarcastically**. EG *'Do you mind if I take notes?' said Stuart sarcastically.*
ADJ QUALIT ⇑ ironic
◊ ADV : USU WITH VB

slogan /sləʊɡəᵊn/, **slogans**. A slogan is a short, easily-remembered phrase which is used in advertising and by political parties and other groups who want people to remember what they are saying or selling. EG *I read with horror the racist slogans scratched on walls throughout the city... E F Schumacher coined the slogan 'small is beautiful'.*
N COUNT

(from *Collins* COBUILD *English Language Dictionary*)

40 Study these ideas and then ask your partners the questions:

Switches and knobs:

Think of the electrical equipment you use:

- How easy was it for you (and the other members of your family) to learn to use each piece of equipment?
- Can you still make them do everything they're supposed to do? Or do you have to consult the instruction booklet?
- Do you have to look at the labels, or can you intuitively see which switch does what? Do they all follow these conventions:
  increase/more ↑ ⤻ reduce/less ↓ ⤴
- And what about the ON switch? Which way does it go: ↓ or ⤴ or ↑ or ⤵ or → or ← ? Does it make a helpful click or not?
- Have you ever used the wrong switch? Was it your fault or the designer's?

Numbers

Make a list of all the numbers you have to remember, or need to look up quite often, e.g. post codes, other people's birthdays, passport number, etc.

- How many are there? How many can you remember without looking them up?
- Have you ever got any of these numbers wrong? Was it your fault or was it a completely unmemorable number?
- Do you have a special technique for remembering numbers?

---

41 These are model answers to the questions in 3.4.

```
Before 1803 it was not against the law for a woman to
   have an abortion.
Before 1832 some women were allowed to vote, but then a
   law was passed disenfranchising all women.
Before the 1831—72 Factory Acts there was no control over
   the hours that women worked in factories or over the
   conditions they had to work under. Moreover, there were
   no limits on night working.
Before 1882, if a woman was married, she didn't have the
   right to own property.
Before 1918 women couldn't vote in elections.

During the wars, women were needed in the factories, and
they took over men's jobs and were given more
responsibility. Nurseries were provided so that mothers
could enter the workforce.  After the wars, when the men
returned from fighting, women had to return to low-status
jobs or to the home as the men reclaimed their old jobs.
The nurseries were closed down and women were now asked
to believe that their children would suffer if they went
out to work.
```

42 Look at this reproduction of a Victorian 'narrative painting'. Tell your partners what you think is the story behind this picture. Their paintings show different parts of the same story. Then work out how the three scenes fit together and what events must have happened in between each scene. Decide on a suitable title for each of the paintings, and for the complete story.

43 Siegfried Sassoon (1886–1967) served as an officer on the Western front in Flanders throughout the war. He survived the war and his collected poems include many written during the Second World War too. He collected and published his friend Wilfred Owen's poems in 1920.

Siegfried Sassoon

309

44   This is the passage on which the notes in 7.8 A are based.

THE GREEN CONSUMER

As we rush towards the end of the century, we are all more concerned about how we live, what we eat, what we consume in all senses of the word. We are concerned about the effects our consumer lifestyle is having on our own health, of course. But we are also concerned about the knock-on effects of what we are doing on the local environment, on people in the Third World and on the planet itself.

One of the liabilities of living in a free society, where almost anything can be advertised and sold, is that false, 'plastic' needs very often force out real needs. But many consumers are no longer prepared to accept this situation: they want to buy responsible products and they want to buy them from responsible companies.

The new breed of Green Consumer is leading this groundswell. They are demanding more information about the environmental performance of products, about the use of animal testing and about the implications for the Third World. They want to know the story behind what they buy. They want to know how things are made, where and by whom. And more and more people are joining their ranks.

We have already seen the effect of concerned consumers on the food industry. People today want to know what is in what they eat and drink.

Now the time has come to mobilise consumer power to tackle an even more important set of problems. This time it is not simply a question of our own personal health, but of the health of the planet itself.

(from the Foreword by Anita Roddick to *The Green Consumer Guide* by John Elkington & Julia Hailes)

45

Don't use aggressive behaviour

People will tend to see you as aggressive and overbearing if you stare at them, raise your eyebrows in disbelief, look at them over the top of your spectacles, or smile in a 'heard it all before' way; or if you point at them, thump your fist on the table, stride around or stand while they are seated; or, if you are seated, lean right back in your chair with your hands behind your head and your legs splayed.

(from *So you think you can cope with customers?* – A Video Arts Guide)

46 Describe the scheme advertised here to your partner. You should do this in your own words, but feel free to quote the odd line if you wish.

Turn your IDEAS into - £££££'s!

Hi! my name's BOB ORTOO and I'm an inventor and a very, very, very rich man.

Want to know how I did it, Eh?

Well, it all happened one day as I was sitting reading a book in my lounge at home in Dollis Hill, London.

I was happily engrossed in Chapter 3 when suddenly the phone rang.

WHAT A NUISANCE!

I had to put down the book, rise from my chair and hurry to the phone in order to answer it.

It was a wrong number, but it set me thinking.

If only I'd had some warning that the phone was about to ring, I could have finished the sentence I was on before going to the phone.

So that's when I invented my 'RING WARNING' device.

A compact box with a buzzer and flashing light that lets you know up to THREE seconds before the phone actually rings. The rest is history, it sold like hot cakes, everyone wanted one and now I'm a MULTI-MILLIONAIRE.

just FROM ONE SIMPLE IDEA

And that's all it takes, just one, simple, easy to make product.

You probably have ideas like that too!

If you have, my book will tell you.

★ HOW TO GET BACKERS.

★ HOW TO MAKE IT CHEAP.

★ HOW TO ADVERTISE IT ON NATIONAL TV FOR ONLY £5 A WEEK.

Never has one book given so much away about the art of successful selling of strange products, and it can be yours tomorrow for just £10.

MAIL COUPON TODAY!

I, I, wow, I just can't believe it.

Send me a copy immediately.

NAME . . . .

ADDRESS . . . .

. . . .

. . . .

PROSPER in BUSINESS

£10

Acknowledgements

The author and publishers are grateful to the authors, publishers and others who have given permission for the use of copyright material identified in the text. It has not been possible to identify the sources of all the material used and in such cases the publishers would welcome information from copyright owners.

The Guardian for the use of the following articles, all © *The Guardian*: 1.2 David Stafford (4.8.91); 3.1 Margaret Horsfield (2.4.91); 7.10 Mark Tran (9.1.90); 8.2 p.114 Andrew Rawnsley (28.11.90); 9.7 Andrew Northedge (24.9.91); 9.9 Graham Wade (24.4.91); 10.4 Rupert Widdecombe (16.8.91); 11.4 Stephen Burgen (28.1.91) (adapted); 18.2E Maev Kennedy (3.1.92); the following journalists and correspondents whose articles and letters appeared in *The Guardian*: 1.4, CA1, CA32, CA34, Mark Wallington, 5.6 Catherine Mant, 6.8 Richard Boston, 12.6 Sir Clive Sinclair and Peter Smee, 14.2 Helen Chappell, 14.4 Jane McLoughlin, 16.2 Michael O'Donnell; 1.6 Guy Hodgson and *The Independent on Sunday*; 7.2 Dave Hill and *The Independent on Sunday*; 8.9 Simon Midgley and *The Independent*; 2.1 review by Maureen Cleave reproduced by permission of *Punch*; 2.4 Jonathan Cape Ltd and the estate of Peter Fleming for the extract from *Brazilian Adventure* by Peter Fleming; 3.4 Rogers, Coleridge and White for the extract from *Women's Rights: A Practical Guide* by Anna Coote and Tess Gill; 3.9A James MacGibbon, the executor, for the poem from *The Collected Poems of Stevie Smith* (Penguin 20th Century Classics) © 1972 Stevie Smith. Stevie Smith: *Collected Poems of Stevie Smith*, copyright © 1972 Stevie Smith, reprinted by permission of New Directions Publishing Corporation; 3.9A, 4.4(2) Tessa Sayle Agency for the poem 'Epitaph' by Christopher Logue and the extract to the Introduction to his book *New Numbers*; 4.2 Hodder & Stoughton Educational Ltd for the extract from *Language Made Plain* by Anthony Burgess; 4.4(1) extract from the Preface to *Communication in Face to Face Interaction* edited by John Laver and Sandy Hutchinson (Penguin Books, 1972), Selection copyright © John Laver and Sandy Hutchinson, 1972, Introduction and Notes copyright © John Laver and Sandy Hutchinson, 1972; 4.4(3) extract from the Introduction to *The English Language* by David Crystal (Penguin Books, 1988) copyright © David Crystal, 1988; 4.6 and 16.1 Innovations International Ltd; 5.3 article by James Allen © *The Daily Telegraph* plc, 1989;

5.9C article by Tom Rowland © *The Daily Telegraph* plc, 1989; 12.2 article by Andrew Marshall © *The Daily Telegraph* plc, 1991; 5.7 and 10.9 Dorling Kindersley for the extract and information from *Save the Earth* by Jonathon Porritt; 5.9A extract from 'Lutheran Pie' reprinted by permission of Garrison Keillor from *We are Still Married* (Viking Penguin, 1989), copyright © by Garrison Keillor; 6.2, CA4, CA19 extract from *The Towers of Trebizond* by Rose Macaulay reproduced with the permission of the Peters Fraser and Dunlop Group Ltd, and © Futura, an imprint of HarperCollins Publishers Ltd; 6.6 the extract from 'The Friendly Sky' from *Hunting Mr Heartbreak* by Jonathan Raban by permission of Harvill, an imprint of HarperCollins Publishers Ltd, excerpts from *Hunting Mr Heartbreak* by Jonathan Raban copyright © 1991 by Jonathan Raban, reprinted by permission of HarperCollins Publishers; 7.6 The Advertising Standards Authority; 7.8 and CA44 Victor Gollancz Ltd, John Elkington and Julia Hailes for the extract from *The Green Consumer Guide* and Anita Roddick for the introduction to the same book; 7.11 *The Bournemouth Advertiser*; 8.1 *The Guardian, The Economist, The Independent, The Sun, The Times, The Mirror* for the mastheads; 8.2, 16.5, 18.4(5), CA13 *The Economist*; 8.4 *The Financial Times* for the masthead; 8.6 Michael Buerk for the article from *Airport* magazine; 9.4 M.A. Uden for the article which first appeared in *The Times*; HarperCollins Publishers Ltd for: 10.6 and 10.10 extracts from *Life on Earth* by David Attenborough, 10.8 extract from *The Stationary Ark* by Gerald Durrell, CA39 extract from *Collins COBUILD English Language Dictionary*; 10.9 Joe Miller for the use of his poem 'If the Earth were ...'; 11.2A extract from *A Dark-Adapted Eye* by Barbara Vine by permission of the Peters Fraser & Dunlop Group Ltd; 11.2B Martin, Secker & Warburg for the extract from *Nice Work* by David Lodge, reproduced with permission of Curtis Brown Ltd, London, on behalf of David Lodge. Copyright © David Lodge 1988; 11.2C Sinclair-Stevenson, part of Reed International Books and Lemon, Unna and Durbridge Ltd for the extract from *Brazzaville Beach* by William Boyd; 11.6(1) William Heinemann Ltd and Viking Penguin for the extract from *The Grapes of Wrath* by John Steinbeck. Copyright 1939, renewed © 1967 by John Steinbeck. Used by permission of Viking Penguin, a division of Penguin Books USA Inc; 11.6 (2) Aitken & Stone for the extract from *The Mosquito Coast* by Paul Theroux; 12.8 excerpt from *The Psychology of Everyday Things* by Donald A. Norman. Copyright © 1988 by Donald A.

Norman. Reprinted by permission of Basic Books, a division of HarperCollins Publishers; 13.2 Rupert Hart-Davis, an imprint of HarperCollins Publishers for the extract from *My Family and Other Animals* reprinted with permission of Curtis Brown Ltd, London on behalf of Gerald Durrell. Copyright © Gerald M. Durrell 1956; Random Century and Georges Borchardt Inc. for the extract from *The Cement Garden* by Ian McEwan, reprinted by permission of Georges Borchardt Inc. on behalf of the author, copyright © 1978 by Ian McEwan; Hamish Hamilton Ltd and G.P. Putnams Sons for the extract from *My Secret History* by Paul Theroux. Reprinted by permission of the Putnam Publishing Group. Copyright © 1989 by Cape Cod Scrivener's Company; 13.4A Martin Secker & Warburg for the extract from *Wilt* by Tom Sharpe; 13.4C Faber and Faber Ltd, Nigel Williams Ltd, Judy Daish Associates Ltd and Faber & Faber Inc. for the extract from *The Wimbledon Poisoner* by Nigel Williams; 13.6 George Weidenfeld and Nicolson Ltd for the extract from *The Millstone* by Margaret Drabble; 15.1 extract from *Hollywood, the Pioneers* by Kevin Brownlow reprinted by permission of the Peters Fraser & Dunlop Group Ltd; 15.7 this extract is reproduced from *The Shock of the New* by Robert Hughes with the permission of BBC Enterprises Ltd; 15.8B Jonathan Cape and the Peters Fraser & Dunlop Group Ltd for the excerpt from *Visions before Midnight* by Clive James; 16.10 William Heinemann Ltd and the Peters Fraser & Dunlop Group Ltd for the extract from *Delight* by J.B. Priestley; 17.2 'Futility' by Wilfred Owen is reprinted from *Wilfred Owen. The Complete Poems and Fragments* edited by John Stallworthy and published by Chatto and Windus; 17.2 George Sassoon and Penguin USA for 'The General' from *Collected Poems* by Siegfried Sassoon.Copyright 1918, 1920 by E.P. Dutton. Copyright 1936, 1946, 1947, 1948 by Siegfried Sassoon, used by permission of Viking Penguin, a division of Penguin Books USA Inc.; 17.3 A.P. Watt on behalf of The Trustees of the Robert Graves Copyright Trust for the extract from *Goodbye to All That* by Robert Graves; 17.6 extract from *The Times Atlas of World History* reproduced by kind permission of Times Books; 18.1 University of Cambridge Local Examinations Syndicate for the answer sheet instructions; 18.2A Victor Gollancz Ltd and Crossroads/Continuum for the excerpt from *Crowds and Power* by Elias Canetti; 18.2B, 18.4, CA9, CA26 Channel Four Television for 'Commuters' and 'Traffic' from *Cities Fit to Live in* by Barrie Sherman, and 'The Refrigerator' and 'The Vacuum Cleaner' by Tim Hunkin from *The Secret Life of the Vacuum Cleaner* ...; 18.2C, 18.6C(2) Andrew Bordiss for extracts from the article which first appeared in the *Sunday Correspondent*; CA2, CA8, CA17, CA45 Methuen London for the excerpts from *So you think you can cope with customers? A Video Arts Guide*; CA7, CA46 Barclays Bank plc; CA24 Agence France Presse; CA25 Oxford University Press for the excerpt from the *Oxford Advanced Learner's Dictionary*; CA28 Nestlé UK Ltd; CA30 Longman Group UK Ltd for the extracts from the *Longman Dictionary of Contemporary English*; CA38 Reuters Ltd.

For permission to reproduce photographs:
pp. 3 (top left), 48 (top right, far right and bottom right), 50, 65, 76 (SmithKline Beecham Consumer Brands/McIlhenny Co.), 191, 203 Jeremy Pembrey; p. 3 (right) Tim Graham/Camera Press, (bottom left) Dave Stewart/Fotofusion; p.11 Michael Steele/*The Independent*; photographs of the interviewees on pp. 14, 24, 66, 73, 95, 118, 135, 147, 174, 221, 226 Peter Taylor; p. 19 Hallam Murray/John Murray Publishers Ltd; p. 24 (left) Douglas Dickens; pp. 48 (top far left and left), 127 (right), 258 (bottom) Bill Godfrey; pp. 48 (bottom left), 189, 287 Leo Jones; p. 51 Neil Libbert/Camera Press; p. 71 by permission of Paulette Maisner; p. 85 Len Bordeaux, Bordeaux Photography Inc., Seattle/Pan Macmillan; p. 88 *The Guardian*; p. 92 Tony Stone Worldwide; p. 94 (top left Michael Short/Robert Harding Picture Library, (right) Robert Harding Picture Library, (bottom left) Peter Francis/Camera Press; p. 96 Enrico Ferorelli/DOT/Colorific!; p. 99 (top) Timothy Woodcock Photolibrary, (bottom) Peter Francis/Camera Press, London; p. 100 Mitsukoshi Ltd for the photograph of Nihonbashi Store; p. 109 *The Bournemouth Advertiser*/Benetton SPA; p. 112 (far left) Stewart Mark/Camera Press Ltd, (others) Conservative Central Office; p.120 BBC Enterprises © BBC 1989; p. 127 (left) Howard J. Davies/Panos Pictures; p.130 (left) Cory Bevington/Fotofusion, (right) Timothy Woodcock Photolibrary; p. 141 Simon Grossett/Frank Spooner Pictures; p. 145 Russell-Cotes Art Gallery and Museum, Bournemouth/photograph by Harold Morris; p. 147 (right) François Gohier/Ardea; pp. 152, 244, 251 (photograph by Max Halberstadt, Sigmund Freud copyrights, courtesy of W.E. Freud), 293, 307 (photograph by Jeffrey Morgan), 309 (painting by Glyn Philpot) - all Mary Evans Picture Library; p. 159 (top left) Liba Taylor/The Hutchison Library, (top right) Michael Harvey/Panos Pictures, (centre left) Abbas/Magnum Photos, (centre right) Ron Giling/Panos Pictures, (main bottom left) Steve McCurry/Magnum Photos, (bottom right) Axandre/Telegraph Colour Library, (inset bottom left) Robin Hanbury-Tenison/Survival International, 310 Edgware Road, London WC2 1DY; p. 176 (top left and right) Dr Jeremy Burgess, (bottom left) David Sharf – all Science Photo Library; p.202 Edward Hopper, American, 1882–1967, 'Nighthawks' (detail), oil on canvas, 1942, 76.2 × 144cm, Friends Of American Art Collection,